FDR'S
FOLLY

ALSO BY JIM POWELL

The Triumph of Liberty: A 2,000-Year History
Told Through the Lives of Freedom's
Greatest Champions

FDR'S FOLLY

HOW ROOSEVELT AND HIS NEW DEAL PROLONGED THE GREAT DEPRESSION

JIM POWELL

CROWN
FORUM

For Marisa, Madeline, Frank,
Justin, Kristin, and Rosalynd

Published by Crown Forum, New York, New York.
Member of the Crown Publishing Group, a division of Random House, Inc.
www.crownpublishing.com

CROWN FORUM and the Crown Forum colophon are trademarks
of Random House, Inc.

Printed in the United States of America

Library of Congress Cataloging-in-Publication Data
Powell, Jim.
FDR's Folly : how Roosevelt and his New Deal
prolonged the Great Depression / Jim Powell
p.   cm.
Includes bibliographical references and index.

ISBN 0-7615-0165-7

10 9 8 7 6 5 4 3 2

First Edition

CONTENTS

INTRODUCTION

———⊳●⊲———

T HE GREAT DEPRESSION has had an immense influence on our thinking, particularly about ways to handle an economic crisis, yet we know surprisingly little about it. Most historians have focused on chronicling Franklin D. Roosevelt's charismatic personality, his brilliance as a strategist and communicator, the dramatic One Hundred Days, the First New Deal, Second New Deal, the "court-packing" plan, and other political aspects of the story. Comparatively little attention has been paid to the effects of the New Deal.

In recent decades, however, many economists have tried to determine whether New Deal policies contributed to recovery or prolonged the depression. The most troubling issue has been the persistence of high unemployment throughout the New Deal period. From 1934 to 1940, the median annual unemployment rate was 17.2 percent.[1] At no point during the 1930s did unemployment go below 14 percent. Even in 1941, amidst the military buildup for World War II, 9.9 percent of American workers were unemployed. Living standards remained depressed until after the war.[2]

While there was episodic recovery between 1933 and 1937, the 1937 peak was lower than the previous peak (1929), a highly unusual occurrence. Progress has been the norm. In addition, the 1937 peak was followed by a crash. As Nobel laureate Milton Friedman observed, this was "the only occasion in our record when one deep depression followed immediately on the heels of another."[3]

Scholarly investigators have raised some provocative questions. For instance, why did New Dealers make it more expensive for employers to hire people? Why did FDR's Justice Department file some 150 lawsuits threatening big employers? Why did New Deal policies discourage private investment without which private employment was unlikely to revive? Why so many policies to push up the cost of living? Why did New Dealers destroy food while people went hungry? To what extent did New Deal labor laws penalize blacks? Why did New Dealers break up the strongest banks? Why were Americans made more vulnerable to disastrous human error at the Federal Reserve? Why didn't New Deal securities laws help investors do better? Why didn't New Deal public works projects bring about a recovery? Why was so much New Deal relief spending channeled *away* from the poorest people? Why did the Tennessee Valley Authority become a drag on the Tennessee Valley?

Curiously, although the Great Depression was probably the most important economic event in twentieth-century American history, Stanford University's David M. Kennedy seems to be the only major political historian who has mentioned any of the recent findings. "Whatever it was," he wrote in his Pulitzer Prize–winning *Freedom from Fear* (1999), the New Deal "was not a recovery program, or at any rate not an effective one."[4]

It's true the Great Depression was an international phenomenon—depression in Germany, for instance, made increasing numbers of desperate people search for scapegoats and support Adolf Hitler, a lunatic who couldn't get anywhere politically just a few years earlier when the country was still prosperous. But compared to the United States, as economic historian Lester V. Chandler observed, "in most countries the depression was less deep and prolonged."[5] Regardless whether the depression originated in the United States or Europe, there is considerable evidence that New Deal policies prolonged high unemployment.

FDR didn't do anything about a major cause of 90 percent of the bank failures, namely, state and federal unit banking laws. These limited banks to a single office, preventing them from diversifying their loan portfolios and their source of funds. Unit banks were highly vulnerable to failure when local business conditions were bad, because all their loans were to local people, many of whom were in default, and all their deposits came from local people who were withdrawing their money. Canada, which permitted nationwide branch banking, didn't have a single bank failure during the Great Depression.

FDR's major banking "reform," the second Glass-Steagall Act, actually weakened the banking system by breaking up the strongest banks to separate commercial banking from investment banking. Universal banks (which served depositors and did securities underwriting) were much stronger than banks pursuing only one of these activities, very few universal banks failed, and securities underwritten by universal banks were less risky. Almost every historian has praised FDR's other major financial "reform," establishing the Securities and Exchange Commission to supervise the registration of new securities and the operation of securities markets, but in terms of rate of return, investors were no better off than they were in the 1920s, before the Securities and Exchange Commission came along.

FDR didn't do much about a contributing factor in the Great Depression, the Smoot-Hawley tariff which throttled trade. Indeed, he raised some tariffs, while Secretary of State Cordell Hull negotiated reciprocal trade agreements which cut tariffs only about 4 percent. FDR approved the dumping of agricultural commodities below cost overseas, which surely aggravated our trading partners.

FDR *tripled* taxes during the Great Depression, from $1.6 billion in 1933 to $5.3 billion in 1940.[6] Federal taxes as a percentage of the gross national product jumped from 3.5 percent in 1933 to 6.9 percent in 1940, and taxes skyrocketed during World War II.[7] FDR increased the tax burden with higher personal income taxes, higher corporate income taxes, higher excise taxes, higher estate taxes, and higher gift taxes. He introduced the undistributed profits tax. Ordinary people were hit with higher liquor taxes and Social Security payroll taxes. All these taxes meant there was less capital for businesses to create jobs, and people had less money in their pockets.

In addition, FDR increased the cost and risk of employing people, and so there shouldn't have been any surprise that the unemployment rate remained stubbornly high. Economists Richard K. Vedder and Lowell E. Gallaway, in their 1997 study *Out of Work: Unemployment and Government in Twentieth-Century America*, reported: "New Deal policies (and some Hoover-era policies predating the New Deal) systematically used the power of the state to intervene in labor markets in a manner to raise wages and labor costs, prolonging the misery of the Great Depression, and creating a situation where many people were living in rising prosperity at a time when millions of others were suffering severe deprivation. . . . Of the ten years of unemployment rates over 10 percent during the Depression, fully eight were during the Roosevelt administration (counting 1933 as a Roosevelt year)."[8] Vedder and Gallaway estimated that by 1940 unemployment was eight points higher than it would have been in the absence of higher payroll costs imposed by New Deal policies.[9]

Economists Thomas E. Hall and J. David Ferguson reported, "It is difficult to ascertain just how much the New Deal programs had to do with keeping the unemployment rate high, but surely they were important. A combination of fixing farm prices, promoting labor unions, and passing a series of antibusiness tax laws would certainly have had a negative impact on employment. In addition, the uncertainty experienced by the business community as a result of the frequent tax law changes (1932, 1934, 1935, 1936) must have been enormous. Since firms' investment decisions very much depend on being able to plan, an increase in uncertainty tends to reduce investment expenditures. It should not be a surprise that investment as a proportion of output was at low levels during the mid-1930s."[10]

Black people were among the major victims of the New Deal. Large numbers of blacks were unskilled and held entry-level jobs, and when New Deal policies forced wage rates above market levels, hundreds of thousands of these jobs were destroyed. Above-market wage rates encouraged employers to mechanize and in other ways cut total labor costs. Many New Deal policies were framed to benefit northern industries and undermine the position of employers in the South, where so many blacks worked. "New Deal labor policies contributed to a persistent increase in African American unemployment," reported economist David E. Bernstein.[11]

When millions of people had little money, New Deal era policies made practically everything more expensive (the National Industrial Recovery Act), specifically maintained above-market retail prices (the Robinson-Patman Act and the Retail Price Maintenance Act) and above-market airline tickets (Civil Aeronautics Act). Moreover, FDR signed into law the Agricultural Adjustment Act, which led to the destruction of millions of acres of crops and millions of farm animals, while many Americans were hungry.

New Deal agricultural policies provided subsidies based on a farmer's acreage and output, which meant they mainly helped big farmers with the most acreage and output. The New Deal displaced poor sharecroppers and tenant farmers, a large number of whom were black. High farm foreclosure rates persisted during the New Deal, indicating that it did almost nothing for the poorest farmers. Historian Michael A. Bernstein went farther and made a case that New Deal agricultural policies "sacrificed the interests of the marginal and the unrecognized to the welfare of those with greater political and economic power."[12]

The flagship of the New Deal was the National Industrial Recovery Act, which authorized cartel codes restricting output and fixing high prices for just about every conceivable business enterprise, much as medieval guild restrictions had restricted output and fixed prices. That FDR approved contraction was astounding, because the American people had suffered through three years of catastrophic contraction. With the National Industrial Recovery Act, it actually became a crime to increase output or cut prices—a forty-nine-year-old immigrant dry cleaner was jailed for charging 35 cents instead of 40 cents to press a pair of pants.

This wasn't full-scale government control as in the Soviet Union, but it came closer than anybody had thought possible. Although the NIRA was struck down by the Supreme Court in May 1935, the New Deal continued to multiply restrictions on business enterprise. "Perhaps the greatest defect in these limited planning measures," wrote economic historian Ellis W. Hawley, "was their tendency toward restriction, their failure to provide any incentive for expansion when an expanding economy was the crying need of the time."[13]

While FDR authorized the spending of billions for relief and public works projects, a disproportionate amount of this money went not to the poorest states such as the South, but to western states where people were better off, apparently because these were "swing" states which could yield FDR more votes in the next election. The South was already solidly Democratic, so there wasn't much to be gained by buying votes there. It was observed at the time that relief and public works spending seemed to increase during election years. Politicking with relief and public works money got to be so bad that Congress passed the Hatch Act (1939).

The New Deal approached its climax in 1938 as Thurman Arnold, head of the Justice Department's Antitrust Division, began to file about 150 lawsuits against companies employing millions of people. Hawley called this "the most intensive antitrust campaign in American history."[14] Whatever the merits of the government's claims, these lawsuits made it politically more risky for businesses to pursue long-term investments, and private investment remained

at an historically low level throughout the New Deal—prolonging the Great Depression.

All the highly publicized relief programs and public works projects couldn't make up for the damage inflicted by New Deal taxes, restrictions, antitrust lawsuits, and the rest. Indeed, the more money the government spent on relief and public works, the more tax revenue it needed, and the more damage done to the economy.

As a cure for the Great Depression, government spending didn't work. In 1933, federal government outlays were $4.5 billion; by 1940 they were $9.4 billion, so FDR more than doubled federal spending, and still unemployment remained stubbornly high. Changes in federal budget deficits didn't correspond with changes in gross domestic product, and in any case the federal budget deficit at its peak (1936) was only 4.4 percent of the gross domestic product, much too small for a likely cure.[15]

The most that could be said in FDR's defense was this, by Donald R. Richberg, former head of the National Recovery Administration: "Although the tremendous expenditures and supports for agriculture and industrial labor that were projected in the Roosevelt administration did not end a huge unemployment problem, they did raise new hopes and inspire new activities among the American people which turned them away for a time at least from even more radical political programs."[16]

FDR had assumed unprecedented arbitrary power supposedly needed to get America out of the Great Depression. Although Democrats controlled Congress, FDR was impatient with American democracy, and he issued an extraordinary number of executive orders—3,728 altogether[17]—which is more than all the executive orders issued by his successors Harry Truman, Dwight D. Eisenhower, John F. Kennedy, Lyndon B. Johnson, Richard M. Nixon, Gerald R. Ford, Jimmy Carter, Ronald Reagan, George H. W. Bush, and Bill Clinton combined. In the name of fairness, FDR saw to it that some individuals were treated much more harshly than others under the federal tax code. NRA codes denied individuals the fundamental liberty to enter the business of their choosing. Compulsory unionism denied individuals the right to work without joining a union. Americans gave up these liberties and more without getting out of the Great Depression, as had been promised. Principal legacies of the New Deal have been a massive expansion of government power and loss of liberty.

FDR's failure to end chronic high unemployment and his increasingly arbitrary tactics were reasons why, after 1936, his political support declined. Republicans gained seats in Congress during the 1938 elections, and they gained more seats in 1940. FDR's own vote totals declined after 1936, and Republican presidential vote totals increased over both those of 1936 and 1932.

FDR didn't make the recovery of private, productive employment his top priority. Along with advisers like Louis Brandeis, Felix Frankfurter, Rexford Tugwell, and Thomas Corcoran, FDR viewed business as the cause of the Great Depression, and he did everything he could to restrict business. His goal was "reform," not recovery. Accordingly, the New Deal taxed money away from the private sector, and government officials, not private individuals, made the spending decisions. New Deal laws determined what kind of people businesses must hire, how much they must be paid, what prices businesses must charge, and it interfered with their ability to raise capital.

The British economist John Maynard Keynes recognized that FDR's priorities were subverting the prospects for ending high unemployment. He wrote FDR a letter which was published in the December 31, 1933, issue of the *New York Times.* Keynes warned that "even wise and necessary Reform may, in some respects, impede and complicate Recovery. For it will upset the confidence of the business world and weaken their existing motives to action. . . . I am not clear, looking back over the last nine months, that the order of urgency between measures of Recovery and measures of Reform

has been duly observed, or that the latter has not sometimes been mistaken for the former."[18]

Newspaper columnist Walter Lippmann observed that New Deal "reformers" would "rather not have recovery if the revival of private initiative means a resumption of private control in the management of corporate business . . . the essence of the New Deal is the reduction of private corporate control by collective bargaining and labor legislation, on the one side, and by restrictive, competitive and deterrent government action on the other side."[19]

The failure of the New Deal seems incredible considering that FDR is widely rated among America's greatest presidents. Moreover, many of the brightest minds of the era were recruited to Washington. FDR, who graduated from Harvard College, filled many of his top positions with graduates of Harvard Law School. They had clerked with the most respected judges of the era. These and other New Dealers were hailed for their compassion and their so-called progressive thinking. They were widely viewed as more noble than the greedy businessmen and reckless speculators who were thought to have brought on the depression. New Dealers wanted to eliminate poverty, abolish child labor, and right other social wrongs. Many New Dealers saw themselves as trying to make the world over. How could such bright, compassionate people have gone so wrong?

This book attempts to explain what went wrong and why. I draw on major findings by economists about the actual effects of the New Deal—how it promoted cartels, imposed confiscatory taxes, made it harder for companies to raise capital, made it more expensive for companies to employ people, bombarded companies with dubious antitrust lawsuits, and relentlessly denounced employers and investors, prolonging high unemployment. Published during the last four decades, these findings have been virtually ignored by pro–New Deal political historians like James MacGregor Burns, Arthur M. Schlesinger Jr., Frank Freidel, William Leuchtenburg, and Kenneth S. Davis. In his autobiography, Schlesinger acknowledged that he "was not much interested in economics." It is remarkable how such respected historians, writing about the most important economic event of twentieth-century American history, could disregard the growing economics literature which challenges their views.

Unless we clearly understand the effects of the New Deal, we cannot say we understand it at all—and more important, what the Great Depression experience means for us now. It would be tragic if, in a future recession or depression, policymakers repeated the same mistakes of the New Deal because they knew only the political histories of the time.

I believe the evidence is overwhelming that the Great Depression as we know it was avoidable. Better policies could have prevented the bank failures which accelerated the contraction of the money supply and brought on the Great Depression. The Great Depression could have been over much more quickly—the United States recovered from the severe 1920 depression in about a year. Chronic high unemployment persisted during the 1930s because of a succession of misguided New Deal policies.

A principal lesson for us today is that if economic shocks are followed by sound policies, we can avoid another Great Depression. A government will best promote a speedy business recovery by making recovery the top priority, which means letting people keep more of their money, removing obstacles to productive enterprise, and providing stable money and a political climate where investors feel that it's safe to invest for the future.

CHAPTER ONE

How Could Such Bright, Compassionate People Be Wrong?

THE GREAT DEPRESSION was a testing time for "progressive" ideas, because practically everything was tried. Some New Dealers were outright socialists, and they had their day. Some New Dealers were advocates of a corporate state, and FDR had a go at that. Some believed the key to good times was compulsory unionism. Those who blamed Wall Street for the Great Depression drafted securities regulations, those who blamed private monopolies unleashed antitrust lawsuits, and those who blamed the "maldistribution of wealth" succeeded in enacting "soak the rich" taxes. Then there were the pump primers who claimed that government spending and budget deficits would bring recovery.

All these ideas were associated with the "progressive" movement. Among its most influential works was journalist Herbert Croly's *The Promise of American Life* (1909). "Traditional American confidence in individual freedom has resulted in a morally and socially undesirable distribution of wealth," he wrote. He denounced "the chaotic individualism of our political and economic organization." Croly warned that the control of wealth shouldn't depend on "the accidental good intentions of individuals" but rather "should be efficiently performed by the state."[1]

World War I gave most Americans their first opportunity to see what a government-run economy would look like, and the "progressives" loved it. The federal government seized control of industries, fixed prices, and ran everything through bureaucracies like the Shipping Board, War Finance Corporation, War Labor Board, and Food Administration. One of the most powerful bureaucracies was the War Industries Board, which regulated all industries producing war materials—some 30,000 items altogether.[2] Inevitably, such power extended far beyond war materials. As historians Samuel Eliot Morison, Henry Steele Commager, and William E. Leuchtenburg reported, "Baby carriages were standardized; traveling salesmen were limited to two trunks; and the length of uppers on shoes was cut down. It was such a regimentation of the economy as had never before been known, and it later served as a model for the New Deal."[3]

The early years of the Great Depression brought many "progressive" solutions modeled after World War I government agencies. Economist George Soule acknowledged, "Many of those who now advocate economic planning have been doing so, in one way or another, since the experiences of 1917–18."[4] Journalist Stuart Chase proposed establishing a Peace Industries Board like President Wilson's War Industries Board.[5]

Columbia University historian Charles A. Beard spoke for many "progressives" when he wrote "The Myth of Rugged Individualism" in the March 1931 *Harper's Magazine*. He said, "The cold truth is that the individualist creed . . . is principally responsible for the distress in which Western civilization finds itself. . . . The task before us, then, is not to furbish up an old slogan, but to get rid of it, to discover how much planning is necessary, by whom it can best be done."[6]

Many "progressives" visited the Soviet Union and came away more convinced than ever that a government-run economy offered the best solution. Stuart Chase wrote *A New Deal* (1932), in which he said that communists didn't need "further incentive than the burning zeal to create a new heaven and a new earth." Chase closed his book by asking, "Why should Russians have all the fun of re-making a world?"[7]

If "progressive" ideas were good, they should have worked. They should have cured the number one social problem of the Great Depression—chronic high unemployment. Republican president Herbert Hoover was discredited, FDR won a popular mandate in 1932, Democrats gained more seats in Congress during the 1934 elections, and FDR achieved an overwhelming victory in 1936. Democrats controlled both houses of Congress throughout the New Deal period. Moreover, control of the White House meant control of patronage—"many thousands of openings available with the pro-liferation of New Deal alphabetical agencies," as historian James T. Patterson put it.[8] In addition, as Virginia's Democratic senator Carter Glass and others acknowledged,[9] billions of dollars in relief and public works spending were deployed to states where it could do FDR the most good during the next election. Although the Supreme Court struck down some early New Deal laws, such as the National Industrial Recovery Act and the Agricultural Adjustment Act, major features were revived in subsequent New Deal laws that the courts upheld, so New Dealers got what they wanted.

"Progressive" ideas didn't fail for lack of talent. Dozens of New Dealers were skilled attorneys trained at Harvard, the most presti-gious institution of higher education in the land. Lawyers from other top-tier universities like Yale, Columbia, and the University of Chicago also joined the government. Some of America's most suc-cessful businesspeople were New Deal advisers. The Great Depres-sion was compared to a wartime emergency, and many New Dealers had served in President Woodrow Wilson's administration during World War I. These people were bright and seasoned; they worked hard and were full of hope. How was it possible for such people to be so tragically wrong?

*   *   *

THE STORY BEGINS with FDR himself. Born on January 30, 1882, he had all the advantages wealth could bring. His father, James, inherited wealth and worked in the railroad and coal mining businesses. FDR attended the best schools, including Groton and Harvard. He briefly practiced law and soon showed a flair for politics. After he was elected to the New York State Senate in 1910, he served as assistant secretary of the navy in the Wilson administration.

His real seasoning came after he was stricken with poliomyelitis at Campobello, New Brunswick, Canada, in August 1921. The disease led to incurable paralysis of his legs; he spent much time in a wheelchair and learned to get around with leg braces and canes. He never walked again without assistance, but he resolved to rise above his disability. "Polio steeled FDR to the hardships of a political career," observed historian Richard T. Goldberg. "He may have become president even if he hadn't contracted polio, but with the disability he became more compassionate, made more widespread contacts, concentrated on his priorities, and learned to bide his time before making a crucial decision. Polio tested and sharpened FDR's basic character. Having emerged from this struggle with courage and optimism, he learned to endure and master the great political crises of his career."[10]

During the 1928 election, Democratic presidential candidate Al Smith failed to carry New York State, but FDR won the governorship by a narrow margin, about 25,000 votes.[11] He won a landslide victory in 1930. By 1932, the depression had dragged on for three years, and the public blamed Hoover. FDR was one of three Democrats seeking the presidential nomination and likely victory in the fall. Al Smith wanted to avenge his 1928 loss to Hoover, and he had the backing of the Tammany Hall machine. Speaker of the House John Nance Garner, a Texan, was the third candidate. Two-thirds of the convention votes were needed to win the nomination. The convention voted three times without producing a winner. If FDR couldn't win on the fourth ballot, his prospects were expected to fade quickly, so his campaign manager, James Farley, struck a deal with Garner to be the vice presidential candidate on FDR's ticket. Then FDR displayed his knack for bold moves. Rather than wait at home for convention representatives to call on him several weeks later, giving him official word of their decision, he boarded an airplane from Albany to Chicago and delivered an acceptance speech. Included were his famous words "There is nothing to fear but fear itself" and "I pledge you, I pledge myself, to a new deal for the American people."

FDR, who embraced "progressive ideas," certainly wasn't a thinker. "Roosevelt responded less to principles than to personalities, and these could be presented best in conversation," observed historian George Martin.[12] Indeed, FDR appeared to be utterly ignorant of economics. He seemed willing to try practically anything as long as it involved more government control over the economy. He was apparently unaware that such policies had been tried before in many other countries—and failed.

It didn't bother him that New Deal policies contradicted one another. When an adviser gave FDR two different drafts of a speech, one defending high tariffs and the other urging low tariffs, FDR told the adviser: "Weave the two together."[13] The Agricultural Adjustment Act forced food prices above market levels, in an effort to help farmers, but higher food prices hurt everybody who wasn't a farmer. The National Recovery Administration forced up prices of manufactured goods, hurting farmers who had to buy farm tools and equipment. Agricultural allotment policies cut cultivated acreage, while the Bureau of Reclamation increased cultivated acreage. Relief spending helped the unemployed, while corporate income taxes, undistributed profits taxes, Social Security taxes, minimum wage laws, and compulsory unionism led to higher unemployment rates. New Deal spending was supposed to stimulate the economy, but New Deal taxing depressed the economy.

Leon Keyserling, a lawyer who helped draft several important New Deal measures, including the National Labor Relations Act, the Social Security Act, and the Housing Act of 1937, acknowledged that FDR could be fickle: "Roosevelt switched to the second New Deal, which switched from the measures like the Agricultural Adjustment Act and the NRA, he switched to a campaign of pillorying business through the royalist phraseology and through the death of the holding companies. This was a political switch associated with his 1936 campaign. Then later on he switched to 'Mr. New Deal is dead; we now have Mr. Win the War.' But these things didn't represent philosophies and schools; they were more or less opportunistic depending on who had his ear at the time."[14]

FDR absorbed the spirit and tactics of class warfare. For instance, Interior Secretary Harold Ickes quoted FDR as saying this about his loyal friend Harry Hopkins, who headed New Deal relief programs: "Harry does get along with the economic royalists. There is something debonair and easygoing about him that makes him personally attractive; he seems to like to accept invitations to expensive homes; he loves horse racing and poker and women, and, except for his social-service and relief records, he would be highly acceptable to this class."[15]

Despite FDR's limitations as a thinker, he was a political genius. He envisioned a new political coalition that could sustain his policies, and he pulled it together. He knew how to inspire loyalty and how to keep people working with him, despite their often bitter disagreements. He knew how to steal the thunder of his political opponents, particularly those on the "left." He became overconfident following his landslide victory in 1936, and a succession of blunders led more and more people to oppose the New Deal, but Republicans didn't come close to finding anybody who could beat him.

FDR had a magnificent tenor voice and projected his personality and program to the American people, who needed somebody to believe in. "Thoroughly experienced public speaker though he was," observed speechwriter Samuel Rosenman, "he was generally very nervous as the time to get up to deliver his speech drew near.

He seldom found any pleasure at a meeting or at a banquet until his speech had actually begun. He would nervously smoke cigarette after cigarette. His hand would shake as he drank water. While waiting to be introduced, he would fidget in his chair. Once he had gotten to his feet and said, 'My friends,' he was a changed man—relaxed, in perfect touch with his audience, every fiber concentrated on what he was saying and in the effect it was producing—all traces of nervousness gone."[16]

WHEN FDR NEEDED advice about government finances, he turned to his neighbor and friend Henry T. Morgenthau Jr. more than anyone else. Morgenthau served as FDR's Treasury secretary for eleven years, almost the entire time that FDR was president. Historian John Morton Blum described Morgenthau as "a tall man, heavy but not stout, squinting a little behind pince-nez, seeming therefore to frown, but given sporadically to a wide slow smile."

Born in New York City in 1891, the son of a successful Manhattan real estate investor, Morgenthau took a while to find his way. He went to Phillips Exeter Academy but dropped out after two years. In 1904, he entered Cornell University and studied architecture (his father considered it useful for a real estate career),[17] but he quit after three semesters. Then he worked at the Henry Street Settlement House, which had been started by Lillian Wald to help poor, mostly Jewish immigrants on Manhattan's Lower East Side. "The settlement house movement," explained historian George Martin, "which was spreading rapidly in the United States, was originally inspired by an English model, the Toynbee Hall [founded 1884] in London. The idea was that men and women who had recently graduated from the universities would make a 'settlement' in a slum, share the problems of the poor and work with them to reform neighborhood conditions. . . . The American settlements, however, developed differently from the English. Their emphasis shifted from education and culture toward social reform, and their leaders often entered politics to demand that sanitation laws be enforced, new parks be opened, and new laws passed."[18] Morgenthau was certainly inspired by Wald's belief that social problems could be cured with more laws.

Later, in Texas recovering from typhoid fever, he became interested in farming and decided to pursue that career since it offered the prospect of independence from his father. He returned to Cornell and studied agriculture. He bought several hundred acres of land in Dutchess County, New York, near East Fishkill.[19]

Morgenthau met his neighbor FDR at a Hyde Park luncheon in 1915. FDR encouraged him to run for sheriff and remembered that "He is an awfully nice fellow." Apparently the two men kept in touch, and in 1920, when FDR won the Democratic nomination for vice president, Morgenthau directed the Democratic campaign in Dutchess County.[20] Morgenthau and his wife often accompanied FDR, playing Parcheesi at Hyde Park and cruising in the Florida Keys. Elinor Morgenthau worked with Eleanor Roosevelt, urging that women register to vote. FDR and Morgenthau supported Al Smith's losing bids for the presidency in 1924 and 1928. After FDR was elected New York's governor in 1928, he named Morgenthau as his conservation commissioner, and Morgenthau served until FDR went to Washington. Then FDR made Morgenthau chairman of the Federal Farm Board and governor of its successor, the Farm Credit Administration. When, in November 1933, FDR's first Treasury secretary, Federal Reserve Bank of New York governor William Woodin, took a leave of absence because of failing health, Morgenthau became acting secretary of the Treasury. By January 1934, it became clear that Woodin couldn't return, and Morgenthau was named Treasury secretary.

During his first four years, Morgenthau seemed to be an unquestioning New Deal loyalist, even when he advocated policies that didn't work. Not until the economic collapse of 1938 did Morgenthau break ranks and publicly suggest that the administration would need to stop hammering business if there were going to be a sustained recovery of private employment. Nonetheless, he remained Treasury secretary until the end, leading the charge for skyrocketing taxes to finance the war effort.

THE NEW DEAL gave away billions of dollars for various relief programs, and Harry Hopkins was in charge of those. He was utterly loyal to FDR, he had a keen sense of what FDR wanted, he was industrious in trying to do it, and he became one of FDR's most trusted advisers.

"You could mark him down as an ulcerous type," remarked Dr. Jacob Goldberg, who had worked with him in New York City. "He was intense, seeming to be in a perpetual nervous ferment—a chain smoker and black coffee drinker. He was always careless in his appearance. Most of the time he would show up in the office looking as though he had spent the previous night sleeping in a hayloft. He would wear the same shirt three or four days at a time. He managed to shave almost every day—usually at the office."[21]

Hopkins was born in Sioux City, Iowa, in 1890, the son of a harness maker who believed in the Democratic populism of William Jennings Bryan. After graduating from Grinnell College, he got a job in a New Jersey summer camp run by Christadora House, a charitable institution serving poor children, and he became a full-time social worker at Christadora House. Drawn to politics, he helped the campaign of New York mayoral candidate John Mitchel, who won and named Hopkins executive secretary of the Board of Child Welfare. He wasn't pleased, however, that the New York press described participants in his programs as "leaning on their shovels." In April 1917, he started working for the Red Cross in New Orleans, then Atlanta. He then moved on to the Association for Improving the Condition of the Poor, in New York. He took over management of the Tuberculosis Association, spent its $90,000 surplus, incurred debts, and arranged mergers with the New York

Heart Association, the Associated Out-Patient Clinic, the Allied Dental Clinic, and the Children's Welfare Clinic.[22] Hopkins was a rising star of the welfare movement.

Hopkins met FDR before the future president was running for governor of New York. In August 1931, FDR established the Temporary Emergency Relief Administration, and Hopkins was recommended for the job of executive director. He accepted and won FDR's loyalty by doing whatever he wanted. When FDR remarked that slum boys might work to preserve forests, Hopkins and Conservation Commissioner Morgenthau arranged to have some 10,000 boys commute to Bear Mountain, north of New York City, where they planted trees. This program became a model for the New Deal Civilian Conservation Corps and the National Youth Administration.[23]

Hopkins played a minor role in FDR's presidential campaign and was on the sidelines during the transition. He hoped to conduct some kind of relief effort on a national scale, but he wasn't called to Washington until March 22, 1933, when he was named the head of the Federal Emergency Relief Administration. During his first two days on the job, newspapers reported that he had disbursed $5 million.[24] After FERA had spent its appropriation, Hopkins managed the Civil Works Administration, then the Works Progress Administration, and had a hand in the National Youth Administration. Although he was honest, he did help steer spending in ways that would help Democrats.

In December 1938, after bad health and the death of his second wife led Hopkins to limit his responsibilities, FDR appointed him secretary of commerce. During World War II, he handled missions to British prime minister Winston Churchill and Soviet boss Joseph Stalin.

FDR LOOKED TO another social worker, Frances Perkins, for his secretary of labor, and she held this post for more than twelve years, until after his death. Perkins emerged as the leading administration champion of compulsory unionism, minimum wage laws, and Social

Security. "Brisk and articulate, with vivid dark eyes, a broad forehead and a pointed chin, usually wearing a felt tricorn hat," wrote historian Arthur M. Schlesinger Jr., "she remained a Brahmin reformer, proud of her New England background . . . and intent on beating sense into the heads of those foolish people who resisted progress. She had pungency of character, a dry wit, an inner gaiety, an instinct for practicality, a profound vein of religious feeling, and a compulsion to instruct."[25]

Fannie Coraline Perkins was born in 1880 in Boston. Her father, Fred, was a clerk for the Jordan Marsh store and later moved the family to Worcester, where he started a stationery business. She entered Mount Holyoke, the first American college dedicated to the education of women, and there in 1902 she heard a talk that changed her life. The speaker was forty-three-year-old Florence Kelley, national secretary of the National Consumers' League, which campaigned for the elimination of "sweatshops" and child labor.[26] Kelley, a socialist, had worked at Jane Addams's Hull House, where the mission was to enlighten the educated classes and improve the lives of poor Italians, Greeks, Slavs, and Jews who lived around Chicago's South Halsted Street.[27]

Perkins, following her graduation, taught successively at Protestant schools in Worcester, Monson (Massachusetts), and Lake Forest (Illinois), but her dream was to work in a settlement house. She got a job at Chicago Commons, a settlement house in a neighborhood of Polish, Irish, German, and Scandinavian immigrants. Thousands of these people, children as well as adults, worked long hours for little money in the garment industry, and Perkins was shocked. Perkins helped out at Hull House. She counseled troubled families, helped them collect their pay, and attended meetings of people who believed that labor unions would be the salvation of the world. She joined the Socialist Party.[28]

She served on the commission that investigated the fire at Manhattan's Triangle Shirtwaist Company, where 146 female garment workers died. The vice chairman of the commission was Alfred E.

Smith, Democratic majority leader in the New York State Assembly. After he was elected governor in 1918, he appointed Perkins to the New York State Industrial Board, which monitored factory conditions. A decade later, Governor Roosevelt made her the state industrial commissioner. He subsequently chose her to be his secretary of labor and the first woman to hold a cabinet-level position in the federal government.

A NUMBER OF FDR's most important New Deal policies were the work of some leading academics who served as his "brain trust"— the phrase seems to have been coined by *New York Times* reporter James Kieran.[29] The man who put together the "brain trust" was Columbia University law professor Raymond Moley. Officially, he was assistant secretary of state, but he drafted speeches, analyzed issues, and made recommendations to FDR. He played a major role during the One Hundred Days. By the summer of 1933, however, Moley had a falling-out with Secretary of State Cordell Hull, who insisted that Moley be dismissed. FDR offered him a post in the Justice Department, but the disillusioned Moley left the administration to become the editor of *Today*, a pro–New Deal magazine that merged with *Newsweek*, and he became increasingly critical of the New Deal's antibusiness policies.

Later, Samuel Rosenman recalled a White House dinner he attended with FDR and Moley: "That night in the small family dining room, for the first and only time in my life, I saw the President forget himself as a gentleman. He began twitting Moley about his new conservatism and about the influence of his 'new, rich friends' on his recent writings, which had been very critical of the Administration. The President grew angry, and the exchanges between them became very bitter. . . . Moley resented this, and said something to the effect that Roosevelt's inability to take criticism was leading him down the wrong paths."[30]

Moley was born in 1886 in Berea, Ohio. After graduating from Baldwin-Wallace College, he got a teaching job. "Meanwhile," Moley recalled, "I had absorbed the ideas and spirit of the Progressive movement, although I was never an admirer of Theodore Roosevelt. I doubted his sincerity and was repelled by his ham acting. I preferred Wilson's more intelligent approach to reform. And he was a Democrat!"[31] From 1919 to 1923, Moley served as director of the Cleveland Foundation, which sponsored studies about Cleveland community issues. The most impressive of the studies, the Cleveland Crime Survey—crime had become a big national issue because of Prohibition—led Moley to collaborate with Harvard Law School professor Felix Frankfurter. The study was highly enough regarded that Columbia University hired him as a law professor in 1923. He wrote two books about criminal justice, *Politics and Criminal Prosecution* (1928) and *Our Criminal Courts* (1930).

During the mid-1920s, while doing work for the National Crime Commission, Moley met Louis Howe, a former newspaperman who had become ghostwriter and political strategist for FDR back when he was a New York state senator. In 1928, Howe invited Moley to meet FDR, who had become a Democratic candidate for governor of New York. FDR appointed him to a commission studying a new parole system for New York State.

FOUR YEARS LATER, when FDR set his sights on the Democratic presidential nomination, Samuel Rosenman suggested that FDR assemble a group of professors to help him develop a platform for national issues. Rosenman was a Columbia-trained lawyer who worked with the Tammany Hall Democratic machine, won election to the New York State Assembly, became a speechwriter for FDR, and was appointed by FDR to the New York Superior Court.

Moley asked Adolf Berle Jr., a Columbia Law School professor, if he would be interested in working on issues with FDR. Berle feared that free markets, left to themselves, tend to produce monopolies, and so he called for government control of the economy. For a while, he was a lawyer for the Reconstruction Finance Corporation, and later he was assistant secretary of state.

Born in Boston in 1895, the son of a Congregationalist minister, Berle was a whiz who graduated from Harvard College when he was eighteen and from Harvard Law School at twenty-one. He worked briefly in Louis Brandeis's law firm and gathered intelligence for the U.S. Army during World War I. After attending the Paris Peace Conference, he made news by denouncing the vindictive terms that the Allies imposed on the Germans there. During the 1920s, he tried to decide whether he wanted to do good or do well. He served as a lawyer for Indians, he lived for two years in the Henry Street Settlement (where Henry Morgenthau had worked), and he started a law firm for corporate clients. In 1927, Columbia Law School hired Berle as a professor.

There, with economist Gardiner C. Means, he wrote the influential 1932 book *The Modern Corporation and Private Property*, funded by a Laura Spelman Rockefeller Foundation grant. Berle and Means asserted that the top 200 corporations dominated the American economy, and they claimed that because big publicly held businesses were run by salaried managers, not the shareholders, they were inherently inefficient. Salaried managers cherished perks and didn't want to work hard, and Berle believed that the average shareholder, with comparatively few shares, was powerless. The implication, of course, was that some kind of government intervention was needed to make a capitalist economy more efficient. *Time* magazine described it as "the economic Bible of the Roosevelt administration."[32]

Berle was five feet seven inches tall, and historian Kenneth S. Davis noted that "his narrow-shouldered body had a somewhat unfinished look, as if its growth had been arrested in midadolescence, and his head appeared, by contrast with his torso, abnormally large, which augmented the general impression he gave of physical immaturity, though his general health was excellent."[33] Lillian Wald, founder of the Henry Street Settlement, remembered his "precious loyalty and friendship."[34] William O. Douglas called him "creative, and the essence of integrity."[35] According to British philosopher

Isaiah Berlin, he had a "pleasant, smooth manner, and a vanity which likes to be appeased."[36]

SINCE AGRICULTURE WOULD be a key issue in FDR's 1932 presidential campaign, Raymond Moley thought his fellow Columbia University professor Rexford Guy Tugwell, an economist especially interested in agriculture, ought to be in the brain trust. Tugwell was born in Sinclairville, New York, in 1891. His father, Charles, was in the cattle and meat business, and when Rex was thirteen the family moved near Buffalo, where Charles developed an orchard. In 1911, Rex left western New York to enroll at the Wharton School of Finance and Commerce, at the University of Pennsylvania. One of his professors there was Scott Nearing, a socialist who was to influence many people over the years.

After receiving his B.A. in 1915, Tugwell became an economics instructor at the University of Pennsylvania. He earned an M.A., then began teaching at the University of Washington. He joined the faculty of Columbia University in 1920. There he met John Dewey, who believed that education should discourage individualism and promote collectivism. With his Ph.D. completed in 1922, Tugwell was promoted to assistant professor and became a full professor nine years later. Along the way, he began writing articles for the *New Republic*, which had begun in 1914 and published the work of "progressives" like Walter Lippmann, Charles Beard, and H. G. Wells. Many of Tugwell's friends were socialists in the League for Industrial Democracy.[37] During the summer of 1927, Tugwell visited the Soviet Union with a group of trade unionists and socialists, including Stuart Chase. In *American Economic Life and the Means of Its Improvement* (1928), written with Thomas Munro and Roy E. Stryker, Tugwell expressed admiration for the Soviet Union. Soviet central planning, he said, "appears to produce goods in greater quantities . . . and to spread such prosperity as there is over wider areas of the population,"[38] although he acknowledged that "ruthlessness, a disregard for liberties and rights" also existed.[39] Soon after the presidential election, in January 1933, Tugwell gave an interview with the *New York World-Telegram* in which he urged big tax increases to redistribute the wealth. "Take incomes from where they are and place them where we need them," he remarked.[40] Among FDR's advisers, Tugwell was the best-known advocate of central planning, and his political fortunes rose and fell with the National Recovery Administration, the New Deal's biggest attempt at central planning.

FARM STATE VOTES were crucial for FDR's electoral victories, and he picked Henry A. Wallace, a distinguished agricultural expert, to be his secretary of agriculture. Wallace had been born on an Iowa farm in 1888, and after graduation from Iowa State College, he went to work on *Wallace's Farmer*, a newspaper that his grandfather had started. He promoted hybrid corn to improve productivity, and he urged the government to provide relief for farmers, although he had opposed the Smoot-Hawley tariff (1930), which raised tariffs to record levels. He believed that the future of American civilization depended on continuing the agricultural tradition, and he supported policies that would encourage people to remain in agriculture. He was alarmed about the long-term trend in which more and more people left agriculture to find jobs in manufacturing and services.

As biographers John C. Culver and John Hyde wrote, "Rarely has a public figure's talent so perfectly matched his opportunity. Henry A. Wallace, born to a family whose very mission was the preservation of agriculture, had become the mobilizing general of just such an effort. The prophet of reform had become the agent of change; the thinker had become the doer. Few men knew more about agriculture than Wallace, and no man anywhere burned with greater zeal to rescue farmers from their cruel misfortune. This was Henry Wallace's hour."[41] The biographers expressed admiration for Wallace's "breathtaking energy level": "Operating on four hours' sleep, he regularly put in fourteen- to sixteen-hour days, working past midnight, arising at five, and briskly walking three miles. . . . There was also his extraordinary intellectual self-confidence. Long-time department employees had never seen a secretary deal with scientists and economists on their own terms, or rattle off facts and figures that almost always proved correct. . . . Most striking of all, however, was his zeal and sense of purpose. He brought to his task the solemn dedication of a crusading reformer."[42]

Wallace excelled as a spokesman for big commercial farmers who benefited from his Agricultural Adjustment Acts (1933, 1938), and he began speaking out on a wider range of issues. He supported New Deal policies aimed at city dwellers, cultivated a reputation as an all-around "liberal," won the support of labor unions, and became interested in international affairs. When FDR decided to run for a third term in 1940, he picked Wallace as his running mate. Wallace's views became too much for many Democrats to swallow, and in 1944 the Democratic convention selected Harry Truman for vice president when FDR ran for a fourth term.

MARRINER ECCLES DOMINATED Federal Reserve policy during the New Deal, and he emerged as the earliest advocate of views later associated with the British economist John Maynard Keynes—namely, that government spending, if there's enough of it, might stimulate recovery from a depression.

Eccles was that rarity among New Dealers, a businessman. He was considered politically legitimate because he didn't come from Wall Street. He was born in September 1890, in Logan, Utah, the oldest son of the second family of David Eccles, who had emigrated from Scotland and built successful businesses in lumber, livestock, sugar refining, railroads, and banking. Marriner inherited several businesses and expanded them. During the early years of the Great Depression, First Security Corporation, a bank run by Marriner, his brother George, and Idaho banker E. G. Bennett, remained open despite bank runs. Their bank didn't close until ordered to by FDR's March 1933 executive order. Long before anybody in America heard of Keynes, Marriner became convinced that the key to business recovery was government spending, and he pressed his views on a number of U.S. senators. He came to FDR's attention and helped draft the Banking Act of 1933, which, among other things, authorized federal deposit insurance.

Eccles thought the Great Depression happened because rich people controlled too much wealth. The rationale for this view was that as people earn more income, the percentage that they spend tends to go down, and the percentage saved and invested tends to go up. Eccles believed the key to business recovery was getting more money in the hands of average people, who spend a higher percentage of their earnings. In February 1933, he testified before the Senate Finance Committee and claimed that government spending was the most important policy for recovery.

Eccles moved to Washington in February 1934 and worked as an assistant to Treasury Secretary Henry Morgenthau, analyzing monetary issues. He also drafted the law establishing the Federal Housing Authority (FHA) to guarantee home mortgage loans issued by savings and loan associations. When FDR offered to appoint Eccles chairman of the Federal Reserve Board, he demanded more power over monetary policy. The Banking Act of 1935 made the changes Eccles had demanded. It established the Federal Reserve Board, which gained power at the expense of Federal Reserve regional banks, especially the New York bank. Eccles became the first Fed chairman. He stepped down in 1948, serving as vice chairman until 1951, then returned to private business.

JESSE HOLMAN JONES, another businessman who played a major role in the New Deal, was president of the Reconstruction Finance Corporation, which, during the New Deal, funded the Federal Emergency Relief Administration, the Home Owners' Loan Corporation, the Farm Credit Administration, the Regional Agricultural Credit Corporation, the Federal Home Loan Bank Board, the Federal Farm Mortgage Association, the Federal Housing Administration, the Rural Electrification Administration, and the Resettlement Administration. The RFC helped the Tennessee Valley Authority market electrical appliances through the Electric Farm and Home Authority. Among other government agencies the RFC started were the Export-Import Bank, the Commodity Credit Corporation, and the Federal National Mortgage Association.

"Like few other government officials in American history," observed historian James S. Olson, "he built the RFC in his own image, transforming it from a large, impersonal agency to a personal fiefdom. Jones was a powerful, imposing man. Tall by the standards of the 1930s, his huge chest and larger belly, covered with double-breasted suits, seemed to fill whatever room he entered. He was always in command. The round face topped with fine, grey-white hair was almost grandfatherly in appearance, except for those out-of-place thick, black eyebrows."[43]

Jones was born in 1874 in Robertson County, Tennessee. His family had been farmers for many generations, but his parents wanted him to get a good education, so they moved to Dallas, and his father began working for his brother's lumberyard. Jesse pursued a brief course of studies at Hill's Business College. He joined his uncle's business, did well, and, when his uncle died, acquired control. Meanwhile, he got involved with Democratic politics. He worked in the campaign to elect Woodrow Wilson president, and Wilson offered him the position of secretary of commerce. Jones declined, preferring to manage the Red Cross Military Relief Section in World War I. During the subsequent peace, Jones returned to private business and, among other things, purchased the *Houston Chronicle*. During the 1920s, Jones was a major fund-raiser for the Democratic Party.

In an effort to bring recovery from the Great Depression, President Herbert Hoover established the Reconstruction Finance Corporation to bail out banks. He appointed Jones to one of the Democratic positions on the board. Lending was extended to smaller banks. After FDR became president, he asked Jones to take over as chairman of the RFC. Jones hired many of the brightest New Dealers, including Adolf Berle, Benjamin Cohen, Thomas Corcoran, Jerome Frank, Paul Freund, and Stanley Reed.[44]

Historian Olson observed that Jones "managed to become a major center of power in Washington, the Great Depression's version of what Bernard Baruch had been during World War I," even though he never held an elected position. "Part of the power was simply a by-product of RFC loans. Throughout the 1930s, the RFC made thousands of loans in every congressional district, and those loans had usually gone to people of influence—bankers, businessmen, and political officials representing local government agencies. On any given day there was a line of senators and congressmen waiting outside his office, hoping for a moment to push one or more pending loan applications. Jones was always solicitous of them, always willing to listen, always prepared to turn on the Texas 'good old boy' charm, and always reminding them of pending legislation affecting his baby—the RFC."[45]

LAWYERS WERE HIGHLY visible in the New Deal. The most influential lawyer was Supreme Court justice Louis D. Brandeis, whose house FDR visited soon after the November 1932 presidential election.[46] Brandeis, a tall, trim, earnest man, turned seventy-six that year. He was perhaps the most famous advocate of using government power against businesspeople, whom he blamed for social evils. He came from a family of Austrian Jews who had settled in Kentucky and Wisconsin, where his father built a successful grain-trading business. He proved to be a diligent scholar; he entered Harvard Law School in 1875 and after graduation began practicing corporate law with Harvard classmate Samuel Warren. They prospered—thanks to Warren's connections and Brandeis's command of the details of a client's situation as well as the law.

Brandeis became an advocate of small businesspeople who were struggling to compete against big businesses. He didn't like the trend toward ever larger businesses serving millions of customers at home and abroad. Rexford Tugwell, recalling a conversation with Brandeis, noted in his diary: "Most of our talk concerned industrial philosophy; he arguing that bigness is always badness."[47]

In 1902, after helping to settle a strike at a shoe factory, Brandeis served as an advocate of compulsory unionism. He came to believe more government power could fix whatever was wrong with society, and in 1908 he submitted a brief to the U.S. Supreme Court defending an Oregon law that set maximum working hours for women. Brandeis made a name for himself by devoting only two pages of his brief to discussing legal precedents and over a hundred pages to presenting sociological data that purported to show that women suffered when working long hours.[48] This failure to rely on legal precedent may indicate that Brandeis concluded he couldn't win his case by citing previous court decisions or by arguing that the law was inconsistent with the U.S. Constitution.

Increasingly, Brandeis spoke out against big business. In 1913, he wrote *Other People's Money and How the Bankers Use It*, which denounced Wall Street financiers. President Woodrow Wilson named Brandeis to the U.S. Supreme Court in 1916, and he became a trusted presidential adviser. During the 1920s, Brandeis could be counted on to defend laws giving government more power over the economy. As businessmen became increasingly hostile to New Deal taxes and regulations, Brandeis snarled in a March 4, 1934, letter, "I wish he [FDR] had gone forward long ago with heavy taxation on the rich—reduction of big corporate powers and lessening dependence on banks and bankers. No policy can be safe which leaves the big fellows with the powers they still have. The only safety lies in disarming the enemy."[49]

BECAUSE OF HIS Supreme Court duties, Brandeis didn't spend a great deal of time offering presidential advice, but a number of his disciples did play a major role in the New Deal. Foremost among these was Felix Frankfurter. The five-foot-five-inch Harvard Law School professor had known FDR a long time and placed many of his students and associates in the Roosevelt administration, giving him immense influence. They were referred to as "happy hot dogs."[50]

Born in Vienna in 1882, Frankfurter came to the United States with his parents when he was twelve and lived on New York's Lower East Side. He couldn't speak English. Nonetheless, he graduated from the College of the City of New York, entered Harvard Law School, and subsequently joined a successful New York law firm. He liked politics better and started work in the U.S. Attorney's Office, New York. He became an adviser to Henry L. Stimson, who ran for governor. Stimson lost, but President William Howard Taft made Stimson secretary of war, and he brought Frankfurter to Washington as a law officer. Frankfurter argued cases before the Supreme Court and became friendly with Justices Brandeis and Oliver Wendell Holmes. Brandeis subsequently recommended that Frankfurter accept an offer to teach at Harvard Law School, and he started in 1914. Two years later, with journalists Herbert Croly and Walter Lippmann, Frankfurter launched the *New Republic*, a journal of opinion. He served as a judge advocate in the U.S. Army during World War I, then as chairman of the War Labor Board; during the war he met Assistant Secretary of the Navy Franklin D. Roosevelt.

Frankfurter went on to become one of the most controversial men in America. When Woodrow Wilson's attorney general, A. Mitchell Palmer, conducted raids against alleged communists, Frankfurter represented some of the defendants. He wrote commentary on controversial cases for *Harvard Law Review*, and a number of his lectures were published as books. He helped the National Association for the Advancement of Colored People. He declined FDR's offer to become solicitor general, figuring he would have more independence and ultimately more impact as a law professor. FDR turned to him for advice, and often FDR would tell an administration official, "If you need a very good lawyer, why don't you talk to Felix about it?"[51] He believed law should go beyond logic and precedent and become a tool for social betterment. He despised

Wall Street lawyers who served big business and grew rich. He advocated compulsory unionism and denounced businesspeople—especially bankers and public utilities.[52] In 1934, Frankfurter wrote FDR, hoping for an end to "the naïve talk that continues to go the rounds that the Administration should now concern itself only with 'recovery' and postpone 'reform' until later."[53]

FRANKFURTER'S BEST-KNOWN protégés were Thomas Gardiner Corcoran and Benjamin Victor Cohen. They became known as "the Gold Dust Twins" because they worked so well together, and for a while they lived together in Washington.[54] They drafted the Securities and Exchange Act (1934), the Public Utility Holding Company Act (1935), the Rural Electrification Act (1935), and the Fair Labor Standards Act (1938).[55]

Corcoran "was the aggressive partner of the team, fighting, cajoling, threatening, ready to do almost anything to advance the program," recalled Samuel Rosenman. "He had warmth and wit, and a keen and exuberant mind. Ben was more resourceful, a more careful and astute lawyer and a more philosophical thinker—but shy and reserved and constantly in the background. Tom stormed in and out of the White House with all sorts of news and ideas; but when he wanted a bill drawn or an order dressed up it was to Ben he turned, and Ben did it. Tom blew in and out of a Senator's office demanding a vote for a New Deal measure, having a good reason at the tip of his tongue to overcome any and all objections. But if the Senator wanted a documented brief for the bill or a scholarly statement of its merits, it was Ben who furnished it. . . . Each admired, adored, and respected the other."[56]

Corcoran, whom FDR dubbed "Tommy the Cork," was born in 1900, in Providence, Rhode Island.[57] He graduated from Brown University, and after earning his law degree at Harvard in 1926, he clerked for Supreme Court justice Oliver Wendell Holmes. Corcoran worked for five years as a Wall Street lawyer, gaining expertise about securities and holding companies. Having lost money in the

1929 stock crash and early depression,[58] Corcoran returned to Washington, where he worked for Hoover's Reconstruction Finance Corporation.

FDR asked Frankfurter to take charge of revising federal securities laws, and he delegated the task to Corcoran, Cohen, and James Landis. After a month's work, they produced the Truth in Securities Act (1933), which Congress quickly passed.

Corcoran subsequently left the RFC and became assistant secretary of the Treasury, then special assistant to the attorney general, exerting influence far beyond what might be suggested by his modest titles. In particular, he urged aggressive legal action against employers who were blamed for the Great Depression. He recruited several hundred lawyers to the Roosevelt administration, and they helped reinforce his views.[59]

FDR thought Corcoran would be the right man to help push the Public Utility Holding Company Act through Congress. In addition, he helped draft the Wealth Tax Act (1935), which sent the top federal income tax rate up to 75 percent. Corcoran had a gift for memorable phrases, and he joined FDR's speechwriting team during the 1936 campaign. His most famous contribution was "rendezvous with destiny."[60]

Cohen, the son of a Polish peddler, was born in Muncie, Indiana, in 1894. After graduating from the University of Chicago Law School (with the highest grades ever posted up to that time), he subsequently attended Harvard Law School.[61] There he did work for Frankfurter, who helped him land a job on the Shipping Board in President Woodrow Wilson's administration.[62] Cohen clerked for Julian Mack, a judge on the federal circuit court of New York. Because major bankruptcy cases came before this court, Cohen learned a great deal about corporate reorganization.

Cohen met Brandeis during World War I, and the men shared a passion for Palestine. Between 1919 and 1921, Cohen served as a lawyer for American Zionists. At the Paris Peace Conference, he negotiated parts of the settlement relating to Palestine.

Interior Secretary Harold Ickes appointed Cohen associate general counsel of the Public Works Administration. There he helped draft the Tennessee Valley Authority Act. In 1934, Cohen became counsel to the National Public Power Committee, where he defended the constitutionality of the Public Utility Holding Company Act. He also advised former bootlegger and Wall Street speculator Joseph P. Kennedy, after he became the first Securities and Exchange Commission chairman.

ICKES, LIKE COHEN, was a midwesterner who earned his law degree at the University of Chicago, after completing undergraduate studies there. He was a "progressive" Republican whom FDR tapped to take charge of New Deal public works projects. "Harold Ickes brought to the job," noted historian Linda J. Lear, "unsurpassed energy, ego, and administrative virtuosity. Roosevelt recognized and rewarded Ickes' gifts and tolerated his irascible, pugnacious personality because of them."[63]

Biographer T. H. Watkins described Ickes as "a short, slightly rotund, slightly rumpled character, bespectacled, sandy-haired, and pug-nosed, his square face characteristically fixed in a look that could have been halfway toward a scowl of outrage or hovering on the fringe of laughter—it was always hard to tell which."[64]

Ickes was born in 1874, on a Blair County, Pennsylvania, farm. At sixteen, following the death of his mother and the chronic depression of his debt-plagued father, Ickes sought his fortune in Chicago. He dabbled in Republican politics, starting with the 1897 campaign for mayor of Chicago. He made many friends and earned a reputation for honesty. Over the years, he had become convinced that a key to a prosperous economy was expanding electrical service, and he favored government-run electrical power producers. These views commended him to FDR, who named him secretary of the interior. Title II of the National Industrial Recovery Act, passed in June 1933, authorized a big public works spending program, and Ickes was put in charge of that.

*   *   *

SO THE NEW DEALERS were talented people. They worked long
hours during the years of crisis. They seemed to genuinely care
about the poor. Why, then, did their policies backfire and harm the
very people who were supposed to be helped? How was it possible
that their well-intended policies prolonged the Great Depression?

Some clues came from their way of thinking. New Dealers always seemed to be comparing actual capitalism with ideal government. They judged capitalism by its apparent effects and government
by its announced intentions. They liked to talk about the good that
might result from government spending, and they belittled the harm
that might result from government taxing. They assumed that
greedy private individuals caused the problems of the world, like
sweatshops, child labor, and depressions, and that the best remedies
would come from government officials who were generally presumed to be serving the public interest, not their self-interest. Of
course, New Dealers were aware that some government officials had
their limits, but there didn't seem to be any limits to the good that
government might do if it had enough power. Recalling their days in
President Woodrow Wilson's wartime administration, many New
Dealers thought the depressed economy of the 1930s could be made
to work by establishing bureaucracies and issuing commands. New
Dealers never appear to have considered the possibility that more
power would magnify the harm done by human error or corruption.

CHAPTER TWO

WHAT CAUSED THE
GREAT DEPRESSION?

O N JULY 1, 1927, the passenger ship *Mauretania* docked in
New York, with two powerful men whose names didn't appear on the passenger list. They were Montagu Norman, head of the
Bank of England, and Hjalmar Schacht, head of the German Reichs-
bank.[1] The following day, they went to the Long Island estate of U.S.
undersecretary of the Treasury Ogden Mills. There they made a decision that would help send the stock market to new highs. At the meeting, besides Mills, Norman, and Schacht, were Benjamin Strong,
governor of the Federal Reserve Bank of New York, and Charles Rist,
an economist representing the Bank of France.[2]

Strong, fifty-four, was the key man. "He was over six feet tall
and wiry and weighed about 150 pounds," wrote biographer Lester
V. Chandler. "It was only after tuberculosis forced him to give up
tennis and golf and to adhere to a diet that he gained the plumpness
shown in his later pictures. The flat planes and deep lines of his long
face, dominated by a large nose, suggested purpose, a strong will,
and even a capacity for ruthlessness. . . . Most of the time he was a
man of charm and warmth with a marked capacity for friendship.

He liked people, and they liked him. He had few intimate relationships; and as are some other powerful men he was ill at ease in intimate relationships but warm and charming in a group."[3]

Strong was dedicated to promoting the reconstruction of western Europe, some of which had been devastated by World War I. He was particularly eager to help Britain. Like most other countries, Britain had been on the gold standard, which penalized governments when they inflated their currencies, and Britain went off gold during World War I so that it could print enough money for war costs. After the war, Britain wanted to go back on the gold standard at its original rate, $4.86, because of pride as much as anything else—to show that Britain was still one of the world's greatest powers.

At the time, gold was flowing out of Britain to the United States, where interest rates were higher. Norman asked his friend Strong to keep interest rates low so that gold would flow to Britain, and the resulting demand for the pound would help support it at $4.86. Otherwise, British officials would be under pressure to acknowledge the consequences of wartime inflation and accept a humiliating devaluation. Furthermore, many Americans had substantial investments in British overseas territories (the British Empire) and were concerned about being repaid in devalued British pounds.

Discussions at Ogden Mills's estate made clear that Schacht wouldn't agree to help Britain, and Rist apparently suggested that Emile Moreau, the French inspector general of finances, wouldn't agree to help either, so Strong decided to do what he could on his own. Despite his concerns about the booming stock market, he secured a cut in the discount rate, at which the Federal Reserve Bank of New York would lend money to Federal Reserve member banks, from 4 percent to 3 percent. Then he paid the Bank of England gold to buy 12 million British pounds, supporting the currency.[4] One effect was to make bonds less attractive investments than stocks, and the stock market, which already had had quite a boom during the 1920s, moved higher.

In addition to cutting the discount rate and selling gold, Strong prodded the Federal Reserve Open Market Investment Committee to buy $200 million worth of government securities from banks, injecting that much cash into the banking system. "The easy-money policy," reported Strong's biographer Lester V. Chandler, "seems to have contributed to the quick recovery of business in the United States, and it was clearly of assistance to western Europe. Capital outflows from the United States were stimulated, gold inflows were stopped and some outflows achieved, the pound was so strengthened in exchange markets."[5]

However, as historian James S. Olson explained, government power, in this case the power of central bankers, magnified the consequences of human error: "Federal Reserve officials incorrectly assumed that the method of expanding the money supply guaranteed the uses of the funds. They thought they could discourage speculation with high discount rates while stimulating economic growth through heavy purchases of [securities]."[6]

Much of the easy money found its way into the stock market, and by 1928, a number of Federal Reserve officials had become concerned that stock market speculation was out of hand. The discount rate was raised to 5 percent. In August 1929, following Strong's death from tuberculosis in October 1928 (he was fifty-six), this was raised to 6 percent. According to Milton Friedman and Anna Jacobson Schwartz, in their 860-page *A Monetary History of the United States, 1867–1960*, "There is no doubt that the desire to curb the stock market boom was a major if not dominating factor in Reserve actions during 1928 and 1929. Those actions clearly failed to stop the stock market boom. But they did exert steady deflationary pressure on the economy."[7]

The October 1929 stock crash made clear that the Fed had overplayed its hand. The problem here, as always, was that it takes time for a change in Fed monetary policy to have an effect on the economy, and nobody knows in advance how big the effect might be and how long it might take to become apparent. Without realizing that one measure is having an effect not yet apparent, an anxious central banker could authorize another action that ended up compounding a problem and disrupting the entire economy.

These Federal Reserve policies began a monetary contraction. As the contraction became more severe, it brought on a depression in output, employment, and income. If nothing else had happened, there would have been a depression because of the severe monetary contraction.

As Friedman and Schwartz reported, "The contraction from 1929 to 1933 was by far the most severe business-cycle contraction during the near-century of U.S. history we cover, and it may well have been the most severe in the whole of U.S. history. . . . U.S. net national product in constant prices fell by more than one-third. . . . From the cyclical peak in August 1929 to the cyclical trough in March 1933, the stock of money fell by over a third. . . . At the trough of the depression one person was unemployed for every three employed."[8]

THE DEPRESSION BECAME worse because the monetary contraction put increasing pressure on banks. The number of bank failures increased, in part, because banks operated (and still do) on what were known as fractional reserves. The amount of cash banks kept on hand was a small percentage of what people had deposited. The rest of the money was loaned out to earn interest for the depositors and the banks, often for a number of years. Fractional reserve banking worked fine when the demand for cash was limited, but many banks weren't strong enough to handle massive withdrawals. When banks couldn't raise money by calling in or selling their long-term loans, they failed.

To be sure, bank failures had been accelerating since the end of World War I. During the 1920s, some 600 banks failed annually.[9] "Nearly all the banks that went broke during the ten boom years of the twenties were small," observed Jesse Jones of the Reconstruction Finance Corporation. "Only 12 per cent had a capitalization above $100,000, and 40 per cent were village establishments started with less than $25,000."[10] During the Great Depression, 90 percent of failed banks were in small towns.[11]

Almost all the failed banks were in states with unit banking laws that suppressed competition. Those laws prohibited a bank from opening branches. Country bankers had lobbied for unit banking laws because they were afraid they would be driven out of business if big-city banks opened branches everywhere. But this policy of suppressing competition guaranteed that the country bankers would be highly vulnerable in a monetary contraction. Unit banking laws backfired badly.

Restricted by unit banking laws, small-town banks found it almost impossible to diversify their loan portfolios and their sources of deposits. Bank customers generally preferred working with a local office, which meant that small-town banks couldn't effectively solicit customers in different regions. When a small-town bank's region—say, the Corn Belt—got in economic trouble, the bank was unlikely to survive. Its principal depositors were corn farmers who went broke and needed to draw down their deposits. Corn farmers were also the principal borrowers and couldn't make the payments on their loans.

Small-town bankers thought competition and big-city bankers were their enemies, whereas they should have been most concerned about a monetary contraction. Surviving a monetary contraction required becoming bigger (combining with other small-town banks) and opening branches, thereby diversifying loan portfolios and sources of funds. By successfully lobbying for unit banking laws, small-town bankers helped wipe themselves out.

Ironically, the lobbying success of small-town bankers seemed to have little effect on big-city bankers. While the big-city bankers were denied additional income they might have earned from a branching system, their loan portfolios and depositors were already substantially diversified, since most big cities include a variety of industries. Relatively few big-city banks failed during the Great Depression.

Although the United States, with its unit banking laws, had thousands of bank failures, Canada, which permitted branch banking, didn't have a single failure during the Great Depression. Unrestricted by unit banking laws, Canadian banks diversified their sources of funding and loaned money to a diverse range of borrowers, so they were in a better position to survive if a particular industry or region went through hard times. In Canada, Friedman and Schwartz observed, "10 banks with 3,000-odd branches throughout the country did not even experience any runs, although, presumably as a preventative measure, an eleventh chartered bank with a small number of branches was merged with a larger bank in May 1931."[12]

Friedman pointed out, however, that "Canada experienced roughly the same decline in the quantity of money as the United States and had a depression of essentially the same severity. Had the ... banking structure [in the United States] been the same as Canada's rather than the unit banks, there would have been few if any bank failures, no banking holidays, and yet the depression would have been as serious."[13]

While state unit banking laws caused most of the harm in the United States, federal laws, too, limited the ability of banks to diversify. The 1927 McFadden Act, for instance, empowered the states to restrict the branching of Federal Reserve member banks, and these were prohibited from establishing branches across state lines.

The first banking "holiday" of the Great Depression was declared by Nevada governor Frederick Balzar (who also signed Nevada's open gambling law and six-week divorce law).[14] Balzar's banking "holiday" began November 1, 1932, and lasted twelve days, but it didn't start a trend.[15]

Economic historian Elmus Wicker contended that the banking panic that developed in early 1933 accelerated and spread because one state governor after another ordered bank holidays. Michigan governor William A. Comsock began the stampede with an eight-day bank holiday beginning February 14, 1933. He acted to protect the Guardian Group of twenty-one banks, in which the Ford family had a substantial interest. Since people needed cash and nobody knew how long the banks might be closed, naturally there was a rush to get cash. As governors in Indiana, Ohio, Illinois, and Pennsylvania panicked, increasing numbers of depositors in other states became worried that suddenly they might be cut off from cash, and they sought withdrawals from their banks.

Wicker explained, "Bank moratoria introduced a new source of depositor uncertainty. In the conventional panic depositor uncertainty had its origin in the questionable solvency of more than one bank. Bank moratoria created additional uncertainty among depositors about when and if state banking officials would close all the banks in a particular state. Moreover, the restrictions on deposit withdrawals increased the demands for currency. The bank holiday was the mechanism for transmitting banking unrest from state to state. The declaration of a banking holiday in one state motivated depositors to withdraw deposits from out-of-state banks to meet their immediate transaction needs thereby transmitting withdrawal pressures to contiguous states and to the New York and Chicago money markets. Moreover, depositors in surrounding states became alarmed that similar deposit restrictions would be imposed in their states and would therefore rush to withdraw deposits in anticipation of a bank moratorium."[16]

THE BANK HOLIDAYS and the monetary contraction were embarrassing indictments of the Federal Reserve System, which had been established on November 16, 1914, to keep America's financial system going even in bad times. To be sure, the Federal Reserve didn't start out as a central bank. It was an association of regional Federal Reserve banks and a Federal Reserve Board, which mainly supervised the banks. The Federal Reserve Bank of New York handled such monetary policy as there was. A Federal Open Market Committee and a Fed chairman didn't come until 1935. At its inception, the

Fed was "a strange hybrid, a mixture of private and public management operating with very unclear lines of authority and with very little centralization," according to economist Allan Meltzer. "Each of the twelve Reserve banks was expected to be semi-autonomous, setting its own discount rate and free to decide whether it wished to participate in system policies." Although this comment suggests the situation would have been better with more Fed centralization, Meltzer stressed that Fed officials misinterpreted the data they were looking at. They didn't understand that the contracting money supply was a danger sign.[17] So regardless of how much or little centralization there might have been, if officials in charge were misinterpreting data, there could be terrible consequences. The Great Depression was a government failure.

Benjamin Strong's successor at the New York Federal Reserve Bank, George Harrison, was an amiable lawyer and administrator. He urged other Federal Reserve bankers to provide more aggressive support for the banking system, but they rebuffed him, and after a while he stopped pushing his views.[18] Fed governor Roy Young resigned, his place taken by investor and entrepreneur Eugene Meyer, who had made a fortune estimated at over $40 million and then during World War I served on the War Industries Board and the War Finance Corporation. Meyer, wrote biographer Merlo J. Pusey, "was known as a man of ideas, a brilliant conversationalist, and a generous benefactor."[19] But Meyer couldn't persuade his fellow Fed governors to inject more cash into the financial system, either.

What were the other Fed governors thinking? Friedman and Schwartz explained that while New York was a U.S. money market and a world money market, "The other Banks were much more parochial in both situation and outlook, more in the position of reacting to financial currents originating elsewhere, more concerned with their immediate regional problems, and hence more likely to believe that the Reserve System must adjust to other forces that it could and should take the lead. They had no background of leadership and national responsibility. Moreover, they tended to be jealous of New York and predisposed to question what New York proposed."[20]

In addition, the Fed subscribed to what was known as the "real bills" doctrine: The primary purpose of the Fed was to help member banks provide for the needs of trade. The Fed would consider helping a bank only if it were a member of the Federal Reserve System, if it were basically sound, and if it had a significant portion of assets in commercial paper (short-term loans to businesses). From the Fed's point of view, as the economy contracted, less bank credit was needed to meet the needs of trade.[21]

Also, keep in mind that the Federal Reserve Board was a committee of seven bank officials. Each considered himself an equal of the others, an important man in his own region of the United States. Committees tended to move slowly, and it was always easier to do nothing than agree on bold action. Inertia was a perennial problem. Friedman and Schwartz noted that the Board hadn't previously taken the lead for Fed policy: "It had been primarily a supervisory and review body."[22]

In 1932, a number of congressmen criticized the Fed for not acting, and it did make some big purchases of government securities, thereby injecting cash into the banking system. It was slow to have an effect, and the Fed didn't take further action.[23] Fed officials failed to understand, as Friedman later documented, that a change in the money supply could take many months, perhaps a couple of years, before having a measurable impact on the overall economy.

BECAUSE THE GREAT Depression occurred despite the presence of the Federal Reserve System, most economists at the time concluded that monetary policy was ineffective. Nobody seemed to realize that monetary policy hadn't really been tried. As a consequence, economists turned their attention to other possible cures for the depression, particularly government spending. The importance of monetary policy wasn't fully appreciated until Friedman published his findings in the 1950s and 1960s.

When *A Monetary History of the United States* was published in 1963, the prevailing view in the economics profession, the view associated with Keynes, still was that changes in the money supply didn't have much effect on changes in the economy. Most books about the Great Depression have repeated the views of FDR and his New Dealers, that the Great Depression was caused by wild speculators, crooked bankers, and rich people hoarding their money rather than spending it. These views have continued to appear even in recent history books. For instance, in *FDR* (1985) biographer Ted Morgan railed against "economic royalists" much as FDR did.[24] Kenneth S. Davis's *FDR: The New Deal Years, 1933–1937* (1986) didn't mention Friedman's findings.[25] Nor did Frank Freidel's *Franklin D. Roosevelt: Rendezvous with Destiny* (1990) or T. H. Watkins's *The Great Depression: America in the 1930s* (1993).

Meanwhile, Friedman seems to have convinced most economists that changes in the money supply have at least some influence on changes in the economy, even if not everybody considers money the most important single factor. Keynesian economist James Tobin concluded his twenty-one-page article about the work in the *American Economic Review* by saying, "This is one of those rare books that leave their mark on all future research on the subject."[26] Nobel laureate Robert Lucas cited "its beautiful time series on the money supply and its components, extended back to 1867, painstakingly documented and conveniently presented." Writing in the *Journal of Monetary Economics,* he reflected on the book thirty years later: "Such a gift to the profession merits a long life, perhaps even immortality. But I think it is clear that *A Monetary History* served the purpose that any narrative history must serve: It told a coherent story of important events, and told it well." As for the main contention that monetary fluctuations explain major economic events, Lucas added, "I will say that I find the argument of *A Monetary History* wholly convincing . . . I find their diagnosis of the 1929–33 downturn persuasive and indeed uncontested by serious alternative diagnoses, and remain deeply impressed with their success in explaining the remarkable events of these four years."[27]

Peter Temin, of the Massachusetts Institute of Technology, was among the best-known dissenters from the Friedman view of the Great Depression. Temin's views were generally associated with those of Keynes. Temin made a case that a drop in consumer spending best explained the contraction between 1929 and 1933. What caused that? Temin believed there wasn't enough data to be sure, but he ended up agreeing that the Federal Reserve was a principal culprit.[28]

Economist Paul Krugman went so far as to say that "Nowadays practically the whole spectrum of economists, from Milton Friedman leftward, agrees that the Great Depression was brought on by a collapse of effective demand and that the Federal Reserve should have fought the slump with large injections of money."[29]

The Federal Reserve might have contributed to the Great Depression merely by undermining the apparent urgency of major banks to take initiative and organize bailouts as had been done in the past. As economists Thomas E. Hall and J. David Ferguson explained, "The very existence of the Federal Reserve caused banks to wait for the central bank to act and not turn to the solution they had devised in the face of the banking crises of the nineteenth century. . . . The clearinghouse banks [which process checks for other banks] looked to the Federal Reserve to act and did not create clearinghouse certificates or lend to the banks under pressure of withdrawals. They stood by and waited forlornly for the rescue that never came."[30]

CHAPTER THREE

WHAT DID FDR BORROW

FROM HOOVER?

PRESIDENT HERBERT HOOVER understood even less about the catastrophic contraction than did the Federal Reserve Board, which had helped bring it about. Nonetheless, he took action. He didn't stand idly by, as some critics suggested, watching passively as America sank into a depression.

"Herbert Hoover was intelligent, experienced, humane, the best product of what we have referred to as the old conscientiousness," historian Page Smith wrote. "He was, in practical fact, one of the best known and most admired men in the world: the Great Engineer, the Great Humanitarian. His liberal credentials were unimpeachable."[1] In 1920, FDR himself had described Hoover as "certainly a wonder," adding "I wish we could make him President of the United States. There could not be a better one."[2]

Born the son of a Cedar County, Iowa, Quaker blacksmith on August 10, 1874, Herbert Clark Hoover grew up poor. Both of his parents died by the time he was ten. He went to live with his uncle in Oregon and then entered Stanford University. After graduation, he worked in a California mine and became a mining engineer. He helped develop coal mines and port facilities in China. Back in the United States, he started his own engineering consulting firm, which prospered; and during World War I he was able to focus his time on war relief. He formed an organization that helped arrange travel to the United States for some 120,000 Americans who were stranded in Europe. Then Hoover organized the Commission for the Relief of Belgium, helping to save many lives. After the United States entered World War I, Hoover headed the federal Food Administration—which President Woodrow Wilson established with an executive order. The Food Administration gained control over the distribution of food. Hoover had many dealings with other wartime agencies, particularly the War Finance Corporation, the War Industries Board, and the War Trade Board. Along with others who served in Wilson's wartime administration, Hoover had concluded that the vast power of the U.S. government could do wonders during an emergency.

HOOVER EMBRACED THE idea, too, that America could get out of a depression by maintaining high wages—which meant "purchasing power" to help businesses recover. Hardly anybody seems to believe the "high-wages" doctrine anymore, so it's hard to appreciate the influence this once had. Henry Ford helped popularize the idea in 1914, when he announced that he had started paying his employees $5 a day—about double the prevailing wage rate. During the 1920s, Ford began paying $6 per day; and as the Great Depression set in, he upped this to $7 per day. He was one of the world's richest men, so it appeared that high wages were a formula for successful business.[3] Ford explained in *My Life and Work* (1922), "If we can distribute high wages, then that money is going to be spent and it will serve to make storekeepers and distributors and manufacturers and workers in other lines more prosperous and their prosperity will be reflected in our sales. Country-wide high wages spells country-wide prosperity."[4]

A number of economists of the day defended the high-wage doctrine. For instance, J. A. Hobson wrote in 1930, "Increased purchasing power by high wages is seen to be essential."[5] According to Irving Fisher (1930), "the underlying theory [of expanding] the purchasing power of the masses of the consumers [is] altogether sound."[6]

Though not a great orator, Hoover wasn't at all the helpless figure portrayed in some history books. He called conferences of industrial leaders and urged them to maintain high wages. Among the leaders were Henry Ford, Alfred Sloan (General Motors), Julius Rosenwald (Sears, Roebuck), Walter Teagle (Standard Oil), and William Butterworth (United States Chamber of Commerce). Hoover believed that the brunt of the contraction should hit profits rather than wages.[7]

Some perceptive observers recognized that Hoover's effort to maintain wages above market levels was a disaster. John T. Flynn, writing in the January 1933 *Harper's Magazine*, insisted that "Prices must come down to bring goods closer to the size of the available income. . . . income itself must be freed for purchasing by the extinguishments of excessive debts. Whether we like it or not, this is what takes place. Any attempt to hold up prices or to save the weaker debtors necessarily prolongs the depression."[8]

The fundamental fallacy in the high-wages doctrine was it didn't increase total purchasing power (the money supply). If businesses increased the amount of money paid out as wages, then employees had more money to spend, but businesses and their shareholders had less money to spend. A high-wages policy might affect the distribution of business revenue, not the total amount of purchasing power in an economy.

HOOVER THOUGHT GOVERNMENT spending could help get America out of the depression. He urged state governors to spend money on public works projects. New York governor Franklin D. Roosevelt pledged his support.[9] But not much came of this,[10] presumably because governors had other budget priorities. In any case, public works projects tended to require people with construction skills, so they weren't an effective way to help unskilled poor people.

Hoover increased farm subsidies, but the fundamental problem was that too many farmers were cultivating too many acres. American agriculture had expanded dramatically when World War I disrupted production in Europe. The grain that Russia used to supply, for instance, had to come from the United States, Canada, and Australia. The revival of European agricultural production after the war meant there was overcapacity elsewhere.[11] In addition, many countries didn't end all the government controls that had multiplied during World War I, and afterward many markets were substantially closed to exports, including American agricultural products.

Because American farmers lobbied aggressively for subsidies to avoid as many cutbacks as possible, they continued to be burdened with excess capacity and low prices during the 1920s. As late as 1926, President Calvin Coolidge agreed to support government purchases of cotton with the aim of maintaining cotton prices. Hoover, who was then secretary of commerce, administered programs to subsidize farmers. In 1930, Congress authorized the Federal Farm Board to increase its farm subsidies by about $100 million. The biggest program involved wheat. The unintended consequence was more farm surpluses, further depressing agricultural prices.[12]

MEANWHILE, IN 1929 the House Ways and Means Committee followed up a statement that Hoover had made during the recent campaign, on October 28, 1928, that he would welcome higher tariffs for agricultural commodities. But it soon became apparent that higher tariffs couldn't be limited to agricultural commodities. Every conceivable interest group wanted higher tariffs to prevent American customers from buying things made outside the United States. As a lobbyist for the Silk Association remarked, "I have never felt that it was a consistent position for one man to try and advocate duties for his own products and object to duties for another person." By the time the hearings had concluded, there were nearly 20,000 pages of testimony.[13]

On June 17, 1930, Hoover signed the Smoot-Hawley tariff, which raised import duties an average of 59 percent[14] on more than 25,000 agricultural commodities and manufactured goods.[15] The U.S. stock market plunged, and more than sixty countries retaliated with restrictions against whichever products would inflict the worst losses on Americans—typically products very different from those affected by Smoot-Hawley. In this way, the tariff led to random damage to economies everywhere.

The Smoot-Hawley tariff began by outraging the United States' neighbors. "The tariff on halibut was doubled, thus offending the eastern provinces of Canada," explained Joseph M. Jones Jr. in his classic study, *Tariff Retaliation*. "The tariff duties on potatoes, on milk, cream, buttermilk, skimmed milk, and butter were all radically increased, thus antagonizing the populations of Quebec and Ontario; the prairie and western provinces were provoked by increased duties on cattle, fresh meats, wheat and other grains; British Columbia and Alberta were infuriated by increases in the duties on apples, logs, and lumber."[16]

In Britain, long the greatest champion for free trade and prosperity, Smoot-Hawley helped provoke a protectionist reaction that led to the Import Duties Act (1932), the country's first general tariff law in more than a century. Part II of the Import Duties bill provided 100 percent tariffs on goods from countries like the United States that penalized British goods.[17]

Because the Smoot-Hawley tariff excluded cork, which accounted for more than half of Spain's exports to the United States, Spain increased tariffs on American cars by 150 percent, enough to shut American cars out of the Spanish market. The Smoot-Hawley tariff hit Italy's principal exports to the United States, including raw cotton, wheat, copper, and leather; and Italy retaliated by more than doubling its tariffs on American cars. Sales of American cars in Italy subsequently dropped 90 percent. Italy also increased tariffs on American radios more than 500 percent. France responded to the

Smoot-Hawley tariff with import quotas that together with its tariffs, business taxes, and other obstacles shut American goods out of
the French market. By 1934, France had restricted the import of
more than 3,000 items with quotas. Austria cut imports from the
United States with a tax on American cars and a licensing scheme
that discriminated against American movies. The Smoot-Hawley
tariff affected just about every Swiss export to the United States,
watches in particular. A tenth of the Swiss population was involved in
the watch business, and 95 percent of Swiss watches were exported.
There was popular support for a Swiss boycott, expressed by this edi-
torial in the *Gazette de Lausanne*: "we ask all the INDUSTRIALS,
ARTISANS, MERCHANTS, AND CONSUMERS to ban from their
OFFICES, FACTORIES, WORKSHOPS, GARAGES, STORES, and
HOMES all merchandise coming from the United States."[18]

Smoot-Hawley probably encouraged many governments to interfere with economic life in other ways. While the principal factor
in such interference was lobbying by local interest groups seeking to
suppress competition, Smoot-Hawley made the task easier by inflaming nationalist sentiment against the United States. For instance,
exchange control involved government restrictions on the freedom
of people to obtain foreign currency for travel or trade. "The years
from 1931 on," explained historian Margaret S. Gordon, "wit-
nessed a revival of exchange control on an unprecedented scale. Few
indeed were the countries which succeeded in passing through the
'great' depression without resort to some exchange restrictions,
if only for a short period, and in many countries severe and far-
reaching systems of control were adopted. The technique of restriction was refined and elaborated, and a complicated mass of
administrative regulations grew up. . . . In addition, exchange control has, for a number of countries, become a convenient weapon of
commercial policy, often discriminatory in nature." By 1935, exchange controls had been enacted in Afghanistan, Argentina, Austria, Bolivia, Brazil, Chile, China, Colombia, Costa Rica, Cuba,
Czechoslovakia, Danzig, Ecuador, El Salvador, Finland, Germany,

Greece, Hong Kong, Hungary, Iceland, Japan, Latvia, Lithuania, Luxembourg, Mexico, Netherlands, New Zealand, Nicaragua, Paraguay, Poland, Rumania, Uruguay, Venezuela, and Yugoslavia.[19] Exchange control on a large scale hadn't been commonplace for perhaps 400 years.

Smoot-Hawley was particularly destructive because the United States was the world's largest creditor. While demanding that debtors make their payments, the United States made it more difficult for them to do so. Farmers, who had lobbied so hard for Smoot-Hawley, saw their exports plunge from the 1929 pre–Smoot-Hawley $1.8 billion to $590 million just four years later.[20] This contributed to the catastrophic downward spiral of business nearly everywhere.[21]

Infinitely worse than the loss of export sales were the political consequences of these trade restrictions run amuck. By spreading misery abroad, higher U.S. trade barriers provoked mass xenophobia and set the stage for brutal dictators. "The high tariff," recalled FDR's undersecretary of state, Sumner Welles, "rolled up unemployment in Great Britain and in Western Europe. [It] encouraged the German government to adopt its autarchic economic policy, which in turn was a contributing factor in bringing about the second World War."[22]

DEMOCRATS AS WELL as Republicans seemed oblivious to the unfolding catastrophes abroad. They focused on the domestic crisis. Hoover authorized the President's Emergency Relief Organization to help coordinate local, private relief efforts. As a result, some 3,000 relief committees were formed across the United States. But funds were limited, and some 7 million people remained unemployed.[23]

Because so many home buyers defaulted on their mortgages during the Great Depression, Hoover aimed to strengthen savings and loan associations by signing into law the Federal Home Loan Bank Act on July 22, 1932. This established the Federal Home Loan Bank System, which was intended to support S&Ls much the way the Federal Reserve System was supposed to support commercial banks. A Federal Home Loan Bank Board chartered and regulated federal S&Ls. The United States was divided into twelve FHLBS districts, each with a Federal Home Loan Bank authorized to borrow money based on federal credit and lend to federal S&Ls in its district. In exchange for this support, S&Ls were restricted to making mortgage loans, and they could solicit business only within fifty miles of their home office. S&Ls weren't permitted to diversify their portfolios by issuing mortgages in other regions or serving other kinds of borrowers.[24]

In fact, S&Ls had sought the limits on their market area. Back in the 1890s, national savings and loan associations solicited deposits by mail and issued loans through networks of branch offices, and local savings and loan associations fought back by lobbying their state legislatures for market area restrictions that would stop the competition from national associations. This lobbying effort was comparable to that of small-town commercial bankers who sought state unit banking laws aimed at preventing big-city banks from opening branches.

Hoover urged bankers to form a National Credit Corporation that might raise $500 million from strong banks and use the proceeds for helping banks in trouble. He suggested that the NCC should be empowered to borrow another $1 billion. He told members of Congress that if the NCC weren't enough, he would consider rechartering the War Finance Corporation.[25] Hoover's friend Eugene Meyer, who had been a director of the War Finance Corporation, warned that more would be needed than the NCC could provide.

Some business leaders were lobbying for a scheme involving government-enforced cartels. Among the best-known advocates was General Electric president Gerard Swope. He urged that antitrust laws be suspended and that the government support businesses that wanted to pursue "cooperative planning" rather than the "uncoordinated, unplanned, disorderly individualism" of free markets."[26] Swope urged that "the industry no longer operate in independent

units, but as a whole, according to rules laid out by a trade association of which every unit employing over fifty men is a member—the whole supervised by some Federal agency like the Federal Trade Commission."[27] General Electric chairman Owen Young more candidly acknowledged that government planning of the economy involved "the voluntary surrender of a certain amount of individual freedom by the majority and the ultimate coercion of the minority."[28]

Newspaper columnist Walter Lippmann recognized what all this involved: "Centralized control is of the very essence of planning. For how else can 'a plan' be put into effect?" In June 1933, Swope's idea became the National Industrial Recovery Act, the climax of FDR's First New Deal.

But despite the enormous influence of World War I experiences on the thinking of Hoover and his associates, he wasn't willing to go as far as Swope wanted. In January 1932, Congress passed the Reconstruction Finance Corporation Act, which authorized the lending of taxpayer money to banks and later other businesses. The first president of the Reconstruction Finance Corporation was Eugene Meyer.

"The RFC was a direct descendent of the War Finance Corporation," explained historian James S. Olson. "Like the WFC, it had eight divisions: auditing, legal, treasury, secretarial, agency, examining, statistical, and railroad. Like the WFC, the RFC had thirty-three local offices to evaluate loan applications. Eugene Meyer recruited WFC people to staff the RFC."[29]

During the first half of 1932, the RFC loaned about $1 billion, an estimated 80 percent to banks and railroads.[30] Some of the loans went to banks headed by leading Republicans, like Charles Dawes's Central Republic Bank (Chicago) and Joseph R. Nutt's Union Trust Company (Cleveland).[31] Many of the loans were kept secret, but of the disbursements that are known, most went for repaying debt, the rest for making improvements. As a result of criticism of RFC lending practices, it began lending to agricultural credit organizations and to states for public works projects and unemployment relief.[32]

Regardless of how the RFC was administered, it didn't come close to compensating for the blunders of the Federal Reserve, which had triggered the monetary contraction and stood by as it worsened. The less than $1 billion of RFC loans was dwarfed by the one-third contraction of the money supply that the Federal Reserve didn't do much about.

Economist Joseph Russell Mason made the case that the RFC undermined many of the banks it intended to help. "There exists no evidence that loan assistance had any positive effect on bank survival," he explained. He went on to say that because the RFC required banks to reserve a significant portion of their assets as collateral for RFC loans in 1932, survival actually became more difficult. "I attribute the destabilizing influence to the over-collateralization of loans, wherein the RFC created liquidity problems for the banks it sought to assist," Mason maintained.[33]

Next came the Emergency Relief and Construction Act (July 1932), America's first federal law providing for unemployment relief. States borrowed money from the RFC and expanded their relief programs from $547,000 in 1930–1931 to $57 million in 1931–1932 and $90 million in 1932–1933.[34]

CONCERNED ABOUT BUDGET deficits because of increased spending, Hoover urged Congress to enact higher taxes, and the result was the Revenue Act of 1932, one of the biggest tax increases in American history. "The range of tax increases was enormous," wrote economic historian Murray N. Rothbard. "Many wartime excise taxes were revived, sales taxes were imposed on gasoline, tires, autos, electric energy, malt, toiletries, furs, jewelry, and other articles; admission and stock transfer taxes were increased; new taxes were levied on bank checks, bond transfers, telephone, telegraph, and radio messages; and the personal income tax was raised drastically as follows: the normal rate was increased from a range of 1^{1}/2 per cent to 5 per cent, to 4 per cent to 8 per cent; personal exemptions were sharply reduced, and an earned credit of 25 per cent eliminated; and surtaxes were raised enormously, from a maximum of 25 per cent to 63 per cent on the highest incomes. Furthermore, the corporate income tax was increased from 12 per cent to 13¾ per cent, and an exemption for small corporations eliminated; the estate tax was doubled, and the exemption floor halved; and the gift tax, which has been eliminated, was restored, and graduated up to 33½ per cent. . . . The raising of postal rates burdened the public further and helped swell the revenues of a compulsory governmental monopoly."[35] All this meant that consumers had less money to spend, and investors had less money to help finance business recovery and productive jobs.

These new federal taxes came on top of state and local taxes, which had increased sharply, and the pain was worse because of the monetary contraction—people had less money. Historian David Beito reported, "As a percentage of the national income, perhaps the most pertinent measure of the burden's impact, taxes nearly doubled from 11.6 percent in 1929 to 21.1 in 1932. In just three years, the tax load on the American people increased more than it had in the 1920s. Not even during World War I had taxes ever taken such a large percentage of the national income. Taxes at the local level more than doubled, rising from 5.4 percent of the national income in 1929 to an unheard of 11.7 percent in 1932. Surging even faster, state taxes went from 1.9 percent in 1929 to 4.6 percent in 1932."[36]

To protect themselves, people increasingly held on to whatever money they had, and Hoover thought that was unpatriotic. He denounced "hoarders" for threatening America's credit system. He urged people to put their money in U.S. Treasury securities rather than private investments that would make it possible to create more productive jobs.[37]

Tax revolts occurred across the United States. Increasingly, when the local government officials gave up trying to collect taxes from delinquent farmers, there were auctions for the right to collect whatever revenue might be extracted, but the auctions were often disrupted. Journalist Anne O'Hare McCormick reported, "Wherever you go you run into mass meetings called to protest against taxes. . . . taxpayers are wrought up to the point of willingness to give up public services."[38]

The National Association of Real Estate Boards helped form local chapters to fight high taxes. According to some estimates, there were more than 1,000 taxpayer organizations. In New York City, Beito reported, "The West Side Taxpayers' Association (WSTA) led off the militant forces with a resolution in March 1932 encouraging taxpayers to withhold their 1932 taxes. As a corollary, it called for reductions in municipal salaries, the lowering of assessments to reflect market value more nearly, and a boost in fares to make the subways self-supporting." People elsewhere organized tax strikes. Voters approved ballot initiatives limiting taxes.[39]

The best-documented tax revolt was in Chicago. On a single day, November 29, 1930, some 4,000 taxpayers filed protests with the Board of Review. Tax collections were suspended for two years, but it proved difficult to get people back in the habit of paying. The Chicago Association of Real Estate Taxpayers (ARET), promoted by the radio broadcasts of John M. Pratt, expressed solidarity with those who refused to pay their taxes, and it filed nine lawsuits involving thousands of plaintiffs who challenged the legitimacy of the taxes. A lower court ordered the Board of Review to hear appeals from an estimated 30,000 taxpayers. ARET opened 161 branch offices throughout Chicago where taxpayers could sign up to support its efforts. One of the ARET cases was rejected by the Illinois Supreme Court, but in a non-ARET case County Judge Edmund Jarecki declared that 1928 and 1929 tax assessments were invalid, because they were applied unequally.[40]

One political response was a plan drafted by D. F. Kelly, a director of Continental Illinois Bank, which would replace the elected Board of Review with a Tax Board of Appeals, whose two members would be appointed and perhaps less responsive to popular pressures against taxes. Labor unions representing government employees supported the Kelly plan, while unions representing private sector taxpayers opposed it. Bankers refused to extend more credit to the city government unless it had more assurance of collecting taxes, and Chicago's major newspapers all backed the government.[41]

Chicago mayor Anton Cermak threatened to withhold government-provided water and police protection from those who didn't pay taxes. He asked newspapers to refuse advertising from tax protesters. They did, and they proceeded to donate space for advertising "Pay Your Taxes Savings Clubs," to help get people in the spirit of paying taxes. Cermak appealed to Washington for a bailout, but members of Congress wanted to know why the feds should give the city money when bankers considered it a bad credit risk. The government began to prevail, though, when the Illinois Supreme Court overturned Judge Jarecki's decision because it seemed impractical to apply tax assessments equally.[42]

By 1933, the tax strike faded because the U.S. Supreme Court declined to hear a key case. But ARET had demonstrated widespread opposition to taxes. ARET drew members from all over Chicago, people of low as well as high incomes, and they had successfully resisted powerful politicians far longer than anybody would have thought possible.

MEANWHILE, HOOVER JOINED those denouncing the stock market. He encouraged a Senate investigation of Wall Street practices. The New York Stock Exchange was pressured to restrict short-selling, which involved borrowing stock and selling it, then buying it back later, hopefully at a lower price. Short-sellers had long been blamed for accelerating stock market declines, when in fact they helped assure that there would be buyers during declines— enabling those who wanted to sell to do so. They had an incentive to be buyers of stock when large numbers of people were trying to liquidate their positions and get out of the market. Without short-sellers, more people would have been stuck with worsening stock positions.

One of Hoover's last measures was a revision of the bankruptcy law that weakened the rights of creditors. It enabled debtors to stretch out their payments without having to hand over assets that had served as security. In cases involving a number of creditors, a majority could deny a minority the right to pursue the settlement that best served their interest. Many states similarly undermined the rights of creditors and went on to suspend the repayment of debts.[43]

Looking back later on what he had done, Hoover took pride in launching "the most gigantic program of economic defense and counterattack ever evolved in the history of the Republic."[44] If there were any benefits from these policies, they were dwarfed by the monetary contraction that the Federal Reserve did little to stop, and the crisis worsened.

Hoover's political skills weren't up to the crisis. He lacked the ability or inclination to give reassuring speeches. The summer of 1932 was a disaster for him. Some 20,000 World War I veterans gathered in Washington to demand about $1 billion of veterans' benefits from the federal government.[45] The benefits weren't due to be paid until 1945,[46] but the veterans, referred to as the Bonus Army, were unemployed and needed money. They camped along the Anacostia River in Maryland. Hoover provided tents, cots, food, and medical care, but since veterans' benefits already accounted for a quarter of federal spending, he was worried about spending more. After the U.S. Senate voted 62 to 18 against accelerating veterans' benefits, all but about 10,000 demonstrators returned home. Those who stayed were angry and rioted. Two demonstrators were killed by local police, and Hoover was asked for help. The U.S. Army disbanded the demonstrators, some of whom were clubbed and tear-gassed.[47] By ordering the action and defending it afterwards, Hoover gave the appearance of being cruel. This bloody episode compounded his serious political problem—the continuing depression. Although he had nothing to do with bringing it on, his failure to end it promptly doomed his chances for reelection and forever tarnished his reputation.

CHAPTER FOUR

WHY DID NEW DEALERS BREAK UP THE STRONGEST BANKS?

O N MARCH 5, 1933, the day after FDR was sworn in, he issued Presidential Proclamation 2038, convening a special
session of Congress. The next day, he cited President Woodrow
Wilson's Trading with the Enemy Act and issued Presidential Proclamation 2039, which ordered all banks—already closed—to remain
closed until March 9. Then he issued Presidential Proclamation
2040 to keep the banks closed a while longer. Because the Trading
with the Enemy Act applied only to wartime, what FDR had done
was illegal, and he urged Congress to pass the Emergency Banking
Act, which amended the Trading with the Enemy Act to apply "during time of war *or during any other period of national emergency
declared by the president*" (revised text in italics). Title I of the
Emergency Banking Act sanctioned FDR's order extending the
"bank holiday" after he had done it.

FDR's bank holiday was little more than a symbolic gesture.
Many historians and biographers have made extravagant claims
about it; for instance, historian Henry H. Adams wrote that "The

bank holiday proclaimed after the inauguration and the banking reform measure saved the whole system of credit and monetary exchange."[1]

FDR's extended bank holiday made life tougher for everybody. Banks needed permission from the secretary of the Treasury to do anything.[2] Businesses were undoubtedly reluctant to accept checks because banks couldn't clear checks. "Subway tokens, stamps, and IOUs took the place of money," observed historian Page Smith.[3] By contrast, during the banking panic of 1907, when J. Pierpont Morgan himself had taken charge of a successful bank rescue operation, some banks did close their doors temporarily, but they continued clearing checks so that people could pay bills. Morgan maintained the mobility of deposits.

Title II of FDR's Emergency Banking Act gave considerable discretionary power to the comptroller of the currency, who, as conservator of national banks, could reorganize banks without going through established bankruptcy proceedings. The Emergency Banking Act also authorized the printing of Federal Reserve notes backed not by gold but by government bonds, which meant that the government could print as much money as it wanted and wouldn't be limited by the amount of gold available. In addition, the Emergency Banking Act authorized the Fed to lend banks money against a wider range of bank assets.[4]

Title III of the Emergency Banking Act amended the Reconstruction Finance Corporation Act, authorizing the RFC to lend as much as $1 billion to banks that, though temporarily strapped for cash, were considered basically sound.[5]

How was FDR able to move so fast with the Emergency Banking Act? Work on it had actually begun during the last days of the Hoover administration, and some of Hoover's top officials had stayed on to help finish it, notably Treasury Secretary Ogden Mills, Undersecretary of the Treasury Arthur Ballantine, and Comptroller of the Currency Francis G. Awalt.[6]

At 10 P.M. on Sunday, March 12, 1933, the day before banks were scheduled to start reopening, FDR went on the radio to deliver the first of his "fireside chats." With a personal manner and confident, soothing voice, he explained what he was doing about the banking crisis. The "chat" went on for thirteen minutes and established FDR as a masterful communicator. However disruptive the New Deal turned out to be, most people were glad that he was at least doing something and keeping them informed.

In this fireside chat, FDR said that only sound banks would be reopened. But, Jesse Jones reported, "It developed that probably no fewer than 5,000 banks required considerable added capital to make them sound. . . . It could easily be charged, and properly so, that a fraud was practiced on the public when the President proclaimed during the bank holiday broadcast that only sound banks would be permitted to reopen. It was not until the late spring of 1934, nearly fourteen months afterward, that all the banks doing business could be regarded as solvent."[7]

SMALL UNIT (ONE office) banks, which accounted for about 90 percent of bank failures, began lobbying for federal deposit insurance to assure customers that they needn't worry about their deposits.[8] Big banks with many branches didn't seek such insurance since they had a diversified business and were financially sound. Federal deposit insurance became the cause of Henry Steagall, who hailed from Ozark, Alabama, and was chairman of the House Banking and Currency Committee.

Because deposit insurance had been tried before in a number of states, the 1933 congressional debates revealed a good understanding of the issues involved. Fourteen state governments, every one with unit banking laws, had previously offered deposit insurance, and all but three were associated with large bank failures. The three exceptions, Indiana, Iowa, and Ohio, involved a small number of banks and an agreement that if one of them incurred losses, creditors would be paid in full by the other banks. Consequently, there was a strong incentive to minimize losses.[9]

These bank failures spurred lobbying for *federal* deposit insurance, an idea that had first been proposed back in 1886. As economist Eugene White noted, between then and 1933, about 150 bills for federal deposit insurance had been proposed, but they never went anywhere. The proposals typically involved a fixed rate and little regulation. In effect, high-risk banks would have been undercharged, and low-risk banks would have been overcharged. Such proposals came from unit banking states concerned about the vulnerability of their banks, whose loans and deposits could be devastated by local economic problems. But representatives and senators in branch banking states, whose banks were prudently diversified, didn't want to be overcharged, so they successfully resisted federal deposit insurance until 1933.[10]

The debate revealed much concern about adverse selection, which meant the worst risks tended to be the ones who wanted insurance the most. If policies were sold only to those who wanted insurance, a portfolio would become loaded with bad risks, requiring very high premiums to be financially sound. Moreover, insurance had to be priced according to the risks of individual policyholders. Undercharging bad risks meant subsidizing the very practices that increased risks. Overcharging less risky banks (to subsidize more risky banks) would give less risky banks an incentive to drop the insurance, jeopardizing funds available to pay insurance claims.

The Banking Act of 1933, which became known as the Glass-Steagall Act, was signed into law on June 16. The provisions that Henry Steagall supported set up the Federal Deposit Insurance Corporation on a temporary basis to guarantee the first $2,500 of deposits in Federal Reserve System member banks ($5,000 after July 1, 1934). The FDIC was established on a permanent basis by the Banking Act of 1935. Ironically, as economist Carter Colembe observed, "Deposit insurance was not a novel idea. It was not untried. Protection of the small depositor, while important, was not its primary purpose. And finally, it was the only important piece of legislation during the New Deal's famous 100 Days, which was neither requested nor supported by the administration."[11]

Federal deposit insurance, it should be noted, didn't stop bank failures. Banks continued to fail. Since depositors no longer worried about losing their money, though, there weren't any more serious bank panics. A major effect of deposit insurance was to transfer the cost of bank failures from depositors to taxpayers.[12] The full consequences of federal deposit insurance didn't become apparent until the 1980s, when bailing out savings and loan associations cost $519 billion.

BESIDES DEPOSIT INSURANCE, the Banking Act of 1933 had provisions that made it illegal for commercial (deposit-taking) banks to engage in investment banking (securities underwriting) and for investment banks to engage in commercial banking. These provisions had been drafted by Carter Glass while Hoover was still president, but his bill had repeatedly stalled in Congress. Glass, age seventy-five, had helped draft the Federal Reserve Act two decades earlier when he was a congressman, and he served as President Woodrow Wilson's secretary of the Treasury. "In appearance, Glass was a cartoonist's delight," observed historian James T. Patterson. "No more than 100 pounds, he was but five feet, four inches tall. His white hair stood stiffly and wildly like a porcupine roach; his nose was beaked and crooked. His narrow mouth grimly dropped down at one corner and twisted up at the other."[13] Biographer Lester V. Chandler remarked that Glass was "surpassed by few in the sharpness of tongue and capacity for righteous indignation."[14]

Only the biggest money center banks engaged in both commercial banking and investment banking, which meant Glass-Steagall was aimed at these, the strongest banks in the United States. The best-known example was J.P. Morgan & Company, which subsequently split into the deposit-taking J.P. Morgan & Company and the investment bank Morgan Stanley. Neither was as strong or influential as J.P. Morgan & Company had been before.

The forced separation of commercial banking and investment banking emerged from the "progressive" era campaign against big business, under way for more than two decades. Anything big was considered suspect, if not bad—capable of monopoly and exploitation. The most famous "progressive" attack on big bankers was *Other People's Money and How the Bankers Use It* (1914) by Louis D. Brandeis. He had made his name as a skilled Boston lawyer who took on cases challenging big municipal transit companies, railroads, and insurance companies. He encouraged President Woodrow Wilson to approve the Federal Reserve Act (1913), which gave the federal government control of banking, and he supported the Clayton Antitrust Act (1914) and the Federal Trade Commission Act (1914), which expanded federal government power over big business. In *Other People's Money*, Brandeis denounced "consolidation of banks and trust companies." He cited J.P. Morgan & Company, which "encroached upon the functions" of other companies. He declared that "these banker-barons levy, through their excessive exactions, a heavy toll upon the whole community." He accused big bankers of "despotism" and held them responsible for "the suppression of industrial liberty, indeed of manhood itself." Brandeis liked small things, and he commended developments in Germany—"the 13,000 little cooperative credit associations, with an average membership of about 90 persons, are truly banks of the people, by the people, and for the people."[15]

This "progressive" passion for small banks defied the reality of the Great Depression. As already noted, small-town banks accounted for about 90 percent of the bank failures. These were mostly rural banks that had a single office—they were in states with unit banking laws, limiting a bank to just one branch. Deposits from farmers and loans to farmers dominated the balance sheet of a small bank in a rural area, and it was almost impossible for such a bank to survive when farmers went through hard times. If the primary concern in 1933 was preserving the assets of small depositors—and not the wishes of the country banking lobby, which didn't want competition from big-city bankers—surely breaking up big banks, as the Glass-Steagall Act did, was about the worst imaginable policy. FDR would have done far better to have used the enormous goodwill he had coming into office, together with his formidable skills as a campaigner and a radio speaker, to get rid of unit banking laws and let strong banks establish branches throughout the country, so people everywhere could have had greater peace of mind.

The idea of separating commercial banking from investment banking gained momentum during the "Hearings on Stock Exchange Practices" that had been going on since January 1933 before the Senate Committee on Banking and Currency. These hearings continued until July 1934, generating some 12,000 pages of evidence. Lawyer Ferdinand Pecora was the major interrogator, and the proceedings were usually referred to as the Pecora hearings. He further publicized the findings in his 1939 book *Wall Street Under Oath*. Two principal allegations seemed to support the view that commercial banking should be separated from investment banking. First, commercial banks supposedly faced an inherent conflict of interest when they both served depositors and engaged in securities underwriting. Since underwriting involves buying securities from an issuing company at a wholesale price, reformers thought banks had an overwhelming temptation to move some of this securities inventory by retailing it to the bank's depositors, whether or not the securities were appropriate investments. Second, legislators believed that the securities business exposed commercial banks to excessive risks and contributed to the epidemic of bank failures. Further, reformers suggested that banks made unsound loans to companies issuing the securities they underwrote, in an effort to maintain the prices of those securities. Glass and many others believed that depositors' savings would be safer if commercial bankers stayed out of the securities business.[16]

The most famous witness was Albert H. Wiggin, president of Chase Bank, who admitted that between September and December 1929 he borrowed money from Chase and used it to short Chase stock while maintaining that the bank was perfectly sound. Like every other short-seller, Wiggin expected the price to go down and hoped to profit from it. Wiggin's testimony was considered so damaging that he had to resign. The other major witness was National City Bank president Charles Mitchell, who acknowledged that he sold stock to his wife and bought it back later, to avoid taxes.

Until recently, historians have repeated the allegations as reasons for separating commercial banking from investment banking. Then during the 1980s, economist George J. Benston examined the original sources, namely, (1) allegations made by senators and representatives, published in the *Congressional Record* before the passage of the Glass-Steagall Act, (2) the Pecora hearings, 1933 and 1934, (3) the *Stock Exchange Practices Report* (SEP), 1934, and (4) the Securities and Exchange Commission's *Investment Trusts and Investment Companies Study*, 1940. Benston reported that the endlessly repeated allegations couldn't be documented in the original sources. In addition, he explained why these sources, particularly the hearings, should be viewed with some skepticism: "The congressmen and their staffs structured the hearings, decided which witnesses to call, and conducted the questioning. Witnesses could not confront their accusers. Nor could people with contrary views call rebuttal witnesses. Thus, there is reason to believe that congressional hearings, then as now do not provide a complete or unbiased record of events."[17]

First of all, the sensational cases were notable for being very few in number. The Pecora hearings, by far the most voluminous of the sources, failed to establish that banking abuses were widespread. Second, Pecora didn't show any pattern of banks promoting the securities they had underwritten to the bank's unsophisticated depositors. Third, Pecora didn't provide any evidence that securities underwriting imperiled the soundness of depositor savings.

As for the sensational cases, Benston wrote, "The charges against Wiggin and Chase related mostly to Wiggin's intermingling of his personal affairs with those of the bank and company. His tax avoidance does not appear to be reprehensible in the light of analysis [Pecora ignored Wiggin's losses, which legally reduced his tax liability]. Nor was his receipt of fees (probably as a director) from corporations that were customers of the Chase National Bank contrary to ordinary banking practice then or now." As for Mitchell, Benston wrote that "his principal personal 'crime' was in attempting to avoid personal income taxes, which was then and remains now legal." And the allegedly unsophisticated investor, a Mr. Brown who testified that he was bankrupt and sick after National City Bank foisted some bad securities on him, had been a successful businessman with over $100,000 to invest (equivalent to over $700,000 today), so he was hardly a novice. The only example cited of a big bank that got in financial trouble because of affiliates was the Bank of the United States, but its failure in 1930 had nothing to do with securities underwriting. Its affiliates engaged mainly in real estate speculation—assets that could never be sold quickly to raise cash. Benston noted that the allegation of widespread abuses "rests on the dubious activities of three banks and their affiliated investment companies." [18]

None of the witnesses testifying on behalf of the Glass-Steagall Act—and these included the chairman of the Federal Reserve Bank of New York and the controller of the currency—mentioned securities business as a factor in any bank failures.[19] For instance, when Senator Glass asked Comptroller of the Currency J. W. Pole about the causes of recent bank failures, he replied: "Well, 90 per cent of the banks are in the small rural communities. Economic changes have put these small communities within easy distances of the larger commercial centers where the banks are stronger and more efficient in every respect, and as a consequence . . . [the small country] bank is not able to maintain itself."[20]

Discussing the 1934 *Stock Exchange Practices Report*, Benston observed that it "does not show the banks transferred or sold the securities of their troubled borrowers to the investment companies they sponsored." According to his study, "There is no evidence that the investment companies took their sponsor-banks' illiquid (in the sense of worth less than face value) loans, made loans to bank customers at less than market rates, or purchased slow-moving or less-than-good (or, for that matter, any) securities from the bank or its securities affiliate, whether underwritten by them or not. . . . I cannot determine from this record how many or what proportion of commercial banks engaged in abusive practices."[21]

Other studies have failed to implicate securities underwriting in bank failures. Benston cited a 1931 Federal Reserve study of 105 member banks that failed in 1931. "The principal cause of the failures was poor and dishonest lending practices, particularly 'lax lending methods,' 'slack collection methods,' 'unwise loans to directors and officers,' and 'lack of credit data,'" Benston wrote. "These four criticisms accounted for 68 percent of the examiners' criticisms of lending policies. . . . Finally, the 50 bond issues contributing to the greatest depreciation to the portfolios of the 105 banks were analyzed. . . . 85.1 per cent of the total depreciation was due to bonds in three groups of industries: public utilities (37.6 per cent), industrials (33.0 per cent), and railroads (14.5 per cent). Both public utilities and railroads were regulated by government agencies."[22]

SINCE THE CASE for breaking up the strongest banks turns out to have been much weaker than historians have reported, Benston became suspicious about what was actually going on. He observed that two of the biggest lobbyists for Glass-Steagall were the Investment Company Institute and the Securities Industry Association, representing securities dealers and investment firms that would benefit by eliminating commercial banks as competitors. Indeed, since the late 1920s, commercial banks had achieved an increasing presence in the securities business, and they posed a competitive threat to securities dealers and investment firms.[23]

The securities business contracted with just about every other business during the Great Depression, and Benston suggested that Glass-Steagall reflected "a willingness by both investment and commercial bankers to eliminate competition for a shrinking market and to secure other benefits and avoid more restrictive legislation."[24]

Other recent investigations have found that investors fared better with securities issued by big banks that both served depositors and engaged in securities underwriting. Randall Kroszner and Raghurm Rajan reported in *American Economic Review* that they gathered data on securities issues during the 1920s and compared the performance of issues underwritten by universal banks (which engaged in both deposit taking and securities underwriting) versus those issued by investment banks (which engaged only in securities underwriting). Universal banks underwrote very few stocks during the 1920s, so the data involved bonds. Kroszner and Rajan found that 40 percent more of the bonds issued by *investment* banks—the kind of banks approved by Senator Glass—went into default.

How could this be? Kroszner and Rajan explained a likely answer: "Investors realize that some [universal bank] affiliates may be less forthcoming than independent investment banks in communicating information about issue quality, due to possible conflicts of interest. They will be most wary when there is little public information about an issue, as in the case of small issues by little-known firms." Consequently, suspicious investors were reluctant to bid for bonds they knew little about and had less confidence in, and when they did bid, they offered less money for such bonds than for well-established, less risky issues. In an effort to avoid the investor discount, due to suspected conflict of interest, universal banks might have avoided new issues by little-known firms and favored issues by "blue chips" that were beyond suspicion. Indeed, Kroszner and Rajan found that universal banks underwrote securities by older, larger firms than investment banks.[25]

Why was it that universal banks underwrote very few highly speculative stock issues? Companies that could borrow money from a universal bank, Kroszner and Rajan suggested, might have had less need to raise money through a stock issue than companies that didn't have good banking relationships. Conversely, companies with good banking relationships were more likely to get capital needed to survive difficult times—contributing to lower default rates for the bonds of these companies.[26]

In a related study, Eugene White reported that during the 1920s, before the passage of the Glass-Steagall Act, banks that both served depositors and engaged in securities business were less likely to fail than banks that didn't engage in securities business. White went on to say that "while 26.3 percent of all national banks failed in this period [1930–1933], only 6.5 percent of the 62 banks which had [investment] affiliates in 1929 and 7.6 percent of the 145 banks which conducted large operations through their bond departments closed their doors." The reason for the greater safety of universal banks, White suggested, was diversification."[27]

While breaking up big universal banks, the Glass-Steagall Act had no impact on the small unit banks that failed by the thousands. These banks typically didn't engage in corporate underwriting. Incredibly, as Benston noted, the Glass-Steagall Act "did not change the most important weakness of the American banking system—unit banking within states and the prohibition of nationwide banking." In fact, he says, "This structure is considered the principal reason for the failure of so many U.S. banks, some 90 percent of which were unit banks with under $2 million of assets."[28]

CHAPTER FIVE

WHY DID FDR SEIZE EVERYBODY'S GOLD?

EARLY ON, FDR became convinced that to solve the country's financial crisis, the federal government had to gain total control over money. The Federal Reserve seemed to have been powerless during the contraction, so FDR asserted the power of the presidency. He began demonizing gold.

Why gold? For centuries, people have viewed gold as the ultimate store of value, something to buy that can help preserve savings when governments depreciate coins and currency. Gold is a beautiful, lustrous metal. It's durable. It doesn't break, burn, or corrode. Brilliant gold coins have been recovered from sunken treasure ships after several hundred years beneath the sea. Gold is malleable, and ever since the days of ancient Egypt, people have shaped gold into splendid coins, jewelry, and sculpture. Perhaps the most beautiful American coin is the gold "double eagle" ($20 gold piece) with a bold relief "Liberty" design by the famous sculptor Augustus Saint-Gaudens. Because gold is rare, it has been a far more reliable store of value than paper money, which can be inflated at the whims of politicians. The *maravedi* gold coin remained the standard of value in the Arab world for more than 400 years. Florence began issuing the gold florin in 1252, and it was a standard of value for 300 years.[1] Perhaps the world's most widely recognized gold coin is the British gold sovereign, which, first issued in 1489, has been minted in Australia, India, and South Africa as well as Britain; in fact, basically the same reverse design (Saint George slaying a dragon) has continued for almost 200 years.[2] Throughout history, when people have felt threatened by inflation, devaluation, and monetary crises, they have turned to gold.

FDR was under considerable pressure to pursue inflation, especially from farmers who wanted higher agricultural prices. But inflation was difficult as long as the United States remained on the gold standard. The U.S. Treasury was obligated to give anybody as much gold as they wished at $20.67 per ounce. If the federal government began inflating the supply of paper dollars, people would naturally anticipate devaluation and begin turning in dollars, hoping to get as much gold as possible before the price went up.

In Presidential Proclamation 2039, March 6, 1933, which declared the national "bank holiday," FDR asserted that gold "hoarding" was "unwarranted" and had brought on the "emergency." The proclamation claimed the legal authority of the Trading with the Enemy Act (October 6, 1917), which provided fines of $10,000 or as much as ten years in prison for anyone convicted of doing business with an "enemy" of the United States.[3] A subsection of the Trading with the Enemy Act authorized the president "under such rules and regulations as he may prescribe" to ban "any transactions in foreign exchange, export or earmarkings of gold or silver coin or bullion or currency . . . by any person within the United States." Presidential Proclamation 2039 made it against the law until March 9 for any bank to "pay out, export, earmark, or permit the withdrawal or transfer in any manner or by any device whatsoever of any gold." Thus did FDR make outlaws of ordinary citizens whose "crime" was to protect their assets with gold.

FDR understood that he must apply the full force of federal power to suppress the natural desire for gold in troubled times. The Emergency Banking Act, signed into law March 9, amended the Federal Reserve Act by adding a new subsection (n), which empowered the secretary of the treasury to demand that all Americans surrender their gold and receive paper money. The following day, FDR issued Executive Order 6073, which prohibited the removal of gold "from the United States or a place subject to the jurisdiction thereof."

In his first fireside chat, delivered on March 12, FDR didn't say a word about his backstage maneuvering to seize gold. He remarked that "hoarding during the past week has become an exceedingly unfashionable pastime." Toward the end of his chat, he said, "There is an element in the readjustment of our financial system more important than currency, more important than gold, and that is the confidence of the people."

Less than a month later, on April 5, 1933, FDR issued Executive Order 6012, which expropriated privately owned gold. He ordered Americans to surrender their gold to the government by May 1, 1933. Violators would be subject to a $10,000 fine or as much as ten years in prison.[4]

FDR spent part of his May 7 fireside chat putting his spin on the gold situation. He said that if Americans were free to buy gold, there soon wouldn't be any left; and therefore, in the interest of fairness, he denied gold to everybody.[5] Of course, it was nonsense to suggest that there soon wouldn't be any gold. Gold markets have flourished around the world for thousands of years. Gold has endlessly changed hands. People have obtained gold during the worst wartime conditions when it was forbidden. Resourceful smugglers have defied the death penalty to deliver gold. Journalist Timothy Green reported that a favorite smuggling technique involved "a thin canvas or nylon corset, bearing thirty or more one-kilo bars of gold slotted neatly into rows all around the garment, strapped to the torso."[6] Green went on to say that "Gold travels amid a clutter of goats and pilgrims on Arab dhows in the Arabian gulf, or hidden in the engine casing of freighters outward bound from Hong Kong. One shipment of movie projectors into India was ingeniously filled with canapé-sized bars of gold, while 560 cans of motor grease swung ashore in Yokohama docks were laced with over one million dollars in gold. Tins of condensed milk make an excellent hideaway because the thick white goo of the milk stops the gold from rattling. Best of all are golden nuggets shaped like a pigeon's egg, which can be carried internally. Women, they hasten to explain in smuggling circles, can carry twice as many of these eggs as men."[7] So much for FDR's professed concern that free people wouldn't be able to buy gold.

What about existing contracts that people had voluntarily agreed to, specifying payment in gold? FDR persuaded Congress to overturn those contracts and wipe out the gold clause. The Joint Resolution of June 5, 1933, provided in part that "(a) Every provision contained in or made with respect to any obligation which purports to give the oblige a right to require payment in gold or a particular kind of coin or currency or an amount in dollars of the United States measured thereby, is declared to be against public policy; and no such provision shall be contained in or made with respect to any obligation hereafter incurred. Every obligation, heretofore or hereafter incurred, whether or not any such provision is contained therein or made with respect thereto shall be discharged upon payment, dollar for dollar, in any coin or currency which at the time of payment is legal tender for public and private debts."[8]

This was an extraordinary succession of commands, by whatever name. There weren't any congressional hearings, even though the issue was one of fundamental importance—namely, the seizure of private property from peaceful people who hadn't done anything wrong. Congressional debate was perfunctory, and when members were asked to vote, they often didn't have a printed copy of the law they were voting on. FDR's display of arbitrary power and his brazen disregard of contractual obligations undoubtedly made investors less willing to fund growth and jobs, making recovery from the depression more difficult.

MEANWHILE, FDR SHOCKED many of his advisers by signing an amendment to the Agricultural Adjustment Act, proposed by Oklahoma senator Elmer Thomas, authorizing the Treasury to issue more paper dollars and empowering the president to fix the price of gold. Raymond Moley explained, "The purpose was to give the President discretionary authority among a selection of methods to promote a rise in prices, especially farm prices. . . . There was a preponderant sentiment in Congress for almost any sort of device to raise prices and correct the devastating deflation, which had gone on since the dawn of 1930."[9]

The dollar plunged on currency markets. Officials in Britain, France, and other countries were alarmed, since their currencies became more expensive in terms of dollars, making their goods more expensive for Americans to buy, to the extent Americans were buying much at all from overseas. Farm commodities prices rose as the dollar depreciated on world markets in May and June 1933.[10]

But in July, gold prices rose, and stock prices and farm commodities prices fell.[11] Farm prices continued in a general downtrend for several months. "If we don't keep the price of wheat and cotton moving up, we shall have marching farmers," FDR reportedly told banker James Warburg, a presidential adviser.

It became increasingly apparent that the National Recovery Administration was failing to revive industrial production and employment, the Agricultural Adjustment Administration wasn't raising farm incomes, and cutting the dollar loose from gold didn't seem to be working, either. So FDR became interested in a Cornell professor's ideas for raising farm incomes. The professor was agricultural economist George Frederick Warren. "He was a stocky, smooth-faced man approaching sixty," journalist John Brooks wrote, "who peered through round spectacles with narrow black rims with a steady, vacuous gaze slightly reminiscent of Calvin Coolidge's, and, invariably, carried a clutch of pencils with the ends sticking out of the breast pocket of his coat. He was given to careless dress, homely witticisms, and pithy, irrefutable sentences like 'Here is a farm, here is a farmer, and here are the facts.'"

Warren had written *Alfalfa* and *Some Suggestions for City Persons Who Desire to Farm*, but it was his book *Prices*, written with his Cornell colleague Frank A. Pearson, that caught FDR's attention. Warren had noticed that when gold prices go up, the prices of other commodities tend to go up, too, and he concluded that rising gold prices *caused* higher farm prices. Accordingly, he recommended, "The price level must be raised to the debt level or the debt level lowered to the price level. Unless the price of gold is raised, the process of bankruptcy and deflation has been only temporarily arrested. This is not a matter of psychology or confidence. It is a grim reality that, at present values of gold and commodities, many of the debts are more than the properties are worth." Warren became one of FDR's close advisers, and FDR arranged to have him use an office at the Department of Commerce.

Most economists seemed to agree with him that the prices of gold and farm commodities often rose together, but they denied that gold was the *cause*.[12] Warburg called Warren's doctrine "almost ridiculous." As Warburg recalled a White House presentation, "The meaning of Warren's charts and graphs—to Warren—was that the price of commodities went up and down automatically with the price of gold. Therefore all one had to do to control the price of commodities was to control the price of gold. . . . I pointed out that Warren's graphs represented only the prices of commodities with an international market. They did not show that milk or eggs or beef were affected by the ups and downs of the dollar in terms of gold. . . . I asked Warren whether, in his opinion, it was the domestic price for gold or the world price that governed domestic commodity prices. He said it was the domestic price—that each country could regulate its commodity price level by regulating its gold price. . . . I said to the

President that . . . the domestic price of gold would not influence anything except the position of the domestic gold miners."[13]

In August, FDR told Henry Morgenthau, then head of the Farm Credit Administration, that he wanted the Treasury Department to buy gold, generating upward pressures on the price. Amidst his haste to take away the right of Americans to own gold, however, FDR had forgotten to officially proclaim the state of emergency that his own Emergency Banking Act had said was necessary. So on August 28, 1933, FDR issued Executive Order 6260, which revoked his executive order of April 5 (seizing privately owned gold). Then the executive order declared a state of emergency and reissued all the gold prohibitions.[14] The next day, FDR issued Executive Order 6261, which required U.S. gold producers to sell all their output to the secretary of the treasury, at a price determined by the secretary.

On Sunday, October 22, FDR delivered a fireside chat to the nation, announcing his gold-buying binge: "Our dollar is now altogether too greatly influenced by the accidents of international trade, by the internal policies of other nations and by political disturbance in other continents. Therefore the United States must take firmly in its own hands the control of the gold value of our dollar. This is necessary in order to prevent dollar disturbances from swinging us away from our ultimate goal, namely, the continued recovery of our commodity prices. . . . I am going to establish a Government market for gold in the United States. Therefore, under the clearly defined authority of existing law, I am authorizing the Reconstruction Finance Corporation to buy gold newly mined in the United States at prices to be determined from time to time after consultation with the Secretary of the Treasury and the President. Whenever necessary to the end in view, we shall also buy or sell gold in the world market."[15]

FDR imagined he could fix the world gold price from his bedroom. Morgenthau reported that when he visited FDR on Friday, November 3, he suggested a 10- or 15-cent rise from the previous day, and FDR decided on a 21-cent rise. Morgenthau asked the rationale for 21 cents, and FDR reportedly replied that "three times seven" is a lucky number. [16] Moley remarked, "Roosevelt gravely marred his image as a responsible statesman, by the early-morning bedside guesses with Morgenthau about what the price of gold was to be 'that day.'" [17]

BUT FARM COMMODITIES prices declined. Warburg observed, "By this time it was evident that marking up the gold price on a blackboard each day had little or no significance." [18] FDR demanded answers from Warren. The professor replied that the government must buy more gold overseas! Purchases would be made through the Federal Reserve Bank of New York, and the first were made on November 2. [19] New York Fed president George Harrison tried to convince central bank officials in Britain and France that FDR wasn't engaged in monetary nationalism intended to harm their interests. But the continued rise in gold prices and consequent fall in the dollar against major currencies outraged the British and French, who feared that with their currencies becoming more expensive, their producers would be priced out of world markets.

While FDR's gold-buying gambit cost the U.S. Treasury millions of dollars and impaired relations with other countries, it didn't do much to raise prices of U.S. farm commodities. Nonetheless, FDR seemed pleased because of reports that American farmers were less rebellious than they had been earlier in the year.

There was increasingly vocal opposition to the gold buying, however. Harrison warned that further depreciation of the dollar would impair the government's ability to raise money by issuing bonds. Undersecretary of the Treasury Dean Acheson resigned in protest against FDR's efforts to depreciate the dollar. Bernard Baruch, an FDR adviser, wrote an article for the *Saturday Evening Post* blasting FDR's policy. Al Smith, FDR's rival for the Democratic presidential nomination, declared that he supported "gold dollars as against baloney dollars." [20]

In his letter published in the *New York Times* on December 31, 1933, John Maynard Keynes said it was "foolish . . . to believe that there is a mathematical relation between the price of gold and the prices of other things."[21] He added, "In the field of gold-devaluation and exchange policy the time has come when uncertainty should be ended. This game of blind man's bluff with exchange speculators serves no useful purpose and is extremely undignified. It upsets confidence, hinders business decisions, occupies the public attention in a measure far exceeding its real importance, and is responsible both for the irritation and for a certain lack of respect which exists abroad."[22]

The American Federation of Labor cosponsored a big rally at Manhattan's Carnegie Hall opposing further depreciation of the dollar. This rally was countered by a bigger rally at the Hippodrome, for depreciation; and among the speakers was Father Charles Coughlin, head of the Radio League of the Little Flower. According to Warburg, Coughlin's anti-Semitic outbursts had the unintended effect of inflaming public opinion against FDR's efforts to push up prices by devaluing the dollar.[23]

Warren's gold manipulation policy petered out in December. "During the whole month," Warburg wrote, "the price was raised only once, from $34.01 to $34.06 on December 18. Commodities declined a little."[24]

Meanwhile, the first victim of FDR's gold prohibition was attorney Frederick Barber Campbell. Before FDR had become president, Campbell deposited twenty-seven gold bars (worth about $200,000) at Chase National Bank, which agreed to return the bars on demand. On September 13, 1933, Campbell wanted his gold bars, but Chase officials, citing Treasury regulations, told him they would have to report the existence of this gold by September 18. Campbell demanded his gold on September 16, but Chase refused, citing the succession of executive orders. Ten days later, Campbell filed suit to enforce his contract with Chase, in the Southern District of New York. Then a grand jury returned a criminal indictment against him for failing to report his gold by September 18. In an effort to block this action, he filed a lawsuit against the United States attorney for the Southern District of New York. All this litigation came before Judge John M. Woolsey, who embraced the gold seizures.[25] On December 28, after the Campbell case had concluded, Secretary of the Treasury Henry Morgenthau Jr. issued a formal requisition order for most of the remaining privately owned gold in the United States.

When the time came to deliver his first State of the Union address, in January 1934, FDR offered a new spin. Gone was the claim that gold buying would push up farm commodities prices, and instead he suggested his concern was stabilizing the value of the dollar.

On January 31, FDR signed into law the Gold Reserve Act, which sanctioned what he had already done by executive order—namely, forbidding private ownership of gold money. The Gold Reserve Act also empowered FDR to devalue the dollar from $20.67 per ounce of gold (the official mint price for a century) to $35 per ounce, which he did by issuing a proclamation.[26]

Even though his gold-buying scheme failed, the government kept all the gold it had taken from private individuals. FDR ranked among history's biggest hoarders, with an estimated 190 million ounces of gold worth $7 billion after the dollar devaluation. FDR undoubtedly hoarded gold for the same reasons that the mercantilist kings of the sixteenth, seventeenth, and eighteenth centuries hoarded it: Gold was the ultimate money, and for a ruler money meant power.

CHAPTER SIX

WHY DID FDR TRIPLE TAXES DURING THE GREAT DEPRESSION?

F ROM THE VERY beginning of his administration, FDR attacked investors and employers. He blamed them for the Great Depression. In his first inaugural address, he declared: "Rulers of the exchange of mankind's goods have failed, through their own stubbornness and their own incompetence, have admitted their failure, and abdicated. Practices of the unscrupulous money changers stand indicted in the court of public opinion, rejected by the hearts and minds of men. . . . The money changers have fled from their high seats in the temple of our civilization."[1]

The business community, generally eager to get along, pursue business, and avoid taking moral stands, was pitifully inept when FDR launched his moral crusade against free markets. After the November 1934 elections, U.S. Chamber of Commerce president Henry Harriman pleaded, "All we want, all we can ask for and all the country needs is a thorough spirit of cooperation. And when I say 'cooperation' I mean a condition in which government does not attack business and business does not attack the government."[2]

FDR sought more power over the economy. Washington, he insisted, should treat the Great Depression "as we would treat the emergency of a war." He called for "national planning" of transportation, communications, and public utilities. He warned that if Congress didn't do what he considered necessary, "I shall ask the Congress for the one remaining instrument to meet the crisis—broad Executive power to wage a war against the emergency, as great as the power that would be given to me if we were in fact invaded by a foreign foe."[3]

A helpless Henry Harriman hailed FDR's National Recovery Administration and the Agricultural Adjustment Act as "extraordinarily daring experiments," but the National Association of Manufacturers was willing to lead the opposition against New Deal assaults on economic liberty. NAM president Robert Lund, of Lambert Pharmaceutical, denounced compulsory unionism. One study of NAM positions found that it opposed thirty-one of FDR's thirty-eight major New Deal proposals between 1933 and 1941.[4] NAM directors declared, for instance, that "Pouring public funds into pump-priming projects, no matter how freely, cannot provide permanent jobs and economic stability if private enterprise is not encouraged simultaneously to proceed and expand. On the other hand, if all possible encouragement is given to private enterprise, then little, if any, pump-priming will be necessary."[5]

The New Deal was the American version of the collectivist trend that became fashionable around the world, so it perhaps shouldn't be surprising that New Deal utterances by FDR and his advisers sometimes sounded similar to fascist doctrines associated with Italian dictator Benito Mussolini. This, of course, was before Mussolini launched an aggressive foreign policy and allied with Hitler. Mario Palmieri's *The Philosophy of Fascism* (1936), published in Chicago by the Dante Alighieri Society, described ideas remarkably similar to those promoted by the New Dealers: "Economic initiatives cannot be left to the arbitrary decisions of private, individual interests. Open competition, if not wisely directed and re-stricted, actually destroys wealth instead of creating it. . . . The proper function of the State in the Fascist system is that of supervis-ing, regulating and arbitrating the relationships of capital and labor, employers and employees, individuals and associations, private in-terests and national interests. . . . More important than the produc-tion of wealth is its right distribution, distribution which must benefit in the best possible way all the classes of the nation, hence, the nation itself. Private wealth belongs not only to the individual, but, in a symbolic sense, to the State as well."

Like FDR, Mussolini believed that individualism was old-fashioned, an obstacle to progress. Palmieri quoted Mussolini as saying, "Anti-individualistic, the Fascist conception of life stresses the importance of the State and accepts the individual only insofar as his interests coincide with those of the State." Again, Mussolini: "Liberty is not a right but a duty . . . the individual, left to himself, unless he be a saint or a hero, always refuses to pay taxes, obey laws or go to war."[6]

To be sure, the early New Deal abounded with mixed signals. While FDR denounced employers and investors, he promoted the National Recovery Administration, which established cartels domi-nated by big business. The more than 700 industrial codes protected old companies against new competition. But when the U.S. Supreme Court struck down the NRA and a number of other early New Deal measures for violating the Constitution, the policies penalizing em-ployers reappeared in other forms.

BECAUSE OF THE 1929–1933 monetary contraction, people had less money in their pockets, and effective tax rates would have in-creased even if the nominal tax rates had stayed the same. But FDR pushed for higher tax rates. First came liquor taxes. Congress had already (February 20, 1933) passed a bill that would repeal federal prohibition of alcohol in nineteen states without Prohibition laws;

and when this bill was ratified by the states, Washington would immediately began to collect liquor taxes—which had never been eliminated. To raise even more money from the sale of alcoholic beverages, FDR secured passage of the Beer-Wine Revenue Act on March 22, 1933. The following year, on January 11, 1934, Congress passed the Liquor Taxing Act, which nearly doubled the tax on distilled liquor from $1.10 per gallon to $2, and legislators substantially increased the wine tax as well. In addition, there was a $5 per gallon tariff on imported alcoholic beverages,[7] and FDR wasn't about to eliminate that.

Besides liquor taxes, FDR secured higher excise taxes on tobacco and gasoline. The National Industrial Recovery Act imposed a 5 percent tax on corporate dividends, and it reduced deductions for business and capital losses. The Agricultural Adjustment Act added a tax on the millers that ground wheat into flour,[8] and there were special punitive taxes on farmers who produced more than the government permitted; for instance, 33.5 percent of the value of tobacco above quota and 50 percent of the value of cotton above quota was taxed. Finally for 1933, tax historian Sidney Ratner noted, "an excess-profits tax of 5 per cent was placed on corporate net income in excess of 12 per cent of the last declared value of the corporation's capital stock."[9]

The Revenue Act of 1934 hit higher income people harder. "The arrangement in structure," explained Ratner, "resulted in making the personal income tax more sharply progressive through a decrease of taxes for those with incomes between $5,000 and $9,000 and an increase for those with net incomes above $9,000." In addition, there wasn't any provision for carrying forward net losses to future years; while FDR wanted to share in everybody's capital gains, Ratner added, he didn't want to share their losses: "Attempts were made to restrict deductions for taxes, contributions, and losses from wagering transactions and sales or exchanges of property between members of a family and between an individual

and a corporation in which he owned more than 50 per cent of the outstanding stock. To prevent individuals with large incomes from incorporating and escaping the surtax on portions of the corporate income not paid out to individuals through dividends, salaries, interest, or any other medium, an additional surtax was levied on the undistributed net income of personal holding companies. The rates were 30 per cent on the first $100,000 of undistributed net income and 40 per cent of the amount in excess of $100,000. . . . . The federal estate tax, which had been increased in 1932 through the superimposition of an additional tax upon the 1926 tax, was raised still higher in 1934 . . . to 60 per cent."[10] And as if FDR hadn't learned anything from Hoover's disastrous experience with the Smoot-Hawley tariff, the Revenue Act of 1934 introduced tariffs on coconut and other oils imported from the Philippines (a goody for farm lobbyists).

Apparently FDR was spurred by the pie-in-the-sky crowd to seek even higher taxes. Dr. Francis Townsend promoted what became Social Security by claiming that a $200-a-month government-run retirement scheme funded by a national sales tax would cure depression, unemployment, and other social problems. Louisiana senator Huey Long touted his "Share-Our-Wealth Club," promising "Every Man a King" on $2,500 a year. The Catholic priest Charles Coughlin established the National League for Social Justice, demanding "social taxation" and "control of private property for the common good."

David Lawrence, founder of *U.S. News & World Report*, warned, "Confiscation of wealth may satisfy the vengeful in us. It may sooth a retaliatory spirit. But it is the path of national suicide. . . . There must always be the reward motive. To many people it is but another way to set goals of human ambition. . . . When government kills the opportunity to earn, it sounds the death knell of the opportunity to serve."[11]

Although FDR had stated in his January 1935 budget message that there wouldn't be any new taxes, on July 19, 1935, he suddenly demanded new taxes in a message to Congress that appealed to envy. He called for "a wider distribution of wealth" via graduated taxes on individuals and corporations. He denounced "the transmission from generation to generation of vast fortunes." Accordingly, he proposed that death taxes take as much as 86.88 percent of estates, a move that was considered particularly obnoxious by many people because confiscatory taxes had already been paid on incomes before any proceeds could go into an estate.[12] FDR proposed raising the rates on income above $100,000, and the top rate went up to 75 percent, compared to Hoover's top rate of 63 percent.[13]

Economist Benjamin M. Anderson observed that for "a vigorous man fifty-five years old," these new taxes would have "paralyzing" results: "More than three-fourths of any profits which he might have from a new venture would be taken away from him by income taxes. Any losses which he might incur from a new venture would be his own. . . . It was a painful thing to watch him turn his energies from creative production to consultation with tax lawyers as to how he could save as much as possible for his heirs."[14]

The Revenue Act of 1935 didn't prove to be very effective at raising federal revenue or redistributing the wealth.[15] But it did send a clear signal to employers and investors that they were under attack. Such taxes encouraged them to conclude that they would be foolish to put their money at risk.

As if all this weren't bad enough, in 1936 FDR signed into law a graduated undistributed profits tax that penalized companies for building up savings essential for investment. Companies that retained 1 percent of their net income would see 10 percent of it taxed away. Companies that retained 70 percent of their net income would see 73.91 percent of it go to the government.[16] Although big businesses paid more in undistributed profit taxes, smaller businesses were probably harder hit because the best way they could get capital was to accumulate profits. Smaller businesses were less likely to qualify for bank loans than big businesses, and smaller businesses generally couldn't raise money by issuing stock or bonds.

Treasury Department officials were aware the undistributed profits tax had the potential for disrupting the economy. In a Treasury memo, one official (Mr. Upham) reported to another (Mr. Magill):

> Nearly every banker I visit gives me numerous illustrations drawn from among the customers of his own institution of business concerns which have abandoned expansion plans because of the penalties and rigors, as they see it, of the UP tax. Moreover, in numerous instances I encounter the business men themselves. Let me cite briefly examples.
>
> (1) In New Orleans is a banker who has $30,000 to set his two sons up in business. He is completely discouraged about starting them in business because if they lose money, they stand a loss of 100 per cent, and if they make money, they cannot build the business institution into a constantly increasing unit by adding to surplus without paying a penalty rate and they cannot distribute to themselves as stockholders and owners without paying a personal income tax so high that it is a discouragement to their business initiative and interest in operating a business at all.
>
> (2) The president of a very substantial concern in Kansas City with branches in more than a dozen states has had in contemplation the establishment of a number of new branches—which would mean the employment of construction labor and the permanent addition of employees to the payroll of his company. He has abandoned all of his plans for new branches due almost entirely he says, and I think honestly, to the UP tax . . .

In his study *The Undistributed Profits Tax*, economist Alfred G. Buehler warned that the tax would discourage businesses from making investments. "To the extent that the undistributed profits tax deprived business of funds needed for expansion," he wrote, "it will slow up business improvement, dampen the spirits of businessmen, and tend to reduce the long-run profits of business."[17]

*   *   *

ACCEPTING THE 1936 Democratic presidential nomination, FDR delivered a speech that again demonized investors and employers. He employed one attack after another, clearly suggesting that the United States was a politically risky place to be making long-term investments for growth and jobs. FDR lashed out against "economic royalists . . . the privileged princes of these new economic dynasties, thirsting for power, [who] reached out for control over government itself." In FDR's view, "They created a new despotism and wrapped it in the robes of legal sanction. In its service new mercenaries sought to regiment the people, their labor, their property . . . this new industrial dictatorship. . . . Against economic tyranny such as this, the American citizen could only appeal to the organized power of government. . . . we seek to take away their power."[18] Throughout the 1936 election campaign, FDR kept up the attacks on investors and employers.

When, in 1937, tax revenues were less than the Treasury had anticipated, Morgenthau branded as "fascists" those who had worked hard, honestly, and lawfully and believed they had a right to keep more of their money. "The question," he said, "is whether we are going to have a Fascist government in this country or a government of the people, whether rich men are going to be able to defy Government and refuse to bear their burdens."[19]

At the administration's suggestion, Congress established a Joint Committee on Tax Evasion and Avoidance, and it scheduled hearings from June 17 to June 28. Thurman Arnold, a Wyoming-born, Harvard-trained lawyer in the Justice Department, helped prepare evidence and testimony. During the hearings, the Treasury Department named sixty-seven "large, wealthy taxpayers who, by taking assets out of their personal boxes and transferring them to incorporated pocketbooks, have avoided paying their full share of taxes." Alfred P. Sloan, for instance, had paid taxes on 60 percent of his income, given half of the rest to charity, and set up a corporation to own his yacht, to minimize the tax hit.[20] FDR's class-war strategy was probably aimed not just at generating more tax revenue but also at regaining some of the popularity FDR had lost because of his court-packing scheme and the wave of sit-down strikes that in the spring of 1937 disrupted major industries.

Former Treasury secretary Andrew Mellon was singled out, too. He had established a charitable trust, giving it five paintings estimated to be worth $3 million and taking a deduction from his taxes (at his death in August 1937, his art collection became the basis for the National Gallery, and he left funds to cover the construction of the building). Mellon also reduced potential estate taxes by making substantial gifts to his children. The Treasury charged him with tax fraud and demanded $3 million in taxes and penalties. Robert Jackson, a zealous New Deal attorney, handled the government's case. Morgenthau declared, "I consider that Mr. Mellon is not on trial but Democracy and the privileged rich and I want to see who will win." While the Board of Tax Appeals found Mellon not guilty of tax fraud, it ruled that because of errors in his tax return, he owed the government more than $480,000.[21]

The result of all the publicity was the Revenue Act of 1937. Historian W. Elliot Brownlee explained, "The measure increased taxation of personal holding companies, limited deductions for corporate yachts and country estates, restricted deductions for losses from sales or exchanges of property, reduced incentives for creation of multiple trusts, and eliminated favors for nonresident taxpayers."[22] Moreover, the government began collecting payroll taxes for Social Security in 1937—as a withholding tax, it set a precedent for the withholding of federal income taxes in 1943.[23] From the very beginning, Social Security wasn't deductible from the federal income tax.

While it's true that the New Deal's "soak the rich" taxes yielded far less revenue than the high rates would suggest—only about 5 percent of Americans paid the federal income tax, for instance[24]—these taxes surely discouraged employers from making investments. As E. I. DuPont de Nemours president Lammot DuPont testified before a Senate hearing, "If an investment proves successful, most of the profit goes to the government. If unsuccessful, the individual bears all the loss; the investor hesitates to wager several to one on a venture attended with such risk."

These New Deal taxes came on top of increasing state taxes during the Great Depression. Sixteen states enacted personal income taxes, and fifteen enacted corporate income taxes.[25] Moreover, historian James T. Patterson reported "a mushrooming of regressive sales taxes," whereas "before 1932 a few [states] had enacted merchants' or manufacturers' license taxes which had passed along higher prices to consumers." In addition, states introduced or raised excise taxes on gasoline, liquor, tobacco, soft drinks, and oleomargarine (this last, of course, a special benefit for dairy farmers concerned about losing butter business). Overall, state taxes doubled during the Great Depression: State tax revenues soared from $2.1 billion in 1930 to $4.1 billion in 1940.[26]

At the same time that FDR raised taxes, he demonized public utilities. He claimed that holding companies gained control of utilities and drained away their funds, imperiling the public.[27] He proposed that the government break up utility holding companies. This became the Public Utility Holding Company Act (1935).

ALTHOUGH THE PUBLIC had blamed businesspeople for the Great Depression, and FDR's business-bashing speeches had worked many times, the chronic high unemployment and the severe recession of 1938 led increasing numbers of Americans to become weary of the New Deal. The high hopes of the One Hundred Days were long gone. More and more people realized they wouldn't get real jobs unless employers were permitted to make money.

Support developed in Congress to repeal the undistributed profits tax and the capital gains tax. Joseph Kennedy and Harry Hopkins testified against the undistributed profits tax.[28] Bernard Baruch told the Senate Committee on Unemployment that the undistributed profits tax and the capital gains tax discouraged people from making investments essential for business recovery. Chase National Bank president Winthrop W. Aldrich warned that the undistributed profits tax made it harder for businesses to accumulate capital. Senator Pat Harrison, chairman of the Senate Finance Committee, and Congressman "Mulie" Doughton, chairman of the House Ways and Means Committee, were among those who listened sympathetically to witnesses testifying against New Deal taxes, in particular the undistributed profits tax. Secretary of the Treasury Morgenthau gave speeches about the importance of encouraging private investment, and the Treasury Department invited people to share their views on taxation. There were over a thousand written responses, and Treasury officials held conferences with 280 people.[29] FDR viewed a repeal of the undistributed profits tax as a repudiation of New Deal principles. If Congress went ahead with repeal, he threatened that he would keep it in session until it had increased revenue from other sources.[30]

Some intellectuals expressed critical views. Influential *New York Herald Tribune* columnist Dorothy Thompson warned that the undistributed profits tax was making it harder for the economy to recover from the depression.[31] In a February 1, 1938, letter to FDR, John Maynard Keynes advised, "If you work [businessmen] into the surly, obstinate, terrified mood, of which domestic animals, wrongly handled, are so capable, the nation's burdens will not get carried to market; and in the end public opinion will veer their way."[32]

To be sure, other New Dealers besides FDR remained adamant that employers must be taxed to the hilt. Among the diehards were Federal Reserve chairman Marriner Eccles, Securities and Exchange Commission economist Leon Henderson, and New Deal lawyer Benjamin Cohen. But the momentum was for repeal. On June 16, 1939, the Ways and Means Committee reported a bill to the House that included a number of pro-business features, including a flat 18 percent corporate income tax and no extension of the undistributed profits tax. The House passed the bill 357 to 1. The Senate Finance

Committee reported a similar bill, and the Senate passed it, slightly amended, without a roll call. Following a House-Senate conference, the Revenue Act of 1939 became law without FDR's signature.

The undistributed profits tax was only one tax among many that had helped prolong chronic high unemployment, but at least there seemed to be recognition that taxes cannot be endlessly increased without consequences. Tax historian Randolph E. Paul, who advised FDR about tax policy during the late 1930s and early 1940s and viewed tax cuts as "business appeasement," reported, "In the opinion of the committee taxes could not be imposed without economic repercussions, and it was wise to take them into account in reaching tax decisions. . . . the committee recognized the difficulties and dangers inherent in the deliberate use of taxation to achieve a given economic effect and the possibility of exaggerated notions of its potentialities and inadequate appreciation of its limitations. The nonfiscal objectives of taxation should therefore be clearly in the public interest and the limitations of our knowledge and ability to forecast consequences should be acknowledged."[33]

Despite the end of the undistributed profits tax, New Deal policies had taken their toll. Opinion surveys of private sector employers suggested widespread fear of the federal government because of FDR's policies. An American Institute of Public Opinion poll reported that a majority of employers anticipated more government control of the economy in the future. Employers felt so much hostility from the Roosevelt administration that according to an October 1940 *Fortune* poll, 77 percent were reluctant to get involved with the government's rearmament effort.[34] A December 1940 *Fortune* poll asked whether it made sense to invest for expansion, and 61 percent of employers said "only in war industries." Finally, in a November 1941 *Fortune* poll, 93 percent of employers said they expected their property rights to be undermined and also anticipated the possibility of a dictatorship.[35]

As economist Robert Higgs reported, net private investment fell by $3.1 billion during the 1930s.[36] Economist Lester Chandler ob-

served, "The failure of the New Deal to bring about an adequate revival of private investment is the key to its failure to achieve a complete and self-sustaining recovery of output and employment."[37]
FDR tax adviser Randolph E. Paul had acknowledged much worse,
that FDR's tax policies "intensified the depression they were working to correct."[38]

WHY WAS SO MUCH NEW DEAL RELIEF AND PUBLIC WORKS MONEY CHANNELED AWAY FROM THE POOREST PEOPLE?

T HE MOST HUMANITARIAN New Deal programs involved relief and public works, yet evidence indicates that these programs probably prolonged high unemployment. According to the U.S. National Resources Planning Board, between 1933 and 1939, 42.6 percent of federal relief and public works expenditures were paid for by tax increases, and 57.4 percent were paid for by borrowing money—which, of course, ultimately had to be paid out of future taxes.[1]

Each dollar taxed meant a working person had a dollar less to spend on his or her own. The person who earned a dollar didn't spend it; instead, someone in government spent it on relief, but total spending probably wasn't much different than before. Many economists would add that when taxes get high enough—remember, FDR tripled taxes during the Great Depression—they undermine the incentive of people to work hard. So to the extent that taxing one more dollar did this, the economy was worse off than before the spending that demanded the taxes.

When the government borrowed money to pay for relief and public works, there were similar complications. Borrowing meant issuing bonds. The board of governors of the Federal Reserve System reported that between 1933 and 1939, almost 89 percent of government bonds were bought by banks and insurance companies.[2] They were under pressure to get a return on their money like everybody else, so they probably weren't sitting with idle bundles of currency in their vaults. The money that banks and insurance companies were giving the government to buy its bonds probably would otherwise have been available in the private sector to buy corporate bonds or make loans. Indeed, in 1940 the *Harvard Business Review* published a report, "Small Business Wants Capital," about the difficulty small companies had borrowing money from banks during the New Deal era.[3] Economist Lewis Kimmel conducted a survey which found that a high percentage of manufacturing companies were denied bank loans.[4] Government borrowing was apparently "crowding out" private sector borrowing, making it more difficult for businesses to get money needed for recovery.

The Civilian Conservation Corps was one of FDR's first proposals for relief, offered March 9, 1933. He said he hoped to enlist a million young men at $1 per day. Because of opposition from labor unions, which feared this would depress private sector wages, the CCC wasn't signed into law until March 31. Like so many other aspects of the New Deal, the CCC reflected the impressions of those who had worked in World War I government agencies. The CCC was run very much like the army. Unemployed single men between eighteen and twenty-five enlisted for a six-month term and could renew three times, for a total of two years. They went to army training camps such as Fort Dix in New Jersey, where they had five days of training based on military routine. They were transferred to a company and reported to a subdistrict which, in turn, reported to a district headquarters, corresponding with army commands. The men wore army uniforms, were driven around in army trucks, slept in military-style open barracks, and were commanded by regular and reserve military officers as well as civilian CCC officers.[5]

The CCC men worked primarily in wilderness areas, planting trees, trying to control tree diseases, and building fire towers and truck trails that might be used for fighting forest fires. In state and national parks, the men built paths, picnic areas, and other facilities. CCC officials claimed they imparted useful skills like reading. The CCC was expensive, costing over $2 billion between 1933 and 1939, and a disproportionate amount of money went to western states.[6]

THE PUBLIC WORKS Administration, established in June 1933, built roads, school buildings, and much more complex projects like dams, warships, and submarines. The 100-mile-long causeway through the Florida Keys, New York's Triborough Bridge, the Grand Coulee Dam, and the aircraft carriers *Yorktown* and *Enterprise* were PWA projects. These required considerable advance planning, which meant they took years to finish. Much of the money was spent on materials. PWA projects tended to employ architects, engineers, and higher-wage, skilled construction workers rather than the poorest, unskilled people who were looking for work.[7] PWA projects were also slow to get going because of the management style of PWA head Harold Ickes.

Harvard University economics professor Douglass W. Brown, writing in 1934, recognized the inherent limitations of public works as a depression remedy: "Experience indicates that work undertaken directly by governmental bodies for this purpose in the United States is never likely to be particularly efficient. 'Working for the city' all too frequently connotes sloth, political intrigue and security from overinquisitive supervision. Overhead—particularly of the human variety—is almost sure to be expensive. Frequently, also, the projects themselves are likely to be of little value, especially if hurriedly selected and carried out. The letting of contracts involves delay and may invite corruption." [8]

Newspaper columnist Walter Lippmann offered an even tougher assessment in 1934: "The P.W.A. as an instrument of recovery must be put down as worse than a failure. It can be shown, I think, that Mr. Ickes has created an organization and a procedure which is a vast improvement on the old pork barrel and has thus made a useful reform in the normal procedure of the Federal government. But as an emergency device for creating work and priming the pump, P.W.A. has a sorry record. The amount of net additional employment created is negligible. What is much worse, the P.W.A., by a wholly misconceived policy as to wages, and handicapped by the mistakes of the N.R.A. in fixing prices, has tended to peg construction costs at a level where private re-employment is not profitable. . . . in the South workers on P.W.A. projects were paid $1.00 an hour while union men on private construction were striking for 75 cents an hour. . . . [the errors of the P.W.A.] arose from a failure to recognize that in a depression men cannot sell their goods or their service at pre-depression prices. If they insist on pre-depression prices for goods, they do not sell them. If they insist on pre-depression wages, they become unemployed." [9]

But PWA projects had much political value. James Farley, postmaster general and chairman of the Democratic National Committee, recalled, for instance, "On May 19, 1936, the President and I went over the entire political situation. He said he thought he would take another boat trip off the coast of Maine as he had done in 1932, following the convention. Then he could inspect PWA projects and flood damage in New England. He thought he might follow the inspection pattern in other states. . . . 'And, of course, there won't be anything political about the inspection trips.' He gave me a broad wink and threw back his head and laughed." [10]

Where did PWA money come from? As previously noted, Congress appropriated some. Hundreds of millions more came from the Reconstruction Finance Corporation, which bought bonds issued by the PWA. The RFC turned out to be the behind-the-scenes banker of the New Deal. Soon after its powers were expanded by the Emergency Banking Act of 1933, it became clear to many in Congress "that here was a device which would enable them to provide for activities that they favored for which government funds would be required, but without any apparent increase in appropriations, and without passing an appropriations bill of any kind to accomplish its purposes," reported Chester Morrill, secretary to the Federal Reserve. "After they had done that, there need be no more appropriations and its activities could be enlarged indefinitely, as they were almost to fantastic proportions."[11] Historian James S. Olson noted that "the Reconstruction Finance Corporation financed a host of other New Deal agencies because its huge reserves and fiscal independence gave Roosevelt the power to act without specific congressional authorization."

The RFC provided $40 million to the Farm Credit Administration, $44 million to Regional Agricultural Credit Corporations, $55 million to the Federal Farm Mortgage Corporation, $83 million to the Federal Housing Administration, $125 million to Federal Home Loan banks, $145 million to the Federal Farm Loan Commissioner, $175 million to the Resettlement Administration, $200 million to the Home Owners' Loan Corporation, and $246 million to the Rural Electrification Administration. The RFC supplied $1 billion to the Works Progress Administration, so it could begin work soon after it was set up in 1935.[12]

Invariably, politics influenced the way PWA money was spent. For instance, FDR hated Robert Moses, the New York City parks commissioner, who was a strong-willed Republican. In 1934, New York mayor Fiorello LaGuardia named Moses to the board of the Triborough Bridge Authority, which managed the bridge complex being built by the PWA—this was the largest PWA project in the East. When FDR learned about the Moses appointment, he asked Ickes to meet with LaGuardia and demand that Moses be removed. However, Moses refused to resign quietly. He told LaGuardia that if

he were forced out of the Triborough Bridge Authority, he would resign as parks commissioner, too, and let the public know that he
was being forced out. FDR urged Ickes to take a stronger line, and
Ickes refused further federal payments for bridge construction until
Moses was out. At the November 21 meeting of the PWA board,
Ickes vetoed all projects for New York City. LaGuardia told Moses
the whole city shouldn't suffer because of his position on the Triborough Bridge Authority, but Moses replied he couldn't be fired unless
legal charges were filed against him.

On December 26, 1934, Ickes issued Administrative Order
Number 129, which said that no PWA money would be advanced
for a project if any of the top officials held another public office. Although Moses wasn't named, the order was clearly aimed at him,
because of his position as parks commissioner. Then Ickes offered a
compromise: He would lift his ban on further PWA-funded New
York City projects if LaGuardia promised not to reappoint Moses
as parks commissioner when his current term expired.[13]

Moses went public with the story, and the Roosevelt administration was denounced by almost all the New York newspapers and
dozens of civic groups like the Long Island Chamber of Commerce,
the Park Association of New York City, the City Club, the Bronx
Board of Trade, the Elmhurst Manor Community Council, the Jackson Heights Taxpayers Association, the Astoria Property Owners'
Association, the Madison Manor Civic Association, the Automobile
Club of New York, the Alliance of Women's Clubs, the New York
Chapter of the American Institute of Architecture—147 organizations altogether.[14]

Every day, the White House received more mail protesting FDR's
efforts to inject politics and personal hatred into the way public
works money was spent. Some members of the House of Representatives discussed a congressional investigation of Administrative Order
Number 129. In the Senate, Louisiana's Huey Long suggested an investigation of James Farley, for which he would seek testimony from
Robert Moses. Then FDR's Democratic rival Al Smith issued a state-

ment to reporters that, among other things, called Ickes' administrative order "narrow, political and vindictive." He expressed amazement that FDR would be involved in such a devious scheme. FDR resolved the controversy by approving a letter drafted by LaGuardia, suggesting that the administrative order shouldn't be applied retroactively to current directors of the Triborough Bridge Authority.[15]

CONGRESS PASSED THE Federal Emergency Relief Act (FERA) on May 12, 1933. Ten days later, Harry Hopkins was sworn in as chief administrator of the program. FERA offered matching grants (one federal dollar for every three dollars appropriated by states) and direct grants for states that demonstrated they couldn't appropriate money for relief. Matching grants meant that more prosperous states, which could more easily afford to make the payments, attracted a disproportionate share of FERA money.[16]

Because so many states wouldn't participate, direct grants became the principal type of federal funding.[17] Hopkins had considerable discretion in disbursing funds, and one consequence, as economist Jim F. Couch reported, was that poorer states had to contribute a higher proportion of funding than wealthier states. Couch reported that Pennsylvania, better off than Tennessee, had to contribute 10 percent of federal funding, whereas Tennessee had to contribute 33 percent.[18]

FERA had some 150,000 administrative jobs, resulting in a mad scramble to control this patronage. North Dakota governor William Langer was convicted of misappropriating FERA funds and went to prison.[19] Although Hopkins was honest, FERA involved government bureaucracies loaded with political hacks and crooks. Lorena Hickock, Hopkins's chief field representative, reported, "Texas is a Godawful mess. As you know, they're having a big political fight in Austin. . . . there's been nothing but delay, confusion, and politics—politics first, last and always."[20]

Since the complex PWA projects were taking so long to get going, and many states were reluctant to cooperate with FERA—

which in any case had spent its $500 million appropriation by October 1933—Hopkins proposed another program that would be under more direct federal control and would offer easy work to help desperate people get through the winter. Accordingly, on November 28, 1933, FDR, by executive order, established the Civil Works Administration, which aimed to shift about 4 million people from relief rolls to job rolls for about fifty days. There wasn't any time to teach skills. Nor was there a list of projects. Some 800,000 people were on the CWA payroll within ten days and 2 million within two weeks.[21] CWA people "labored on public works, taught school, performed in the arts—or, where projects had been ill conceived, did no more than rake leaves," explained historian Frank Freidel. "The made work was often conspicuous—the term 'boondoggling' came to be applied to it."[22] For writers, artists, sculptors, musicians, and scholars, the CWA offered the Arts Program, whose projects included a study of ancient safety pins.[23]

Complaints about the CWA grew. Historian Kenneth S. Davis reported, "Trouble arose from the fact that CWA's wage and hour provisions did not conform with those of the NRA codes. . . . In the South CWA workers were receiving only a little less for a twenty-four to thirty-hour week than cotton mill workers were supposed to get for a forty-hour week under the cotton industry code."[24] FDR considered this a temporary program and ordered it virtually shut down by March 1934.

AFTER A YEAR and a half of these programs, the unemployment rate was still about 22 percent.[25] The 1934 elections, which gave Democrats two-thirds majorities in both houses of Congress, enabled FDR to aggressively expand public works projects. The idea, as ever, was that such projects would create jobs (again, not counting jobs destroyed by taxes that reduced private sector spending). The Democratic Congress gave FDR a blank check, the Emergency Relief Appropriations Act of 1935. Then on May 6, 1935, FDR issued Executive Order 7034 to establish the Works Progress Administration. Financially, it was a federal program that didn't call for any state matching funds.

"The most powerful criticism directed against the work relief bill," wrote Walter Lippmann, "is that it permits the President to spend nearly five billion dollars at his discretion. . . . Only three or four years ago Vice-President Garner sponsored a public works bill in which Congress undertook to name every village that was to have a post office and every creek that was to be dredged, to say how much must be spent at each project, and what wages were to be paid. Yet here is a bill which allows the President to select the projects, determine what shall be spent, and to fix the wages. It is a tremendous reversal. The pendulum has swung from one extreme to the other, from the extreme of dictation by Congress to the extreme of dictation by the Executive."[26]

Getting congressional funding required giving states the power to administer the WPA, which meant hiring people and controlling patronage. Indiana Democratic county chairman V. G. Coplen told FDR's 1932 and 1936 campaign manager, James Farley, "What I think will help is to change the WPA management from top to bottom. Put men in there who are . . . in favor of using these Democratic projects to make votes for the Democratic Party."[27] In West Virginia, supporters of Governor Herman Kump battled with supporters of Senator Matthew Neely. Harry Hopkins's field representative, Lorena Hickock, observed, "It is just one awful political mess. A Kump controlled relief administration out to wreck a Neely-Nolt controlled works progress administration. I declare I don't know who is worse." Hickock reported that "Our chief trouble in Pennsylvania is due to politics. From the township to Harrisburg, the state is honeycombed with politicians all fighting for the privilege of distributing patronage."[28]

Journalist John T. Flynn reported many cases where relief and public works money was channeled not to the needy but to political supporters. In Kentucky, for instance, Hopkins saw to it that WPA money went to those who would support the candidate FDR supported for the U.S. Senate, A. B. "Happy" Chandler. Apparently pressure was brought to bear on the 17,000 people getting government checks in Kentucky's first WPA district. There, Flynn wrote, "Another WPA official who was the area engineer, managed a thorough canvass of the workers in Pulaski and Russell counties. . . . It became part of Mr. Hopkins' WPA organization in Kentucky to learn how many of the down-and-out had enough devotion to Franklin D. Roosevelt to be entitled to eat. It was not sufficient for an indigent Kentuckian to be just down and out and hungry. . . . A lady employed in the Division of Employment in WPA District 4 in Kentucky got a letter from the project superintendent asking her for a contribution to the Barkley Campaign Committee. A district supervisor of employment in District 4 talked to her, told her that the election was drawing near and that she might be criticized if she did not contribute since she was employed on WPA, that she should be in sympathy with the program and be loyal and he stated also that he was a Republican but he was going to change his registration. Then he told her she would be permitted to contribute if she liked in the amount of two percent of her salary."[29] And so thousands of people on relief were pressured to kick back some WPA money for the political campaign.

Historian Patterson described the WPA patronage schemes of governors in Florida, Idaho, Nebraska, Ohio, and Oklahoma. He added, "Democrats in New Mexico, where politics were raw and open, were especially demanding. From the start Democratic Governor Arthur Seligman requested—and got—lists noting the political preference of all relief and CCC workers in the state."[30]

In September 1935, FDR began a cross-country trip with Hopkins and Ickes to generate publicity for public works projects, and *Time* reported "the President could use his two prime Relievers to make his tour a happy one by promising Federal gold at strategic points en route."[31] The politically astute deployment of relief and public works money gave FDR considerable advantages in the 1936 presidential election campaign. Virginia's Democratic senator

Carter Glass acknowledged that "the elections would have been much closer had my party not had a four billion, eight hundred million dollar relief bill as campaign fodder."[32]

A sidelight of the WPA was its National Youth Administration. Its grants enabled students to stay in school, and it provided work for recent graduates who couldn't find a productive job. Supposedly the graduates would get some kind of useful training, but a lot of the work involved cleaning parks. "No doubt this approach was of benefit to communities," wrote historian John Salmond, "but it scarcely gave the enrollees the training they needed to find jobs at the end of the emergency."[33]

Revelations that relief and public works money was often being used to serve the interests of FDR and state politicians led Congress to pass the Political Activity Act (1939), better known as the Hatch Act after New Mexico senator Carl Atwood Hatch. It prohibited federal employees, employees of the District of Columbia government, and state and local government employees who administer federal programs from trying to influence the outcome of a political campaign, offer jobs to political campaign workers, or manage a political campaign.

During the Great Depression, politicians were well aware that the New Deal was much more generous toward some states than others. Southern politicians complained that they got very little. Politicians in northeastern states complained that they paid more in taxes than they received in CWA, FERA, and WPA benefits. Hopkins said lower payments were based on lower living costs, and for a long time historians didn't question this.

IN 1969, UTAH historian Leonard Arrington discovered long-lost documents from the little-known Office of Government Reports, which provided more detail about New Deal spending state by state. Apparently the data were generated during the 1940 election campaign to show voters what the New Deal had done for them. Arrington published a preliminary analysis, a major point of which was that western states benefited more than any other region. He ranked states according to the amount of New Deal spending per person, and the top fourteen states were all in the West. Arrington calculated that, on average, a person living in the West received 60 percent more New Deal money than a person living in the South.[34] In a subsequent report, Arrington showed that the average of all New Deal loans and spending per person from 1933 to 1939 was $291. The high was $1,130 in Nevada; the low, $143 in North Carolina.[35]

Other researchers wondered why so much New Deal spending had gone out West, since southern states were poorer. Arrington's student Don Reading conducted a study to see whether the pattern of New Deal spending corresponded with FDR's stated objectives of "relief, recovery and reform." Reading found that higher levels of New Deal spending were associated with larger amounts of government-owned land in a state, perhaps because this meant there were already government offices that could help administer the spending programs. More New Deal spending also went to states where people had suffered larger declines in per person income during the 1929–1933 contraction, *even though such states were comparatively affluent.* Reading showed there was *less* New Deal spending in states with a higher percentage of black residents, a higher percentage of tenant farmers, and lower per person income.[36] In other words, the pattern of New Deal spending for relief and public works *didn't correspond with FDR's stated objectives of "relief, recovery and reform."*

In 1974 came the first of a succession of economic analyses confirming that New Deal spending, though perhaps initially conceived as a humanitarian program, was driven by FDR and state politicians anxious to win states. It isn't enough for a presidential candidate to win the popular vote nationally, because in the United States the president is chosen by the electoral college, where each state has votes equal to the total number of its representation in the House and Senate. Victory goes to the candidate who wins a majority of electoral votes. If the national vote total were all that mattered, a presidential candidate could focus on the most populated states and ignore smaller states, but the electoral college system provides a compelling incentive to court smaller states.

Economic historian Gavin Wright concluded this was exactly what FDR did. Wright performed a statistical analysis of New Deal spending purportedly aimed at helping the poor, and he estimated that 80 percent of the state-by-state variation in per person New Deal spending could be explained by political factors. They were statistically more important than the amount of government-owned land in a state or the 1929–1933 decline in per person income. Wright explained that less New Deal spending went to southern states that gave FDR big winning margins (over 67 percent) in 1932, presumably because he was sure to win those states again. More New Deal spending went to western states where he had won less than 60 percent of the vote in 1932, to help assure victory.[37] After specifically analyzing WPA spending, Wright observed that "WPA employment reached peaks in the fall of election years. In states like Florida and Kentucky—where the New Deal's big fight was in the primary elections—the rise of WPA employment was hurried along in order to synchronize with the primaries."[38]

Economist John Joseph Wallis, in 1984, provided further confirmation that more affluent states received the lion's share of New Deal money. He used the amount of state relief spending as an indicator of affluence, since more affluent states could afford to budget more for relief. Wallis wrote, "In the case where explicit matching grants were written into the authorizing legislation (the Social Security categorical relief programs, early FERA grants, and loosely into a large part of the WPA grants), it was clear that national grants to a state were dependent on state and local relief expenditures. In the remaining programs, FERA, CWA, and part of the WPA grants, it was also apparent (though not legally mandated) that the national policies were to reward states with larger expenditures by making larger relief grants."[39]

In 1991, economists Gary Anderson and Robert Tollison reported that FDR's ambition wasn't the only political factor affecting the pattern of New Deal spending. The seniority of Democratic senators and representatives and their presence on appropriations committees were associated with higher per person New Deal spending in a state. Further, Anderson and Tollison reported that New Deal spending went disproportionately to states where farmland was more valuable.[40]

The biggest losers were in the South, as economists Jim F. Couch and William F. Shughart II reported, too. Their book *The Political Economy of the New Deal* (1998) showed, for instance, hourly pay for "skilled" WPA recipients ranged from 31 cents in Alabama, Kentucky, Tennessee, and Virginia to $2.25 in New Jersey.[41] In an interview, Shughart said, "Our explanation was that Roosevelt was buying votes to ensure his re-election in 1936. The money didn't go South because the South was solidly in the Democratic Party's camp. Those votes were already bought and paid for."[42]

Couch and Shughart went on to analyze state patterns of spending for major New Deal programs—farm programs, the Civil Works Administration, the Federal Emergency Relief Administration, and Works Progress Administration.[43] "The actions taken by Washington during the Great Depression," they wrote, "are frequently cited as the leading example of all the good that can be done by a vigorous and compassionate state and routinely offered as a role model for the governments of today to strive to emulate. The conventional wisdom about the period of the New Deal is that government directed all of its efforts toward rescuing ordinary people from the economic crisis visited on them by Wall Street and that in the process of responding to the emergency, the New Dealers were incapable of considering their own personal interests. . . . But the rhetoric of the New Dealers simply does not match reality. . . . the evidence presented [here] suggests that political self-interest was perhaps the most important motive underlying the administration's spending decisions. A state's popular vote support for FDR in the 1932 presidential election and its importance to the president's Electoral College strategy are consistently significant determinants of the amount of federal aid it received."[44] Such findings go a long way toward explaining why New Deal policies so often had effects that were the opposite of what was intended, harming the very people who were supposed to be helped.

New Deal relief and public works projects had some unintended consequences. Patterson reported that New Deal spending enabled many financially strapped states to cut their own appropriations for relief, education, and other programs, so that New Deal spending might not have resulted in much of a net increase for federal/state spending on relief.[45]

Economists John Joseph Wallis and Daniel K. Benjamin estimated that New Deal spending programs displaced private employment, either reducing the rate of private sector job creation or actually destroying private sector jobs.[46] Economists Price V. Fishback, William C. Horrace, and Shawn Kantor found that "In addition, state and local governments may have reduced their own relief activities once the federal government stepped in. Although the FERA, CWA and WPA were engaged in building infrastructure, these programs do not appear to have had the strong effect on productivity in the county where the money was spent."[47]

After the 1936 election, federal spending got out of hand, so FDR ordered that the WPA budget be cut in half and that the PWA be gradually phased out.[48] The following year, however, the economy tumbled into a severe recession. Some in the Roosevelt administration blamed it on cuts in federal spending, but this amounted to an admission that federal spending failed to bring about a sustained revival of private investment and employment.

One might be tempted to say that even if only a fraction of New Deal relief spending went to the neediest people, it was still worthwhile because they were so desperate. But unavoidable political factors meant that government programs for the neediest cost much more than they should have, and taxes were higher as a consequence. Tax increases meant that consumers had less money to spend, employers had less money to hire people, and the New Deal ended up prolonging high unemployment.

CHAPTER EIGHT

WHY DIDN'T NEW DEAL SECURITIES LAWS HELP INVESTORS DO BETTER?

WALL STREET WAS the top target of New Deal reformers. The hearings Ferdinand Pecora conducted in early 1933 for the Senate Committee on Banking and Currency generated front-page stories about Wall Street double-dealing and tax dodging. The committee issued a scathing report claiming that Wall Street caused the Great Depression: "The excessive and unrestrained speculation which dominated the securities markets in recent years, has disrupted the flow of credit, dislocated industry and trade, impeded the flow of interstate commerce, and brought in its train social consequences inimical to the public welfare."[1]

Seemingly the obvious thing to do was impose tough regulations on Wall Street firms. Yet British economist John Maynard Keynes warned FDR that "even wise and necessary Reform may, in some respects, impede and complicate Recovery."[2]

For starters, nobody really knew whether Pecora's sensational allegations were typical or exceptional cases. In fact, there was reason to believe the level of ethics on Wall Street was probably higher than the level of ethics in Washington. If voters realized they elected a bad politician, they wouldn't be able to turn him or her out of office for one year, two years, four years, or six years, depending on the term of office. Consequently, it was always hard for voters to do anything about bad politicians. On the other hand, an investor could issue a sell order as soon as a problem developed with a stock, regardless of the reason. Although large numbers of small investors might have been unsophisticated and didn't know much about what was going on, big investors made it their business to know. Often only a small number of their sell orders was enough to affect the price and send a signal that something was happening.

FDR and Congress, however, proceeded on the basis of Pecora's colorful cases. New York attorney Samuel Untermyer drafted a securities bill that called for the Post Office to regulate stock exchanges and the marketing of stocks. Raymond Moley thought the bill was a bad idea. Meanwhile, FDR asked Attorney General Homer Cummings to get a bill drafted, and he turned to Huston Thompson, an attorney at the Federal Trade Commission. His idea was to have the Federal Trade Commission regulate the marketing of stocks. Moley sought advice from Harvard Law School professor Felix Frankfurter, and he showed up in Washington with James M. Landis, another Harvard Law School professor, and Benjamin Cohen, who had been a student of Frankfurter's. Cohen and another Frankfurter protégé, Thomas Corcoran, produced a better-drafted bill that called for the Federal Trade Commission to regulate the marketing of stocks. The Senate, which had already started deliberating on the Thompson bill, passed that, while the House, without any hearings, rushed to pass the Corcoran/Cohen bill. In the subsequent Senate-House conference, the Corcoran/Cohen bill replaced the Thompson bill, and both houses of Congress approved it. FDR signed the Federal Securities Act into law on May 27, 1933.[3]

Investors were presumed to be most vulnerable when buying new stock issues, since there was the least information about these, compared with long-traded ("seasoned") issues that had been examined by financial analysts, business journalists, and others. Accordingly, the 1933 Securities Act required that issuers of new securities worth over $300,000, marketed in interstate commerce, register a disclosure statement showing the type of business, description of property, management and promoters, type of security, and manner in which proceeds of the underwriting would be used, as well as detailed financial statements. This information would be made available to investors in a prospectus. The Securities Act was to be administered by the Federal Trade Commission.

Economic historian Lester V. Chandler reported, "The regulations on new security issues were burdensome, especially in the early stages before lawyers, financiers, and corporate officers became accustomed to them, understood procedures, and worked out routines. Compliance was time-consuming and expensive. Also, businessmen were fearful of the civil and criminal penalties that they might inadvertently incur."[4]

Big businesses had money and lawyers available to handle securities registration requirements, but these were a more serious burden for smaller businesses that provided most of the jobs. Consequently, the new securities regulations probably gave big businesses important advantages over smaller businesses in the competition for capital, since smaller businesses were less likely to afford the time and money needed for securities registration.

Moley observed, "The market for new securities was virtually frozen during the year that followed. Bankers and lawyers were unwilling to advise investors to risk entanglement with a law that might be enforced with Draconic severity. For the new members of the FTC were regarded not only as amateurs but also as men possessed of irrational prejudice. . . . as the year passed, even Roosevelt recognized that the act in its existing form was unworkable. . . . Its impact on the economy was negative and it retarded recovery."[5]

Surely a depression was the worst time to do anything that would interfere with the ability of employers to raise capital. The securities regulations were enacted when over 11 million people, 22 percent of the workforce, were unemployed.[6] As for the possibility of fraudulent stock market practices, there were already plenty of laws against fraud.

Corcoran and Cohen went on to draft the Securities and Exchange Act to establish regulatory procedures, and it passed the House 280 to 84. The Senate passed a similar measure, 62 to 13.[7] In the conference to resolve differences between House and Senate versions, the decision was to have the Federal Reserve determine stock margin requirements. Rather than have the Federal Trade Commission administer the Securities and Exchange Act, it was decided to establish a new agency, the Securities and Exchange Commission. The SEC would have five members. The Securities and Exchange Act became law on June 6, 1934.

IF SEC REGULATIONS made it more difficult and costly for employers to raise capital, at least the SEC was assumed to protect investors. But nobody had made clear why state securities regulations apparently had failed to protect investors and how federal securities laws were going to be different. Federal securities laws, after all, weren't the first laws intended to protect investors. Rhode Island had enacted the original "blue sky" law back in 1910—the term *blue sky* refers to laws which, Supreme Court associate justice Joseph McKenna wrote, were intended to outlaw "speculative schemes which have no more basis than so many feet of blue sky."[8] Kansas enacted one in 1911, and by 1918 twenty-seven states had "blue sky" laws. The Federal Trade Commission investigated allegations of securities fraud during the 1920s.[9] Instead of answering basic questions about what a federal law would do to avoid the presumed failure of state laws, one New Deal historian after another simply chronicled the abuses and fraud revealed by the Pecora hearings and took for granted that the availability of all those SEC disclosure statements must have made a difference.

In the first empirical study of the effects of SEC regulations, published in the April 1964 *Journal of Business*, future Nobel laureate George J. Stigler reported that fewer companies raised capital in the stock market after the SEC was established than before.[10] By making it more difficult for companies to raise capital, the SEC seems to have made recovery more difficult and thereby helped prolong the Great Depression.

Stigler focused on the effects of SEC disclosure requirements on new stock issues, because if investors were misled or swindled, the deals were most likely to involve new stock issues. Stigler hastened to add that SEC-mandated disclosures weren't the only source of information about new issues. Investors gathered information from financial analysts, business journalists, and others. In any case, if the SEC really protected investors, the rates of return from new issues should have been higher than they were before the SEC was established.

Comparing rates of return on new stocks issued in the 1920s (the stock market boom before the SEC) and rates of return on new stocks issued in the 1950s (the boom that began long after the SEC was established), Stigler observed that SEC regulations had the effect of eliminating the best-performing stocks as well as the worst performers.[11] His most important finding was that the rates of return on new stocks issued before the SEC was established were very similar to the rates of return on new stocks issued since the SEC has been in operation.

"In both periods," Stigler explained, "it was an unwise man who bought new issues of common stock: he lost about one-tenth of his investment in the first year relative to the market, and another tenth in the years that followed. . . . The averages for the two periods reveal no differences in values after one or two years, but a significant difference in the third and fourth, but not fifth, years. These comparisons suggest that the investors in common stocks in the 1950s did little better than in the 1920s, indeed clearly no better if they held the securities only one or two years."[12] That investor returns in the 1920s and 1950s were similar suggests there cannot have been much abuse and fraud, because losses resulting from abuse and fraud would have reduced the rate of return. Such cases as there were could have been dealt with by enforcing laws already on the books.

The main issue, Stigler concluded, was the extent to which the SEC reduced the efficiency of markets by making it more difficult for companies to raise money. "So far as the efficiency and growth of the American economy are concerned," he wrote, "efficient capital markets are even more important than the protection of investors—in fact efficient capital markets are the major protection of investors."[13]

After Stigler did his work, the most important effort to measure the effects of SEC regulation was by economist Gregg Jarrell, published in the *Journal of Law and Economics* (December 1981). Working with data on industrial company stocks issued between 1926 and 1939, Jarrell confirmed Stigler's finding that the SEC doesn't seem to have improved the rate of return.

If, as many people had claimed, the stock market had crashed and the depression occurred because of stock market abuse and fraud, and if the SEC reduced abuse and fraud, then the rate of return would have improved. That the rate of return didn't improve suggests the SEC was ineffective.

Both before and after the establishment of the SEC, new stock issues were losers during their first year; but held for five years, new stocks were profitable whether they were issued before the SEC existed or after. The five-year rate of return for new issues before the SEC, Jarrell reported, was superior to the rate of return for new issues since the SEC has been functioning. He concluded, "The mandatory registration of new equity issues did not improve the net-of-market returns over five years to investors who purchased the issues."[14] Investors, on average, were a little better off without the SEC!

The main reason investors lost so much money between 1929 and 1933 wasn't stock market fraud or abuse. Rather, the main reason was that the stock market went down. Almost every year during the 1920s, there was a larger volume of new stock issues. In 1921, there was $275 million worth of new stock issues; in 1929, $6.7 billion worth.[15] New stock issue volume had gone up almost twenty-five-fold. If the $6.7 billion of new securities had been issued at the beginning of the period, they would have yielded spectacular returns, and the great majority of investors would have been rolling in money. But, unfortunately, latecomers had terrible timing. The largest volume of new securities was issued during the year the market crashed, and the stock market declined during the next five years. Similarly, the largest volume of investment trust issues came out in 1929 and declined with everything else.

As already noted, major factors bringing on the Great Depression were the severe monetary contraction that the Federal Reserve presided over, unit banking laws that made it almost impossible for small-town banks to diversify their portfolios, high-wage policies that made it more expensive for employers to hire people, the 1930 Smoot-Hawley tariff that throttled trade, and the 1932 tax hikes that took money out of people's pockets. If there had been SEC disclosure statements in 1929, they might have convinced some investors to avoid some of the riskiest stocks, but they wouldn't have told investors to sell all their stocks and stay out of the market for the next several years. SEC disclosure statements offer facts about particular companies, not investment advice. So all the SEC disclosure statements in the world wouldn't have prevented people from losing money during the stock crash and the Great Depression.

One thing the SEC did, however, definitely made investors worse off: It enforced price fixing on Wall Street—the high commissions that investors paid to buy or sell securities. The best one might say about the SEC is it didn't originate the price fixing. This went back a couple hundred years. But the SEC was supposed to be a bold reform reflecting the high-minded principles of Louis Brandeis, Felix Frankfurter, and other "progressives." In fact, for four decades, the SEC helped sustain a cartel of Wall Street firms. As Jarrell explained, SEC-enforced price fixing "restricted trading, enriched brokers, and fostered economic inefficiency."[16] Real reform, free market reform—deregulation, competition, and discount prices—didn't come to Wall Street until May 1, 1975.

WHY DID NEW DEALERS MAKE EVERYTHING COST MORE IN THE DEPRESSION?

THE NATIONAL INDUSTRIAL Recovery Act (NIRA) was FDR's biggest bet, his best hope, the flagship of the New Deal. This scheme for government-enforced cartels was inspired by big bureaucracies that controlled the economy during World War I. Herbert Hoover, Bernard Baruch, and many others had concluded that bureaucracies could work wonders in wartime, and they likened the Great Depression to a wartime emergency. In Europe, the trend was toward government-run economies, and many people in FDR's administration especially admired Italian fascism. *Time* magazine even said, "Possibly Italy's Benito Mussolini will be the Man of the Year when his new Corporative State begins to show results."[1]

In 1931, General Electric president Gerard Swope had begun promoting a similar scheme that won considerable support. Swope, biographer David Loth noted, was "a short, slender man, very quick in his movements, disconcertingly decisive in his speech. . . . Co-workers found him coldly impersonal, impatient and dead set on getting his own way. They said he always was in a hurry."[2]

Swope's idea was to have bureaucratic codes, drafted by trade associations, determine how much each company could produce and what the prices would be. The Swope Plan was debated in newspapers and magazines, even assigned to college students.[3] But it went farther than Hoover was willing to go, and he dismissed it as "the most gigantic proposal of monopoly ever made in history." Hoover accused the U.S. Chamber of Commerce, which embraced the Swope Plan, of "sheer fascism."[4] Swope refused to take no for an answer, and he continued to have a major impact on the debate about depression policy.

In its effort to do something about the depression, the U.S. Chamber of Commerce formed the Committee on Continuity of Business and Employment, headed by Chamber president Henry Harriman. This committee issued its report in October 1931, embracing Swope's basic idea and rejecting free markets: "A freedom of action which might have been justified in the relatively simple life of the last century cannot be tolerated today, because the unwise action of one individual may adversely affect the lives of thousands. We have left the period of extreme individualism and are living in a period in which national economy must be recognized as a controlling factor."[5]

The scheme that emerged from such thinking, the NIRA, was the work of the best brains FDR had assembled. Simon Rifkind, who drafted bills for New York senator Robert F. Wagner, played an important role, as did Leon Keyserling, a lawyer and economist who became an administrative assistant for Wagner. Jerome Frank, a former Chicago lawyer, helped with drafting. Assistant Secretary of Commerce John Dickinson developed ideas. Labor Secretary Frances Perkins was involved. Felix Frankfurter was consulted about the constitutionality of proposed legislation. New York banker James P. Warburg offered an assessment of some of the proposals. Louis Brandeis offered his suggestions. And, of course, FDR's brain trust—Raymond Moley, Rexford Tugwell, and Adolf Berle—were in the thick of the discussions.[6]

A number of different plans were proposed, each with its ardent advocate, and it wasn't apparent how these would come together. Then on April 4, 1933, Alabama senator Hugo Black introduced a bill that would forbid Americans from working more than thirty hours per week. If employers wanted to maintain their current level of output, they would have to hire more people. The idea was to spread the work around, even though this would mean lower incomes for those employed. Labor union bosses backed this bill, but FDR was concerned that if Black's bill became law, it might become difficult to get enough support for the more ambitious measures he thought were needed. So FDR asked Moley to somehow reconcile the plans and come up with a bill fast.

Moley turned to Hugh S. Johnson, a former cavalryman who was recommended to FDR by Bernard Baruch. "Ruggedly built, rough in demeanor, and skilled in picturesque and vituperative invective," observed historian Ellis W. Hawley, "he projected an image of the tough-minded troubleshooter who could cut through the guff and get things done."[7]

Born in Fort Scott, Kansas, in 1882, Johnson went to West Point and served in several U.S. military installations and in the Philippines. He dreamed of fighting in World War I, but he was confined to duty in Washington, D.C.[8] He helped establish military conscription and mobilize millions of young men. Johnson was also the War Department's representative on the War Industries Board. He was eager to apply his wartime experience to the Great Depression.

"There was an unused office in the old State, War, and Navy Building next to mine," Moley recalled. "I dumped all the plans and correspondence on the desk and told Johnson that this ended my responsibility for industrial-recovery planning unless he wanted to consult me to iron out differences with Dickinson and Perkins. It was a hot day. Johnson took off his coat and tie and plunged into a job that was to make him, next to Roosevelt, the most talked-about member of the Administration during the year ahead. For that office was the birthplace of the National Industrial Recovery Act."[9]

Budget Director Lewis Douglas was so excited that he reportedly told FDR: "It is so far reaching, so compelling, so thoughtful, that it takes in every economic factor. I am positive, if it can be developed, that it will do for our economic system in a very short time what could never be done by the public works scheme. It will make all this unnecessary."[10] Many New Dealers shared his view.

FDR signed the NIRA into law on June 16, 1933. The NIRA authorized the Public Works Administration, discussed in chapter 7, and the National Recovery Administration (NRA), which would conduct the Swope-style industrial planning. Chamber of Commerce president Harriman hailed it as the "Magna Carta of industry and labor."[11] Harriman told members of the Philadelphia Chamber that laissez-faire "must be replaced by a philosophy of planned national economy."[12] The NIRA was to run for two years.

The man put in charge of the NRA was Hugh Johnson. *Time* magazine noted that his "scowl, his broad mouth and furrowed brow, his pithy epithets, the daily state of his health and temper, made acres of newspictures, miles of news copy every 24 hours."[13] Historian Kenneth S. Davis observed, "'Old Iron Pants,' as General Johnson was sometimes called, looked the part he played. . . . His gruff, bearlike charm; the torrential energy and prodding local officials into swifter action; the sense of mingled toughness and harassed sensitivity conveyed by his continuously disheveled appearance (his clothes always looked as though they had been slept in); especially his genius for colorful invective . . ."[14]

Johnson's number two man was Chicago lawyer Donald Richberg, a former partner with Harold Ickes, known for his hostility to business. He denounced "rugged individualism" and "traders, pawnbrokers and slave-drivers who have sought the mastery of the world for the witless purpose of squeezing more money out of more men."[15]

Johnson, Richberg, and their cohorts occupied offices in the Department of Commerce Building where Herbert Hoover had once worked. Johnson described his quarters as "the worst-planned and least efficient modern office building in the world."[16] It was curious that Johnson didn't wonder how the very same government, which he believed could save the world, couldn't even get a building right.

The NRA sanctioned labor unions as monopoly bargaining agents in a workplace. Section 7(a) provided "the right to bargain collectively through representatives of their own choosing without interference, coercion or restraint on the part of the employer." "Collective bargaining" meant that if a majority of workers in a company wanted to be represented by a union, then 100 percent of workers must be represented by that union and pay union dues, whether they wished to or not. So 7(a) disregarded the right of individuals to bargain freely on their own.

The NRA pressured labor unions not to strike, but historian Frank Freidel reported that "From the beginning of the NRA, strikes were one of its by-products, as workers sought to attain its specified wages and hours, or began to organize under 7-a. Newspapers gave them large headlines, and middle-class readers, seldom favorable to organized labor, shuddered."[17]

The NRA empowered labor unions to draft codes requiring that industries pay above-market minimum wages. The theory here, embraced by FDR and his New Dealers as it had been embraced by Hoover, was that the depression was caused by falling wages, and if wages could be forced up, the depression would be cured.

THE "HIGH-WAGE" theory was very much in vogue, but many recognized the fallacies. From across the Atlantic Ocean, in Cambridge, England, economist John Maynard Keynes could see the scheme was thwarting prospects of recovery. In a letter to the *New York Times*, published December 31, 1933, he wrote: "I cannot detect any material aid to recovery in N.I.R.A., though its social gains have been large. The driving force which has been put behind the vast administrative task set by this Act has seemed to represent a wrong choice in the order of urgencies. The Act is on the Statute Book; a considerable amount has been done towards implementing

it; but it might be better for the present to allow experience to accumulate before trying to force through all its details. That is my first
reflection—that N.I.R.A., which is essentially Reform and probably
impedes Recovery, has been put across too hastily, in the false guise
of being part of the technique of Recovery."[18]

Harvard University economics professor Edward Chamberlin
wrote in 1934: "The most obvious error in the high wage theory is
its tacit assumption that a high wage rate is identical with a high
total volume of purchasing power in the hands of labor. . . . The
total spending power of labor is the product of the average wage
rate multiplied by the number of laborers employed. High wages accompanied by a large volume of unemployment mean a reduction
rather than an increase in this total." Chamberlin added, "There is
no doubt that the tendency to substitute machinery for labor is
strengthened by artificially high wages. . . . a rate of wages which
is too high may work positive injury to the class it is supposed to
benefit."[19]

Blacks were major victims of the NRA. The labor codes were
drawn up by craft unions that excluded blacks as members and did
everything they could to promote the interests of white workers and
to subvert the interests of blacks, who were seen as competition.
Above-market wages effectively outlawed price competition in labor
markets. Since large numbers of black workers were unskilled, they
couldn't compete on the basis of skills. Their best hope was to offer
to work at a lower rate and get on-the-job experience, which would
increase their skills and their ability to compete. "Because of the
NRA, wages in the South's largest industry, textiles, increased by almost 70 percent in five months," reported law professor David E.
Bernstein. "Employers responded to such massive wage increases by
investing in mechanization and dismissing their unskilled workers.
. . . Southern industrialists called for the government to set a reduced minimum wage for African Americans to preserve their companies' competitiveness and their workers' jobs; with some merit,
they accused northern industrialists of supporting a relatively high

wage scale to retard the flight of low-wage industries to the South." Some 500,000 black workers were estimated to have lost their jobs because of the NRA minimum wage law.[20]

Moreover, by sanctioning compulsory unionism, the NRA labor codes effectively excluded blacks from many jobs. As the NAACP's publication the *Crisis* reported in November 1934: "Daily the problem of what to do about union labor or even about a chance to work, confronts the Negro workers of the country. . . . Seeking to avail itself of the powers granted under section 7A of the NRA, union labor strategy seems to be to form a union in a given plant, strike to obtain the right to bargain with the employees as the sole representative of labor, and then to close the union to black workers, effectively cutting them off from employment."[21] Out of a reported 2.25 million union members in 1933, only about 2 percent were blacks. Despite their differences on other issues, Booker T. Washington, W. E. B. DuBois, and Marcus Garvey were all critical of compulsory unionism.

THE INDUSTRIAL PLANNING portions of the NRA got most of the attention. These mandated that companies cut output and maintain fixed prices. There were some warnings about what would happen. For instance, Harvard University economics professor Edward S. Mason wrote: "The provisions for limitation of output and the raising of prices, if effective, can result only in the further curtailment of our already seriously reduced national income. The power to administer these provisions has not yet been clearly allocated. It may well come to rest in the hands of the trade associations or some other representative of an exclusive business interest. In this case, the codes would serve as the foundation of a cartel type of organization exercising a monopolistic control over price and production."[22]

The first NRA code was developed for the cotton textile manufacturers, many of which were moving from high-cost New England to lower-cost locations in the South. New England labor unions pushed for government-mandated minimum wages that would partially wipe out the cost advantages of the South. The Cotton Textile Institute, dominated by New England firms, agreed to a minimum wage of $13 per forty-hour week in the North and $12 per week in the South; but since this meant increasing costs, they insisted that the NRA maintain minimum selling prices for their goods—in other words, outlaw price competition. In doing so, the NRA disregarded U.S. laws against price fixing.[23]

Weeks passed before there were any more codes—probably in part because it dawned on FDR that raising prices would cancel out the effect of raising wages, and he exhorted businessmen to absorb higher labor costs without raising prices.[24]

Hugh Johnson tried direct mail promotion to businesses. He drafted what was called the President's Reemployment Agreement, which specified minimum wages between $12 and $15 for a work week up to forty-four hours. The mailing urged businessmen to sign it and become NRA "members." He concocted a Blue Eagle insignia based on a Navajo thunderbird, together with the slogan "We do our part." The idea was to have businesses display the Blue Eagle and intimidate dissidents into signing. For further intimidation, he urged consumers to sign pledges that they would buy only from businesses displaying a Blue Eagle: "When every American housewife understands that the Blue Eagle on everything that she permits to enter her home is a symbol of its restoration to security, may God have mercy on the man or group of men who attempt to trifle with this bird!" Millions of Blue Eagle posters were distributed throughout the country. Johnson touted the Blue Eagle in radio talks, rallies, and parades in a thousand cities and towns. The highlight was a parade of a quarter-million marchers down Fifth Avenue in Manhattan—watched by an estimated 2 million people.[25] But outraged at the Blue Eagle propaganda, Henry Ford reportedly said, "Hell, that Roosevelt buzzard! I wouldn't put that on my car!"[26]

Raymond Moley remarked that "Nothing like this, short of war, had been seen in any nation since Peter the Hermit and others incited the Crusades. It submerged all the other activities of the New Deal. Indeed, it almost became synonymous with the New Deal."[27]

Many people were uncomfortable with these tactics. According to pro-FDR historian Kenneth S. Davis, critics cited "the disgust and cynicism that had colored the long-term popular reaction to the propaganda fervors of the Great War" and "pointed to unwholesome similarities between the Blue Eagle and the fasces of Mussolini's Italy, the swastika of Hitler's Germany." FDR, however, backed Johnson, and in one of his fireside chats claimed that the NRA "gives us the means to conquer unemployment."[28]

Much as Gerard Swope had envisioned, each code was drafted by a corporation lawyer who worked for an existing trade association or an association specifically formed to help business owners protect their interests. Proposed codes were judged by an industrial advisory board that had the most influence, by a labor advisory board that had less, and by a consumer advisory board that had virtually no influence at all. Altogether, the NRA produced 550 codes, 200 supplementary regulations, and 11,000 administrative orders that affected 2.3 million employers and 16 million workers.[29] Moley observed that "The concept of recovery as distinguished from reform was forgotten, and the codes, hurriedly drawn, embodied restrictions upon and concessions by industries that had been the subject of debate for many years."[30]

There were some 1,400 NRA compliance enforcers at fifty-four state and branch offices. They were empowered to recommend fines up to $500 and imprisonment up to six months for each violation.[31] On December 11, 1933, for instance, the NRA launched its biggest crackdown, summoning about 150 dry cleaners to Washington for alleged discounting.[32] In April 1934, forty-nine-year-old immigrant Jacob Maged of Jersey City, New Jersey, was jailed for three months and fined for charging 35 cents to press a suit, rather than the 40 cents mandated by the NRA dry cleaning code. Abraham Traube, the president of the Cleaners and Dyers Board of Trade, who had a hand in drafting the code, defended the get-tough policy on discounters by saying, "We think that this is the only way to enforce the NRA. If we did the same thing in New York City we would soon get the whole industry in line."[33]

It's hard now to believe how tenaciously officials interfered with the minutiae of American business. There were NRA codes for artificial flowers and feathers, fabric, auto equipment, mattress covers, light sewing (except garments), breakfast furniture, retail drugs, retail farm equipment, retail solid fuels, rock crushers, truckers, retail lumber and building materials, undergarments and negligees, upholstery and decorative fabrics—NRA officials drafted codes that told these and other industries what to do, and FDR gave each of the codes the force of law by issuing them as executive orders.[34]

Journalist Henry Hazlitt reported in the December 1933 *American Mercury*, "The corset and brassiere industry, while permitting manufacturers or wholesalers to contribute up to 50 percent of the net cost of a retailer's advertising space, prohibits them from paying any of the cost of advertising on 'corsets, combinations, girdle-corsets, or step-in corsets which are advertised for retail sale at less than $2, or on brassieres which are advertised for retail sale at less than $1.'"[35]

"The case becomes much more serious," Hazlitt continued, "when it involves price fixing in a basic industry, for example, that of lumber. Under the code in this industry an agency is set up known as the Lumber Code Authority, Inc., to administer the agreement and to undertake the task of controlling (i.e. restricting) production, and the task of 'cost protection.' The latter, of course, simply means the fixing of prices. The Authority, it is to be observed, is not permitted to fix maximum but only *minimum* prices. It must not allow such prices to fall below 'the cost of production.' . . . It can fix a very substantial minimum price. . . . The home-owner whose house is going to cost him considerably more than heretofore will be glad to notice that foreign buyers will not have to pay these high prices for American lumber: export sales are explicitly excluded from the minimum-price provisions. In other words, where American lumber interests have to meet foreign competition, they will consent to the indignity and the hardship and horrible injustice of selling below cost of production. Anyway, they can take it out of the American consumer."[36]

Ironically, Title I of the NIRA, having to do with industrial codes, undermined Title II, which set up the Public Works Administration, by making construction materials more expensive. The government (PWA) bought materials needed for roads, dams, ships, and other projects from companies whose prices were higher than they would otherwise have been because of the government-enforced codes.[37] In terms of value for money, taxpayers were overcharged.

To the degree the NRA succeeded in raising consumer prices, it intensified the problems of the poor. Eleanor Roosevelt admitted, for instance, that people in Minnesota had difficulty obtaining coal to heat their homes "because of freight rates and a rise in price attributed to the NRA—it now costs $4 a ton."[38]

Businesspeople, many of whom who had originally embraced the NRA, turned against it. Historian Robert M. Collins wrote, "Small businessmen complained bitterly that the competitive edge often enjoyed by smaller firms would be destroyed by NRA compulsion to accept unionization and pay higher wages while being barred from meaningful price competition. . . . durable goods producers found that the codes merely resulted in higher prices for materials without any corresponding advantages. . . . the NRA's labor provisions antagonized businessmen of every stripe. . . . The resulting burst of labor activism caused more work stoppages in 1933 than the nation had experienced in any year since 1921. In 1934 nearly one-seventh of the national work force was involved in industrial conflict."[39]

One of the most common complaints was that NRA codes stopped companies from expanding their output and hiring people. "Relatively new and rapidly recovering industries such as aircraft production and chemicals," reported economist Michael A. Bernstein, "were opposed to NRA guidelines that hampered aggressive action by newcomers. Even within the iron and steel industry, a sector in which the large majority of producers favored NRA controls, smaller firms resisted and protested the efforts of the code authority to restrict capacity expansion, price competition, and marketing offensives." Within the petroleum industry, Bernstein continued, "the large integrated producers favored NRA regulation, especially of output and pricing levels, in order to bolster profits. Smaller independent firms were implacably opposed to such restrictions. In their view, the opportunity to compete offered by depression circumstances could be exploited only by price offensives and marketing practices that were explicitly prohibited by NRA guidelines." Similarly, Bernstein added, "A split developed between the textile firms in the North and those in the South. The latter were younger, leaner, more mechanized, producing for the faster-growing markets of the interwar period, and served by an unorganized labor force. The attempt by the Cotton Textile Institute, the industry's trade association, to implement cooperative agreements to fight the depression was thwarted by the split that developed between the northern and southern mills."[40]

ON MARCH 7, 1934, FDR responded to complaints by issuing Executive Order 6632 appointing the National Recovery Review Board.[41] Headed by famed defense attorney Clarence Darrow, then seventy-seven, it was to investigate whether the NRA, having done so much to throttle competition, was promoting monopoly. A principal finding: "[In] virtually all the codes we have examined, one condition has been persistent . . . the code has offered an opportunity for the more powerful . . . interests to seize control of an industry or to augment and extend a control already obtained."[42]

Opponents of the NRA became more outspoken. Virginia's Democratic senator Carter Glass protested the NRA code that applied to newspapers. He wrote Johnson, "I just want to tell you, General, that your blue buzzard will not fly from the mastheads of my two newspapers." Johnson replied, "We will make an exception of your case. If your newspapers do not wish to display the Blue Eagle they will not be disturbed." But this infuriated Glass: "I do not appreciate your willingness to make exceptions of my newspapers. If this act is constitutional, you have as much authority to enforce it against me as you have against any other person, but because it is not constitutional you have no right to enforce it against anyone. . . . because your job is to enforce the act, you have no authority to make exceptions. I want you to try and enforce it on me. I invite you to send your assistant [Donald Richberg]. But before you send him I want to tell you that when he comes he will be requested to leave, quietly. If he refuses to leave quietly, I will see to it, personally, that he is thrown out."[43]

The best-known opponent of the NRA was Henry Ford, who had initially been sympathetic to FDR. "We know that President Roosevelt wants to do the right and helpful thing," Ford remarked. He remained discreetly silent as Hugh Johnson secured agreement from General Motors and Chrysler to draft a code for the automobile industry. Ford refused to sign it. Johnson claimed that Ford nonetheless "approves of everything done and being done by this administration," a statement that Ford subsequently denied. When Johnson was asked what would happen to employers who refused to sign a code, he snapped, "They'll get a sock in the nose!"[44]

Because General Motors and Chrysler had signed the auto industry code, their dealers displayed Blue Eagle posters, stickers, and other propaganda materials. Johnson made clear that the government would purchase motor vehicles and anything else for that matter only from Blue Eagle businesses that had signed an NRA Code.

This led to some embarrassment when a Ford bid for 500 trucks, ordered by the Civilian Conservation Corps (CCC), was reportedly $169,000 less than the next lowest bid, from Dodge Brothers. The NRA policy meant suppressing low-cost suppliers like Ford and passing along excessive costs to taxpayers, who had enough of their own problems to worry about in the depression. Ironically,

Dodge reportedly paid lower wages than Ford.[45] The CCC went with Ford, the low bidder.

Determined to suppress resistance to the NRA, FDR issued Executive Order 6646 on March 14, 1934. His language was considerably less charming than in his fireside chats on the radio: "No bid will be considered unless it includes or is accompanied by a certificate duly executed by the bidder stating that the bidder is complying with and will continue to comply with each approved code."[46]

Johnson urged the public not to buy from a refusenik like Ford. "I think the American people will crack down on him when the Blue Eagle is on the other cars," Johnson said. Many newspapers joined the effort to intimidate Ford. The *Cleveland Plain Dealer*, for instance, editorialized, "In a fight between the eagle and the flivver, who wins? Our bet is on the eagle . . . because the bird of the air rather than the bird of the roads has the moral backing of the public." The *New York Daily News* warned, "If Mr. Ford can tell it [the New Deal] to go to hell and get away with it, it won't be long before some of the other big boys will do the same thing."[47]

Henry Ford still refused to sanction the NRA with his signature, and some Americans openly admired his courage. The *New York Times* reported that Ford "now has become the bright and shining knight of the motor capital, which watches with approval of some hopefulness his latest tilt with generally accepted standards in his defiance of the NRA." Humorist Will Rogers remarked, "When you start jerking the Fords out from under the traveling public, you are monkeying with the very foundations of American life."[48]

Apparently the public was more concerned about the quality and price of their cars than they were about the NRA, because Ford car sales were up for the year, even though the company could no longer sell to the U.S. government or anybody else who accepted federal money. Ford "had maintained his independence, and he must have suspected that his defiance was not without advertising value," reported Allan Nevins. "Every day brought him reminders of the unique position he had achieved. It was reflected in news stories. Long-standing Ford customers praised his cars. Men, women, and children told him their troubles, sent him poems of praise, and begged for aid in an immense variety of projects. The assumption that Henry Ford could meet any practical problem and even achieve the impossible was widespread and persistent." When Ford was announcing his plans for the next year, which involved selling a million cars, he remarked that the country would be better off "if American industrialists would just forget these alphabet schemes [all the New Deal bureaucracies] and take hold of their industries and run them with good, sound, American business sense."[49]

DESPITE MOUNTING FAILURES and complaints about civil liberties violations, in 1934 FDR still had high hopes for the NRA, but he was increasingly concerned about Johnson being drunk in public and flaunting his mistress, Frances Robinson. Johnson wouldn't leave gracefully, so in August, FDR fired him. Richberg took over the NRA.

In February 1935, FDR asked Congress that it be extended another two years, but both conservative businesspeople and "progressives" like Senator William Norris didn't want any more of the NRA. The Senate supported a ten-month extension, which FDR considered unacceptable.[50]

Opposition to the NRA grew stronger and stronger by the time the U.S. Supreme Court struck it down as unconstitutional on May 29, 1935. Economists at the Brookings Institution declared that "the NRA on the whole retarded recovery."[51] Raymond Moley was among the framers of the NRA who later acknowledged the error of his ways: "Planning an economy in normal times is possible only through the discipline of a police state. . . . Economic planning on a national scale in a politically free society involves contradictions that cannot be resolved in practice. The bones of the Blue Eagle should be a grim reminder of this reality."[52]

CHAPTER TEN

WHY DID THE NEW DEALERS DESTROY ALL THAT FOOD WHEN PEOPLE WERE HUNGRY?

POLITICAL SUPPORT FROM farmers was a major reason why FDR won the 1932 Democratic presidential nomination. Although he was governor of New York, other candidates had the support of industrial and financial interests in the eastern United States.[1] So during his campaign, FDR promised farmers that he would somehow increase their income.

At the time, the approximately 6 million American farmers had been hit hard by the monetary contraction between 1929 and 1933. They were perhaps worse off than most people because they hadn't recovered from the agricultural depression that followed World War I. The war had disrupted European food production and distribution and, as a result, had increased demand for American farm products. Cultivated acreage and output expanded. But then demand for American farm products fell off after the war, as European farming revived; and for a decade American farmers resisted having to cut back. There were still too many farmers and too many cultivated acres when the economy began collapsing in 1929.

Increasing numbers of farmers defaulted on their mortgages and lost their properties, and pressure was building for some kind of relief. Many states enacted mortgage moratoria for up to three years, enabling farmers to retain possession of their properties even though they didn't make their mortgage payments. Farmers showed up at foreclosure sales and exerted strong pressure against bidding by anybody other than an owner, which enabled owners to buy their properties back for a few dollars. Sometimes farmers destroyed shipments of agricultural commodities that undercut their prices.[2]

During the 1920s, farmers had tried a number of schemes aimed at raising their incomes. They formed cooperative associations that would control the marketing of their crops in hopes of realizing higher prices than they would expect on their own, but these associations invariably failed. There were always mavericks who could make more money selling outside the associations. What farmers wanted was compulsion, some way of limiting what everybody produced, to force prices above market levels.

Louisiana governor Huey P. Long, later famous for launching the "Share the Wealth Society," might have been the first to hatch a scheme for government-enforced scarcity. In August 1931, he wrote Virginia senator Carter Glass, "We can restore the prosperity of the South and materially the balance of the world within less than two weeks if the cotton-producing states have Governors and other officials who had the courage to act now and decisively. The only way that this can be done is to prohibit by law at once the raising of a single bale of cotton in all cotton-producing states during the year 1932. . . . if action is immediately taken along this line they will get the benefit of the price that will result from this move."[3]

Montana State College economist M. L. Wilson proposed legislation that would cut American farm production. The idea was to have the Department of Agriculture estimate crop totals for the next year, then assign a share of the crop to each farmer—the farmer's maximum allowable output. Wilson pitched his idea to Congressman Marvin Jones, chairman of the House Agriculture Committee.

Frederick P. Lee, a lawyer who drafted legislation for the committee, came up with the Agricultural Adjustment Act, which combined the ideas of raising tariffs, dumping American farm surpluses on world markets, and telling American farmers how many acres they'd be permitted to plant. The House passed it on January 12, 1933, but the Senate decided to wait and see what President-elect Roosevelt would actually support.

FDR's issues adviser Raymond Moley spoke with his Columbia University colleague Rexford Tugwell, an economist knowledgeable about agricultural issues. He described efforts by Oregon Republican senator Charles L. McNary and Iowa Republican congressman Gilbert Haugen, who, five times during the 1920s, had introduced a bill aimed at dealing with the farm problem. The idea was to cut off the U.S. market from the international market, have a government bureaucracy determine what quantities of farm commodities were needed in the U.S. market, and then dump any additional quantities overseas at lower prices than in the United States.[4] The United States, like many other nations, had enacted antidumping laws, but dumping was what McNary and Haugen contemplated, and this became the basis for plans considered by FDR and his advisers. How they could have even considered such a scheme is incredible, since overseas markets were substantially closed to American agricultural as well as manufactured products.

FDR's new agriculture secretary, Henry A. Wallace, the son of a former agriculture secretary and the unemployed editor of an Iowa farm magazine, had the job of overseeing the revision of the Agricultural Adjustment Act. Wallace sought help from Agriculture Department economist Mordecai Ezekiel and American Farm Bureau Federation attorney Frederick P. Lee. They loaded the bill with authorizations to restrict farm production and purchase farm surpluses. To the extent the resulting law might succeed in raising farm prices, of course, everybody else in America would be worse off, particularly the millions of unemployed industrial workers; but that wasn't the concern of the Department of Agriculture.

Congress passed the Agricultural Adjustment Act on May 12, 1933. It imposed a tax on food processors and disbursed the proceeds to farmers who followed government "guidelines" to reduce their cultivated acreage of wheat, cotton, corn, hogs, rice, tobacco, and milk. The agriculture secretary was authorized to make "marketing agreements" restricting the output of food processors. Finally, the AAA authorized federal land banks to issue bonds that would help refinance farm mortgages.[5] Wallace described the AAA as "a contrivance so new in the field of social relations as the first gasoline engine was new in the field of mechanics."[6]

FDR presented the Agricultural Adjustment Act as an emergency measure, but he envisioned permanent government control of agriculture. The legislation, as originally drafted, provided that it would run for two years, and FDR urged that the law continue to be in effect until the emergency was declared over, whenever that might be. The first AAA report called for emergency measures to become "permanent measures." And in October 1935, FDR acknowledged, "It never was the idea of the men who framed the Act, of those in Congress who revised it, or of Henry Wallace or Chester Davis that the Agricultural Adjustment Administration should be either a mere emergency operation or a static agency. It was their intention—as it is mine—to pass from the purely emergency phases necessitated by a grave national crisis to a . . . more permanent plan for American agriculture."[7]

FDR was persuaded by his Wall Street friend Bernard Baruch to name his associate George Peek to head the AAA. Peek, who was sixty in 1933, had quit Northwestern University after one year to sell farm equipment. During World War I, he worked for the War Industries Board, where he met Baruch and Hugh Johnson. Then he was hired as the president of Moline Plow Company, which was in trouble because of the postwar agricultural depression. "In temperament," wrote legal historian Peter H. Irons, "Peek resembled his friend Hugh Johnson: he was gruff, profane, and unyielding in debate, and preferred the company of 'practical' farmers and businessmen like himself. Despite his big-business background, he shared the Midwest dirt farmer's distrust of bankers and lawyers."[8]

Peek had wanted to be secretary of agriculture and resented Wallace; the two men were soon struggling over policy. Peek wanted to focus on reducing supplies of American farm products by "dumping" them in Europe.[9] American taxpayers would be forced to cover the government's losses on the scheme, and of course it would hurt European farmers. The likely outcome was that European farmers would lobby their governments for subsidies, if they weren't already getting them. Either American farm products would lose their market share in Europe, or American and European governments would escalate destructive trade retaliation, increasingly subsidizing their respective farmers in a struggle for market share, making taxpayers ever worse off on both sides of the Atlantic.

BY THE TIME the AAA became law and key people were recruited, corn, cotton, tobacco, and wheat were already planted, and livestock operations were moving along. The contemplated output restrictions wouldn't take effect until the following year. So some of the New Dealers began to think their only option, if they wanted to force up farm prices soon, was to destroy crops already planted. Wallace prevailed with this view.

Agriculture Department officials signed up about a million cotton farmers, and they were paid $100 million to plow under some 10 million acres of farmland. This forced up prices, and Federal Reserve Bank of St. Louis economist Clifton Luttrell explained what happened: "The early programs had especially damaging effects on the market, since a large portion of the American cotton crop was grown for export and a number of close substitutes were available. . . . Wool, silk, and other vegetable fibers have competed with cotton for ages, and a new and vigorous rival—synthetic fibers—emerged to take an increasing portion of the domestic and world fiber markets after World War II. Due to this elasticity of demand for U.S. cotton, any action to increase American cotton prices provided great incentive to increase cotton production abroad and reduce consumption at home. Thus there was little likelihood that the government would aid cotton farmers successfully. Nevertheless, the government tried."[10]

Moreover, forcing up cotton prices harmed industries using cotton. For instance, reported Luttrell, "the cotton industry was being forced to contract as federal programs priced cotton out of both export and domestic markets." In general, he added, "higher-than-market crop prices reduced domestic consumption, leading consumers to increase the use of substitutes for the specific crops affected."[11]

There was more government-ordered destruction on the farms. Hog farmers were paid to slaughter some 6 million baby pigs. Economic historian Broadus Mitchell noted that "Most of this pork, under agreement of the government with the packers, became fertilizer; less than a tenth was saved as food and distributed in relief." Mitchell added, "Over 12,000 acres of tobacco were plowed under. California cling peaches were permitted to rot in the orchard."[12] Of course, this was just the sort of thing that John Steinbeck protested against in his 1939 novel *The Grapes of Wrath*.

Wallace justified this destruction of crops by blaming the problems of farmers on free markets, but the public focused increasingly on the bizarre contradictions of the government programs. Reported historian John T. Flynn, "We had men burning oats when we were importing oats from abroad on a huge scale, killing pigs while increasing our imports of lard, cutting corn production and importing 30 million bushels of corn from abroad . . . [and] while Wallace was paying out hundreds of millions to kill millions of hogs, burn oats, plow under cotton, the Department of Agriculture issued a bulletin telling the nation that the great problem of our time was our failure to produce enough food to provide the people with a mere subsistence diet. The Department made up four sample diets. There was a liberal diet, a moderate diet, a minimum diet and finally an emergency diet—below the minimum. And the figures showed that we did not produce enough food for our population for a minimum diet, a mere subsistence."[13]

Farm lobbyists were often able to secure passage of state laws as well as federal laws restricting farm production. "In California," reported historian Ellis W. Hawley, "where the producers' associations were particularly strong, the farm forces pushed through an agricultural prorate act, an agricultural adjustment act, a milk control act, and a processed foodstuffs act. In Oregon, Washington, and Idaho 'little AAA' laws were also passed. In Georgia the state commissioner of agriculture could fix prices for fruits, vegetables, and truck crops. In Florida a citrus commission could fix minimum prices. And in Texas the commissioner of agriculture could accept and enforce citrus marketing agreements. Perhaps the most extensive effort at state control, however, was that undertaken in the milk and dairy industry. During the period from 1933 to 1940 some twenty-one states adopted milk control laws, all of them empowering some state agency or board to fix producer prices, and most of them providing for wholesale and retail price fixing, pooling arrangements, production quotas, and entry controls. . . . in most cases they amounted to little more than a public underwriting of private arrangements between producers and distributors."[14]

Reduced farm acreage devastated the poorest farmers, who were sharecroppers. The 1930 census reported there were about a million and a half sharecroppers—671,000 blacks and 937,000 whites. Their estimated annual cash income fell from $735 in 1929 to $216 in 1933.[15] "Although AAA payments could have increased overall farm incomes in a country," reported economists Price V. Fishback, William C. Horrace, and Shawn Kantor, "income inequality was exacerbated as the landowners' incomes increased and the incomes of the much larger group of tenants, croppers and workers declined."[16]

Because sharecroppers didn't provide FDR with many votes, he seemed indifferent to the ways his policies harmed them. As historian

Robert S. McElvaine, an FDR admirer, observed, "He refused to make substantive moves toward improving race relations, and he never endorsed the objectives of such organizations as the Southern Tenant Farmers' Union. . . . very few blacks voted in the South, and poor whites in the region could be counted on to vote Democratic even if the President did not do more for them. A vote-adding machine seemed to be planted in Roosevelt's head. It was always calculating when a decision had to be made."[17]

Natural calamities, explained historian Broadus Mitchell, further cut supplies of agricultural commodities: "The droughts of 1934 and 1936, the former being the more severe, were the worst in seventy-five years. Much of the area between the Appalachians and the Rockies was struck, cutting crops in 1934 by a third and in 1936 by a fifth. This result in general fell in with the crop restriction policies of the Department of Agriculture, and the second drought reduced yields the year after the control features of the AAA had been invalidated by the Supreme Court. The droughts increased prices of farm products, farm incomes and the purchasing power of these incomes. The effects of the droughts on agricultural prices continued beyond the immediate reduction of products, for carry-overs were diminished."[18]

RESTRICTING FARM PRODUCTION wasn't the only New Deal strategy for farmers. On October 16, 1933, FDR issued Executive Order 6340, establishing the Commodity Credit Corporation, which made loans to farmers—with funds provided after farmers delivered their crops to a warehouse or grain elevator. If prices rose, farmers could pay off their loans, reclaim the crops, and sell them at a profit. On the other hand, if prices fell, farmers could cancel their loan obligations, forfeit the crops, and keep the money; it would then be the government's problem to dispose of the surpluses.

While overall farm incomes increased, farmers actually found themselves worse off because FDR's National Recovery Administration had been even more successful in forcing up the prices that consumers, including farmers, had to pay for manufactured goods.[19] Farmers were furious, and there were demands to halt farm mortgage payments and offer other kinds of relief.[20] Many farmers went on strike, withholding their produce from the market. "A farmer picket was shot by a milk truck driver near Madison, Wisconsin," historian Kenneth S. Davis reported. "A farmer who persisted in shipping milk in defiance of the strike was beaten near to death outside Marshfield, Wisconsin. Truckers attempting to bring farm produce into Council Bluffs and Sioux City, encountering road blocks, were forcibly turned back. The great stockyards of Omaha reported a 50 percent decline in truck deliveries to them of cattle and hogs."

The AAA tried forcing up prices with compulsory marketing agreements, but inevitably these favored some parties at the expense of others. As a consequence, there was widespread resistance to the scheme. For instance, according to Davis, the "network of milk agreements in the Chicago area was obviously falling apart." Food processors fought efforts to bind them with AAA marketing agreements and, consequently, to have AAA inspectors go through their financial records.[21]

The more acres one owned and kept out of production, the more subsidies, so big farmers pocketed most of the farm subsidies. Economist Donald Paarlberg explained that despite reformist claims, the AAA benefited some farmers at the expense of others. "The agricultural elite, generally the large landowners," he wrote, "managed to retain most of the program benefits themselves rather than share them with tenants and employees. . . . The top one percent of the farmers got 21 percent of the benefits." The program was preferential, he continued: "They began by designating six 'basic crops'—cotton, corn, wheat, rice, peanuts and tobacco. Dairy products soon joined the group. Left out of the program were more than 100 other crops. . . . More, in fact, was left out than was included. The politically influential basic crops produced only about 20 percent of the agriculture industry's income but received 75 percent of the program benefits. The omitted crops not only were left out; they also had to bear the burden of the increased output that occurred on acres diverted from the basic crops. Producers of cattle, hogs, and poultry had to accept the higher feed cost that resulted from reducing corn acreage, for example."[22]

Despite all these programs, the farm foreclosure rate remained high during the Great Depression, according to economist Lee Alston. He calculated that in 1931, 18.7 out of every 1,000 farms went into foreclosure. The foreclosure rate went up to 38.8 in 1933, but by 1937, it was only down to 18.1.[23] Ever since the end of the U.S. agricultural boom during World War I, there had been too many American farmers, and this was still the case in the late 1930s. Until more farmers decided to pursue some other business, low farm income and high foreclosure rates seemed sure to persist.

Although the AAA reduced the number of cultivated acres, farmers often increased output by giving up their least productive acres and more intensively cultivating their most productive acres.[24] Reconstruction Finance Corporation head Jesse Jones wrote, "Despite . . . payments to cotton farmers to destroy 'every third row,' they had brought to the gins an ever larger crop than that of the previous year."[25]

The U.S. Supreme Court, in January 1936, ruled the AAA to be unconstitutional, citing the tax on food processors, but FDR was determined to maintain government control of agriculture. Accordingly, Congress enacted the Soil Conservation and Preservation Act, and FDR signed it into law on February 26, 1936. This paid farmers for planting acreage with soil-conserving legumes and grasses, thereby reducing the acreage of crops whose output FDR was trying to control.

ON JUNE 3, 1937, FDR signed into law the Agricultural Marketing Agreement Act, which salvaged the marketing orders provision from the Agricultural Adjustment Act. The Department of Agriculture was authorized to issue marketing orders for milk, fruits, vegetables, and specialty crops such as almonds and walnuts. "In their most anticompetitive, anticonsumer form," explained journalist

Michael McMenamin, "they establish production quotas, allocate the quotas among producers, forbid producers to sell more than the amounts allocated, and use the power of the federal government to fine producers who attempt to sell more than their quota."[26]

How did a marketing order originate? A group of growers petitioned the secretary of agriculture. He held hearings to determine how much support there was for a proposed marketing order and how strong the opposition, if any, would be. If the secretary of agriculture thought a proposed marketing order was worth pursuing, then all affected growers voted on it. A marketing order was issued when two-thirds of growers supported it.[27]

Meanwhile, the original Agricultural Adjustment Act was revised to eliminate the feature that the Supreme Court objected to—namely, the tax on food processors that had been paid to farmers. FDR signed the revised Agricultural Adjustment Act on February 16, 1938. It mandated price fixing for dairy products, corn, cotton, and wheat; and it permitted price fixing for butter, dates, figs, hops, turpentine, pecans, prunes, raisins, barley, rye, grain sorghum, wool, mohair, peanuts, tobacco, and several other crops.[28]

Tax historian Sidney Ratner observed, "The AAA of May 12, 1933, and its substitutes, the Soil Conservation Act of February 29, 1936, and the Agricultural Adjustment Act of February 16, 1938, were instrumentalities for subsidizing agricultural landlords and commercial farmers through taxes on the rest of the community."[29] Brain truster Tugwell later acknowledged that it benefited only about 20 percent of American farmers, primarily, as noted, big commercial farmers. Tugwell was aware that the AAA made sharecroppers and tenant farmers worse off.[30]

To be sure, the Department of Agriculture had established the Farm Security Administration, which provided cash to needy families and offered advice about better farming practices. The FSA seemed to be much more important than it actually was, because FSA officials had shrewdly hired outstanding photographers like Roy Stryker, Walker Evans, Dorothea Lange, Gordon Parks, Carl

Mydans, and Ben Shahn to document their work. Some 164,000 of their black and white photographs are at the Library of Congress, and many can be viewed online.

But FSA spending was surprisingly meager, and as was the case with Harry Hopkins's relief spending at the Federal Emergency Relief Administration, the Civil Works Administration, and the Works Progress Administration, a disproportionate amount of money went not to the poorest states but to "swing" states where past elections had been close and where more Democratic votes could assure FDR's victory in the next election. The poorest people, in the South, who already voted solidly Democratic, got less FSA assistance. For instance, figures in the South were $8.12 for Alabama, $7.93 for Arkansas, $5.96 for Missouri, $5.24 for South Carolina, $4.16 for North Carolina, $3.95 for Louisiana, and $3.51 for Georgia. By contrast, total FSA spending per farmer until 1939 was $63.18 in South Dakota, $62.63 in Montana, $60.95 in Maryland, and $59.99 in North Dakota. FSA loans per farmer, similarly meager, were also higher in western "swing" states and lower in the South.[31]

Meanwhile, farm lobbyists were successful in securing more subsidies. The Commodity Credit Corporation began making loans based on above-market prices—for instance, extending loans based on cotton at 10 cents a pound when at the time cotton was actually 7 cents a pound. Naturally, farmers increased their output so they could take it to the government, get a loan based on above-market prices, then cancel their loan obligations, forfeit the crops, keep the money, and let the government worry about what to do with the surpluses. "From August, 1938, to December, 1939," reported historian William E. Leuchtenburg, "the United States dumped 128,200,000 bushels of wheat abroad, during the summer of 1939 at a loss of fifty cents on every bushel. It paid cotton growers an export subsidy of $7.50 a bale. . . . All to no avail. In 1939, after six years of AAA subsidies to cut back production, the cotton carryover was three million bales greater than in 1932. Only the war rescued the New Deal farm program from disaster."[32]

CHAPTER ELEVEN

HOW DID THE TENNESSEE VALLEY AUTHORITY DEPRESS THE TENNESSEE ECONOMY?

O N JANUARY 21, 1933, President-elect Roosevelt met Nebraska senator George W. Norris at Muscle Shoals, Alabama, on the Tennessee River. "His shoulders were slightly stooped and his hair had whitened," noted Norris biographer Richard Lowitt. "He appeared more like a man in his fifties with his unwrinkled skin, clear blue eyes, lithe body, and easy gait. . . . The only thing Norris had in common with the stereotyped portraits of biblical prophets was his white hair, offset by a pair of strikingly black eyebrows. His eyes were kindly and humorous. He had the simple, homely air of 'plain folk.'"[1]

Norris, age seventy-one, was a man to reckon with. After Wisconsin senator Robert M. La Follette died in 1925, Norris became the leading "progressive" in the Senate. He championed government relief for farmers and more power for labor unions, and he was a relentless foe of privately owned utilities, which he viewed as exploiting the public. Born in Sandusky County, Ohio, Norris graduated from Baldwin College and earned a law degree at Valparaiso University. In 1910, as a congressman, he helped topple the entrenched Speaker of the House, Joseph Cannon, and in 1917 he broke ranks with most "progressives" by opposing American entry in World War I.

Although a Republican, he didn't agree with the generally pro-market views of Republicans who occupied the White House during the 1920s. His hatred of privately owned public utilities led him to repeatedly introduce bills to restrict their activities. He believed government should monopolize the generation of electric power. He felt his views were compatible with those of FDR, and he endorsed FDR for president in 1932. FDR called him "the very perfect gentle knight of American progressive ideals."[2]

Muscle Shoals was the focus for controversy about electric power. The story went back to World War I, when E. I. du Pont de Nemours and Company had applied to the government for permission to build a hydroelectric plant at Muscle Shoals to support a factory that would produce nitrates for explosives. The proposal was prompted by the mounting threat of German submarines which sunk ships carrying nitrates from Chile to the United States. Congress was receptive to the idea of a hydroelectric plant but seemed to consider any profit du Pont might make as excessive, and Secretary of the Navy Josephus Daniels thought it would be beneficial to have the government get into the gunpowder manufacturing business. So the government decided to build the facilities without the expertise of du Pont, the world's most experienced gunpowder manufacturer. Unfortunately, the government couldn't provide soldiers with enough clothing, never mind enough gunpowder, and the project was expanded to include two factories, one of which would be built by du Pont. The du Pont plant was finished for $129.5 million and produced 35 million pounds of cannon powder before the Armistice (November 1918), but the government-run factory didn't produce anything at all. "On the basis of the numbers," wrote historian James Grant, "the war effort probably would have been better served if the original Army–du Pont contract had been allowed to stand."[3]

President Woodrow Wilson's Republican successor, Warren Harding, favored selling the facilities to a private bidder. Senator Norris was horrified. In 1921, Norris introduced a bill to keep Muscle Shoals in government hands, but the bill didn't go anywhere. He continued introducing his bill, and Congress passed it in 1928 and 1930, but Presidents Coolidge and Hoover vetoed it. Norris's aim, as a farm-state senator, was to get government-subsidized electricity for farmers. Other politicians supported his bills because the project might be used to produce government-subsidized fertilizer for cotton and tobacco farmers. FDR liked the idea of government-run power generation, and in 1929, as New York governor, he had suggested that the state build dams and power plants on the St. Lawrence River so that his constituents might be charged less for electricity (at taxpayer expense).[4]

FDR thought that Muscle Shoals could become part of a far larger project, embracing the entire Tennessee Valley—an area of more than 41,000 square miles in parts of Alabama, Georgia, Kentucky, Mississippi, North Carolina, and Virginia as well as Tennessee. The project would help control floods, plant trees, reduce erosion, manufacture fertilizers, and, of course, generate electricity, all at artificially low prices subsidized by the 98 percent of the American people who didn't live in the Tennessee Valley.

Asked how he would present this idea, considering the likely resistance to establishing such a big monopoly, FDR replied, "I'll tell them it's neither fish nor fowl. But whatever it is, it will taste awfully good to the people of the Tennessee Valley."[5] The *New York Times* dismissed the idea by saying, "Enactment of any such bill at this time would mark the 'low' of Congressional folly." The TVA would drive the Tennessee Electric Power Company out of business, so its executives spoke out against the TVA bill, as did executives from several other states. Testimony indicated that existing power generation capacity exceeded consumption by more than 60 percent.[6]

Nonetheless, FDR and Norris pushed the bill through Congress, and FDR signed the Tennessee Valley Authority Act into law on May

18, 1933. TVA's billing as a measure to promote recovery from the Great Depression was odd, since FDR, Norris, and others supporting the bill contemplated the construction of dams, power houses, transmission systems, and other projects that would take many years to complete. The contemplated payback period was several decades.

One might have wondered, too, why Norris and other "progressives" were comfortable establishing TVA as a government monopoly, considering how hostile they were to private monopolies. Obviously, it wasn't monopoly they objected to but private ownership. The Tennessee Valley Authority Act outlawed competition with TVA in its territory. The TVA wasn't subject to state or federal regulation. Nor would the TVA have to pay federal or state taxes. On the contrary, the TVA was dependent on congressional appropriations—subsidies from the federal government. During the Great Depression, the population of the Tennessee Valley was estimated to be around 2.5 million,[7] compared to the U.S. population of 130.9 million, reported in the 1940 census,[8] so the 98 percent of the American people who didn't live in the Tennessee Valley were subsidizing the 2 percent who lived there. If it were true that private utilities had overcharged customers, at least private utility customers got something for their money (electricity), which is more than could be said for taxpayers who didn't live in the Tennessee Valley.

THE TVA ACT mandated a three-person board of directors. FDR named hydraulic engineer Arthur E. Morgan as the chairman. He was the former president of Antioch College and an expert on flood control. Historian Arthur M. Schlesinger Jr. described him as a "tall, rangy, gray, impressive man of fifty-five," an ardent believer in central planning and an admirer of utopian socialist Edward Bellamy.[9] Morgan's "ideas on cooperative communal enterprise closely paralleled those of the nineteenth-century Utopian Socialists," wrote historian Thomas K. McCraw. "He brought to the Tennessee Valley Authority a righteous, moralistic sense of high mission and an unequivocal conviction that the world could be rationally remade."[10]

Morgan wanted the TVA to do much more than produce electrical power and fertilizer. He envisioned vast efforts to improve the lives of people in the Tennessee Valley, by expanding into housing, education, and other areas. Morgan contemplated seizing the land of people who didn't want to be "improved" his way.[11] Or as he put it more delicately, "laws of land ownership should be changed so that men shall not be allowed to own and occupy land unless they will manage it in the interest of a permanent agriculture."[12]

The second TVA director was sixty-six-year-old Harcourt A. Morgan (no relation to Arthur), born in Canada and a graduate of Ontario Agricultural College;[13] he did postgraduate work at Cornell, became an agricultural scientist, and served as president of the University of Tennessee.[14] The university's farm extension system provided county agents to help farmers. Harcourt Morgan believed that better agricultural practices were essential if farmers were to improve their lives. He urged crop rotation to help replenish the nutrients in soil, rather than planting of the same crops year after year. He talked to farmers about diversifying their crops and controlling erosion. "With his lanky frame and leathery face," observed historian McCraw, "he seemed the embodiment of the farmers he represented. He spoke their language, and dressed the part, habitually wearing both a belt and suspenders."[15]

The third director, thirty-three-year-old David Lilienthal, was a lawyer who devoted his career to filing lawsuits against public utilities. A protégé of Felix Frankfurter, Lilienthal gained national attention working on the Wisconsin State Utility Commission's successful lawsuits to cut electricity rates. Historian Schlesinger called him "a quiet, solid man, with a round face, spectacles, receding sandy hair, a deceptive gentleness of manner, and a hard precision of mind."[16] He proved to be a skilled promoter and bureaucratic infighter.

All three directors were strong personalities, each claiming their own turf. Arthur Morgan focused on building dams, Harcourt Morgan on agriculture, and Lilienthal on government-subsidized electrical power. They soon began squabbling. Arthur Morgan promoted his vision of the TVA as providing a "designed and planned social order."[17] Lilienthal strongly opposed Morgan's view that investor-owned utilities should be treated with respect. For more than five years, Lilienthal and Arthur Morgan struggled to dominate the TVA, while the Great Depression dragged on. As Arthur Morgan became increasingly frustrated at his inability to achieve a utopian dream, he attacked his colleagues publicly and began lecturing FDR on what he should do. FDR fired him in 1938 and made Harcourt Morgan the chairman. A joint House-Senate committee investigated the charges and countercharges, and 101 witnesses generated 15,470 pages of testimony.[18] After that, the TVA was mainly about generating subsidized electrical power and producing fertilizer.[19]

Lilienthal emerged as the most effective advocate of this government power monopoly. Speaking to audiences in the Tennessee Valley, he asserted, "The Tennessee Valley authority power program is not a taxpayers' subsidy. It is a business undertaking. . . . We are . . . obligated to operate our business on a sound basis." He predicted, "Every one in the Valley will benefit from [the TVA]. . . . the demand for power, obviously, will greatly increase with an increase in industrial activity and an increase in the economic well-being of the people of the Valley." Yet biographer Willson Whitman acknowledged that "every year TVA had to go to Congress for money."[20]

Lilienthal claimed that the TVA had "responsibility to see that things happen—but no powers of compulsion."[21] The act, however, specified that that the TVA had the authority "in the name of the United States of America" to assert the "right of eminent domain," and in purchasing real estate or going through condemnation procedures, "the title to such real estate shall be taken in the name of the United States of America." Furthermore, "in the event that the owner or owners of such property shall fail and refuse to sell to the Corporation at a price deemed fair and reasonable by the board, then the Corporation may proceed to exercise the right of eminent domain, and to condemn all property that it deems necessary."[22]

One of the principal targets of TVA eminent domain proceedings was Tennessee Electric Light and Power Company, which had put up and maintained utility poles for transmission wires. It was owned by the New York–based public utility holding company Commonwealth and Southern, whose president was lawyer Wendell Willkie (a registered Democrat who was to become the Republican presidential candidate in 1940). The "genial, tousle-haired" Willkie battled the TVA in the courts, and altogether nineteen private utilities resisted the expropriation of their assets by the TVA. At one point, thirty-seven injunction lawsuits were under way, defending private property.[23] Ultimately, of course, the private utilities lost.[24]

The TVA served as a producer/wholesaler, selling power to municipally owned power companies, which would handle local distribution. Local governments that weren't already in the power distribution business were encouraged to get in with a loan from the New Deal's Public Works Administration. The TVA undermined local political resistance by paying municipalities some money instead of taxes (the payments were less than the taxes a private utility would have paid). Privately owned utilities found themselves competing with government-run utilities whose rates were likely to be lower because they were taxpayer-subsidized.[25]

Government-owned regional power systems did not materialize in other regions of the country, despite some interest. Interior Secretary Harold Ickes, who wanted the Department of the Interior to control such systems, opposed any such plan. Local people resisted federal control.[26]

As a remedy for the Great Depression, the TVA didn't work. The building of TVA dams, like any other complex public works projects, proceeded slowly. Norris Dam (100 megawatts) and Wheeler Dam (356 megawatts) weren't finished until 1936, three years after passage of the Tennessee Valley Authority Act. Pickwick Dam (220 megawatts) was finished in 1938; Guntersville Dam (102 megawatts) in 1940.[27] Hiwassee (117 megawatts) was completed in 1940; Chicakamauga

(120 megawatts) in 1940. Although building these dams provided work for engineers and skilled construction workers, the dams really came too late to have much impact on the lives of most people in the Tennessee Valley during the Great Depression. The major TVA dam construction programs occurred later.

In addition, as is apparent from these numbers, the depression-era TVA dams were comparatively small. By contrast, Bonneville Dam, in Oregon, opened in 1938 and had a capacity of 5,295 megawatts.[28] Construction on Grand Coulee Dam, in the state of Washington, which had been debated and planned during the 1920s, finally got under way in 1934; the main dam was finished in 1941, and the first five generators began producing 344 megawatts the following year. After World War II, additional generators were built, expanding capacity to 6,809 megawatts.[29] TVA dams were smaller because the rivers were smaller than some of the rivers out West, and in Tennessee gorges tended to be narrower.[30]

Much of the power generated by the dams was used for energy-intensive industries such as those manufacturing fertilizer and aluminum. During World War II, 80 percent of TVA-generated electric power went to the federal government. For instance, Douglas Dam, about twenty miles from Knoxville, generated power for concentrating uranium at the top secret Oak Ridge facility, where scientists conducted research that led to development of the atomic bomb and nuclear submarine engines. In the decade following World War II, the TVA tripled its generating capacity, and about half the power went to the federal government.[31]

TO THE DEGREE the TVA had any impact at all, it appeared to be negative. The most important study of the effects of TVA policies—conducted by energy economist William Chandler in 1983—estimated that in the half century after the TVA was launched, *economic growth in bordering states, where people didn't get their electricity from the TVA, equaled or surpassed growth within the Tennessee*

Valley. Chandler tracked the growth of per person incomes in Tennessee (where everybody received TVA power) and Georgia (where nobody received TVA power), because these states had similar levels of income before the TVA began. By the 1940s, as more and more TVA dams were completed, Georgia began to surpass Tennessee in per person annual income growth, and this was true most years up to 1980, the end of Chandler's survey period. Further, after comparing Tennessee and North Carolina, Chandler reported that "Incomes in both states grew at the same average rates during the first decade of the TVA experiment. Incomes in North Carolina grew faster than in Tennessee in eleven of the twenty years between TVA's creation in 1933 and 1953." Altogether, he concluded, "Among the nine states of the southeastern United States, there has been essentially an inverse relationship between income per capita and the extent to which the state was served by TVA. . . . Watershed counties in the seven TVA states, moreover, are poorer than the non-TVA counties in these states."[32]

How could this be? Why wouldn't cheap electric power help people prosper? Receiving TVA-subsidized electricity gave Tennessee Valley farmers an incentive to remain in agriculture. Throughout the Tennessee Valley, people left farming for manufacturing and later for service industries at a slower rate than was the case in the bordering states of Georgia, North Carolina, and Arkansas. People in these states moved more quickly into manufacturing and service sectors, which offered higher incomes.

The TVA would have failed even if it hadn't provided incentives for people to continue doing what they were doing (small-scale agriculture) rather than pursuing manufacturing and service jobs. It was a fallacy to imagine that one factor—such as electrical power—could bring recovery. All kinds of investments were needed, particularly the investments that people make to improve their own skills. During the 1930s, Western intellectuals were impressed by the Soviet Union's reported gains in steel output, but of course it turned out the Soviet economy was a disaster.[33] During the 1950s, 1960s, and 1970s, so-called development economists suffered from the same illusion that there was a single key to prosperity, and the World Bank spent billions subsidizing the construction of steel plants and other complex projects in Third World countries, none of which brought prosperity.

Ironically, the Tennessee Valley actually lagged other regions in electrification, even though David Lilienthal aggressively promoted electricity and electrical appliances. As Chandler explained, "Rural electrification did not proceed as rapidly in the TVA area as elsewhere nearby. In 1930 Tennessee held a slight advantage over Georgia. About 4 percent of Tennessee's and 3 percent of Georgia's farms had power, compared to 13 percent nationwide. . . . By 1940 Tennessee trailed Georgia in rural electrification. . . . All major TVA states trailed North Carolina, Virginia, and Georgia."[34]

Why were people in the TVA region slower to adopt electricity? Chandler explained that use of electricity correlated with income. The more money people earned, the more electrical appliances they could afford and the more electricity they would tend to use. To the degree that the TVA slowed down the rate of progress, by subsidizing people in existing, low-paying farm work and reducing their incentive to find higher-paying work elsewhere, the TVA undermined a fundamental factor in the demand for electricity.[35]

This view seems to be confirmed by the pattern of water usage in the South. In 1930, about 3 percent of Tennessee farms had running water, which was about the same as Kentucky and North Carolina, and better than Alabama, Arkansas, Georgia, and Mississippi. Two decades after the beginning of the TVA, however, half the farms in the non-TVA states of Georgia, North Carolina, and Virginia had running water, versus only about a third in Tennessee. Incredibly, Tennessee had become a laggard despite over $5 billion of TVA spending on water development during its first two decades.[36]

The TVA system of dams and locks did little to stimulate shipping business on the Tennessee River. Consequently, Chandler wrote, "The citizens of the depression ridden Tennessee Valley got almost no benefit out of the navigation system. . . . The workers might just as well have been digging holes and filling them up. During the Depression, there were thousands of uses for money that would have returned the investment in short order."[37]

Much was claimed about the TVA's contribution to flood control, but this appears to have been vastly exaggerated. An estimated 85 percent of the flood control benefits went to a single city, Chattanooga, which had been hit by the worst floods. Chandler observed, "Without the political force demanding flood control in Chattanooga, the TVA might not have been created. And but for that accident of geology, the Tennessee River cutting through the Cumberland Mountains rather than flowing southward to the Gulf, flooding would not have been so spectacularly newsworthy and therefore political in Chattanooga in the first third of this century."[38]

Second, and most amazing, TVA dams seem to have deliberately flooded more acres than have gained some protection from natural floods. According to Chandler, TVA dams flooded 243,000 acres of land to provide some protection for the 8,750 acres in Chattanooga.[39] Economist John Moore, in a 1967 analysis, reported that TVA dams "permanently flood a total of about 730,000 acres, an area larger than that which the Army Engineers estimated would be flooded by a flood so large that it expected to occur only once in 500 years. They flood an area which is approximately as large as the state of Rhode Island. . . . the permanent removal of so great an acreage of land from productivity and taxation must inevitably have an oppressive effect upon the economy of the region."[40]

Most directly affected by the TVA during the Great Depression were the 15,654 people who were forced out of their homes to make way for dams.[41] Farm owners received cash settlements for their condemned property, but tenant farmers received nothing because they didn't own any land. After chronicling victims of the TVA "population removal program," historians Michael J. McDonald and John Muldowny reported: "TVA's 'social experiment' was a failure."[42]

The Tennessee Valley Authority added to the burdens of taxpayers across the country and, the evidence suggests, did the most harm to people in the valley who were supposed to benefit from it.

CHAPTER TWELVE

WHY DID THE SUPREME COURT STRIKE DOWN EARLY NEW DEAL LAWS?

T HE EARLY 1930s saw powerful political pressures to suppress economic liberty, as the New Deal promoted price fixing and cartels that benefited producer interests at the expense of consumers. But for three years, the U.S. Supreme Court defended economic liberty and struck down one New Deal law after another.

New Deal historians long blamed these adverse Supreme Court decisions on the "Four Horsemen of Reaction," meaning Justices Willis Van Devanter, James C. McReynolds, Pierce Butler, and George Sutherland. The four were sometimes joined by others, particularly Chief Justice Charles Evans Hughes and Justice Owen Roberts. So in addition to 5–4 decisions, a key unanimous decision struck down the National Industrial Recovery Act—even the "progressive" Justices Louis D. Brandeis, Benjamin Cardozo, and Harlan Fiske Stone were on board for that one. An 8–1 decision struck down New Deal restrictions in the oil business. Brandeis wrote the majority opinion striking down the Frazier-Lemke Act that authorized farmers to walk away from their obligations to creditors.

Born in 1859 in Marion, Indiana, Willis Van Devanter brought an appreciation of business risks to the Supreme Court. He graduated from Indiana Asbury (now DePauw) University, then Cincinnati Law School in 1879, and joined his father's law firm. When his father retired, and partner John Lacey was appointed chief justice of the Wyoming Territorial Supreme Court, Van Devanter headed for Wyoming, too. He hunted grizzly bears in the Bighorn Mountains with Buffalo Bill. He handled a great deal of legal business for the two principal interests in Wyoming, cattle operations and railroads.

By 1887, he was a law partner with Charles N. Potter, who brought him into the Republican Party. He was elected to the territorial legislature the following year and played a major role codifying territorial laws, which subsequently became the basis of the state's laws. President William McKinley appointed Van Devanter assistant attorney general in the Department of the Interior. President Theodore Roosevelt nominated Van Devanter to the U.S. Court of Appeals for the Eighth Circuit. He served there for seven years before President William Howard Taft nominated him for the Supreme Court in December 1910. He served twenty-six years, writing 346 majority opinions. He helped draft the Judiciary Act of 1925, which enabled the Supreme Court to handle more cases and eliminate its backlog.

James Clark McReynolds, born in 1862 in Elkton, Kentucky, was a brilliant man and a prickly pear. His father was a physician and planter who didn't approve of compulsory government schools. Young McReynolds graduated from Vanderbilt University and earned a law degree at the University of Virginia. Interested in politics, he went to Washington and served as an assistant to Tennessee's Democratic senator Howell E. Jackson. After two years, he moved to Nashville, where he became a corporate lawyer. He ran unsuccessfully for Congress, then taught commercial law at Vanderbilt, and in 1903 was appointed assistant attorney general in Republican Theodore Roosevelt's administration. There he helped enforce antitrust laws.

Under Roosevelt's successor, Republican William Howard Taft, McReynolds helped break up the tobacco trust.

He remained a Democrat, though, and supported Woodrow Wilson's campaign for the White House in 1912. Wilson named McReynolds attorney general the following year. Although McReynolds's volatile temper and abrasive manner often made enemies, Wilson in 1914 nominated him to fill the vacancy on the Supreme Court that followed the death of Justice Horace Lurton, who, like McReynolds, was from Tennessee. A brash bachelor, McReynolds didn't like the two Jewish justices, Brandeis and Benjamin Cardozo. He wouldn't speak to Justice John Clark, whom he considered unfit for the job. After Justice Stone described one lawyer's brief as dull, McReynolds told him, "The only duller thing I can think of is to hear you read one of your opinions." McReynolds reportedly didn't like female attorneys or tobacco smokers, either.[1]

McReynolds's opinions focused on protecting private property, freedom of contract, and freedom of speech. In *Meyer v the State of Nebraska*, 262 U.S. 390 (1923), he struck down a law that made it illegal to teach a foreign language prior to the ninth grade. In *Farrington v T. Tokushige*, 273 U.S. 284 (1927), McReynolds overturned a law that banned the teaching of the Japanese language. He was horrified at the policies of FDR, whom he called an "utter incompetent."[2]

Having come up the hard way, Pierce Butler cherished individualism and enterprise. He was born in 1866 in Pine Bend, Minnesota. His parents had emigrated from Ireland after the potato famine of the 1840s, and his father operated a tavern before trying to develop a farm on the frontier. Pierce was educated at a small country school where he learned Latin, German, and math. He graduated from Carleton College, studied law at a local law firm, and passed his bar exam. He learned to excel at negotiating settlements in railroad rate cases. As general counsel for the Chicago, St. Paul, Minneapolis, and Omaha Railroad, he became known as one of the best railroad lawyers. In court, he had a reputation for "shredding" witnesses.

President William Howard Taft's attorney general asked Butler to help the federal government prosecute antitrust cases. He took on meat-packing companies, and he later argued railroad cases before the Supreme Court. President Warren Harding nominated him to the Supreme Court in November 1922. During his career on the high court, Butler wrote 323 majority opinions, 44 dissenting opinions, and 3 concurring opinions.

The most impressive thinker was George Sutherland, a champion of natural rights jurisprudence. He believed the most important function of law was to protect individual liberty by restraining government power—historically, the biggest threat to liberty everywhere. Sutherland understood that for ordinary people, economic liberty was generally the most important liberty. Intellectuals tended to rate First Amendment liberties more highly because they spoke out publicly and published their political views, but every individual's livelihood depended on freedom to choose where to work, where to live, where to travel, where to spend money, what to buy, and how much to pay. Freedom of contract was absolutely essential for all these other freedoms. It would be hard to find a Supreme Court justice who ever did a better job defending economic liberty than George Sutherland.

He was born in 1862 in Stony Stratford, England, and his family emigrated to America when he was a child. They moved to Utah, the second state to adopt woman suffrage, and he was educated at Brigham Young University and the University of Michigan.

He returned to Utah, where he began practicing law in 1883. He entered Republican politics, serving in the U.S. House of Representatives (1901–1903) and the Senate (1905–1917). As a U.S. senator, Sutherland had introduced the "Anthony Amendment," the proposed constitutional amendment that would give women the right to vote. "When we have established the righteousness of the case for a Democracy," he declared in a 1915 speech, "when we have proven the case for universal manhood suffrage, we have made clear the case for womanhood suffrage as well."[3]

Defeated during the 1916 elections, he became an adviser to Warren Harding and was nominated to the U.S. Supreme Court soon after Harding was elected president in 1920. Sutherland wrote the majority opinion in *Adkins v Children's Hospital*, 261 U.S. 525 (1923), striking down the Minimum Wage Act of 1918, which applied only to women. The case was argued before the Supreme Court by Felix Frankfurter, who, like his mentor Louis Brandeis, submitted a brief (a thousand pages) full of sociological data.[4]

How could a champion of woman suffrage oppose a minimum wage law for women? The case involved twenty-one-year-old Willie Lyons, an elevator operator who earned $35 per month plus two meals a day at the Congress Hotel in Washington, D.C. The new minimum wage law prevented employers from paying women less than $71.50 per month, and since the going rate for elevator operators was only about $35 per month, she was soon unemployed. If the hotel had persisted in paying her the going rate, it would have been subject to penalties provided by the minimum wage law. Because there wasn't a minimum wage law for men, her job was filled by a man at $35 per month. Thus did a "progressive" law, intended to help protect the "health and morals" of women, throw women out of work.[5]

The Minimum Wage Act of 1918 "is not for the protection of persons under legal disability or for the prevention of fraud," Sutherland wrote. "It is simply and exclusively a price-fixing law, confined to adult women . . . who are legally as capable of contracting for themselves as men. It forbids two parties having lawful capacity— under penalties as to the employer—to freely contract with one another in respect of the price for which one shall render service to the other in a purely private employment where both are willing, perhaps anxious, to agree, even though the consequence may be to oblige one to surrender a desirable engagement and the other to dispense with the services of a desirable employee. . . . surely the good of society as a whole cannot be better served than by the preservation against arbitrary restraint of the liberties of its constituent members."[6]

*   *   *

THE SO-CALLED PROGRESSIVES promoted more and more interference with economic liberty, and Sutherland wrote another landmark decision in *New State Ice Co. v Liebmann*, 285 U.S. 262 (1932). In 1925, the Oklahoma legislature had passed a law declaring that the ice business was "public" and that no firm could enter it without securing a permit. Getting a permit involved hearings where competitors could testify that new firms weren't necessary, and apparently the Corporation Commission denied permits to new competitors.[7] Subsequently, Liebmann, without a permit, bought land and started an ice business. New State Ice Company, in Oklahoma, filed a lawsuit to stop Liebmann from competing.

In Sutherland's words, "A regulation which has the effect of denying or unreasonably curtailing the common right to engage in a lawful private business, such as that under review, cannot be upheld consistent with the Fourteenth Amendment. . . . The control here asserted does not protect against monopoly, but tends to foster it. The aim is not to encourage competition, but to prevent it; not to regulate the business, but to preclude persons from engaging in it."[8]

Justice Brandeis, supposedly the "progressive" defender of the downtrodden, denounced "destructive" competition (offering bargains) and defended government-enforced monopoly in the New State Ice case. "It is no objection to the validity of the statute here assailed that it fosters monopoly," he wrote. "That, indeed, is its design."[9]

Brandeis believed that either a government monopoly or government-controlled private monopoly would mean greater efficiency, less waste, and better living. He assumed government officials had superior knowledge about the desires of customers, the competence of entrepreneurs, the quality of service they offered, the potential of new technologies, and other factors. Brandeis further assumed that established firms contribute more than new entrepreneurs do. Finally, Brandeis assumed that even if government officials knew what they were doing, they wouldn't be corrupted by lobbyists from established firms who wanted to suppress competition. None of these assumptions have turned out to be true.

Brandeis defended the Oklahoma ice monopoly by blaming the Great Depression on what he called "unbridled competition." He insisted, "There must be power in the states and the nation to remould, through experimentation, our economic practices and institutions to meet changing social and economic needs."[10] By "experimentation" he meant the government-enforced monopoly privileges that friends of liberty had fought for hundreds of years. In England, Queen Elizabeth's government had granted a monopoly in the manufacture of playing cards, but that monopoly was struck down in the *Case on Monopolies* (1602). The judge ruled that monopoly was "against the common law and the benefit and liberty of the subject."[11] As long ago as 1776, Adam Smith demolished the case for government-enforced monopolies in *The Wealth of Nations*. U.S. Supreme Court justice Stephen J. Field wrote a dissenting opinion in the *Slaughter-House Cases* (1873), which protested a government-enforced monopoly: "A right to pursue a lawful and necessary calling, previously enjoyed by every citizen, and in connection with which a thousand persons were daily employed, is taken away and vested exclusively for twenty-five years, for an extensive district and a large population, in a single corporation."[12]

The first major New Deal case for which Sutherland wrote an opinion (dissenting) was *Home Building & Loan Assn. v Blaisdell*, 290 U.S. 398 (1934), where the issue was freedom of contract. John H. Blaisdell, a Minnesota man, took a $3,800 mortgage on some land with a fourteen-room house. He and his family lived in three rooms, renting the others. But his tenants lost their jobs, and he couldn't keep up the payments.[13] Home Building & Loan Association foreclosed. Two weeks before May 2, 1933, the redemption deadline provided in his mortgage contract (when he could get the house back by paying the amount due), the state enacted a law extending the deadline until May 1, 1935. As a result of the law, Blaisdell was granted a two-year extension in state court. Home Building & Loan Association protested that the state law violated the U.S. Constitution's impairment of contract clause (Article 1, section 10).

Chief Justice Charles Evans Hughes wrote the majority opinion upholding the Minnesota law. He had served two nonconsecutive terms, first as associate justice, then as chief justice. He was born in 1862 in Glens Falls, New York, a small community on the upper Hudson River. He graduated from Madison (now Colgate) University and subsequently attended Brown University with the idea of becoming a minister like his father. But he discovered baseball, poker, and smoking and decided it would be better to pursue a legal career.

For two decades, he flourished in a New York law firm. Then he opted for an easier life as a lecturer at Cornell University and New York Law School. In 1905, he was appointed by the New York State Legislature to a committee that investigated utility rates for gas and electricity. He exposed pervasive fraud and earned the praise of the state's newspapers. Elected governor of New York in 1906, he pushed for compulsory workmen's compensation, an eight-hour day for railway workers, and government regulation of public utilities. President William Howard Taft nominated Hughes to the Supreme Court in 1910. He served until President Warren Harding persuaded him to become secretary of state in 1921. Then he returned to private law practice for nine years, until President Herbert Hoover nominated him for chief justice. He was a "swing" vote on the Court, often supporting the expansion of government power before the New Deal, joining the "Four Horsemen" against some important early New Deal decisions, and later supporting the New Deal.

In *Home Building & Loan Assn. v Blaisdell*, Justice Hughes acknowledged that the creditor couldn't take possession, occupy, or dispose of the property. The creditor was entitled only to collect rent of $40 per month. Hughes considered this a reasonable position during the Great Depression.

Sutherland's dissenting opinion insisted that lenders deserved equal treatment with borrowers and warned that efforts to disadvantage lenders would almost surely backfire. The more borrowers were allowed to get out of inconvenient contracts, the greater the risks for lenders anxious to be repaid, and the less lending there was likely to be in the future. Sutherland turned out to be right, and business investment remained at historic lows throughout the Great Depression.

In *Nebbia v New York*, 291 U.S. 502 (1934), a Rochester grocer was convicted of selling two bottles of milk for less than the 9 cents per quart ordered by the Milk Control Board (consisting of three officials), which the New York State Legislature had established in 1933.[14] The aim was to protect the profit margins of milk producers and distributors. The grocer claimed the law violated the equal protection clause of the Fourteenth Amendment.[15]

The majority opinion was by Justice Owen J. Roberts, another "swing" vote on the Court. He was born in 1875 in Philadelphia, the son of a Welsh hardware merchant. Owen graduated from the University of Pennsylvania, where he excelled as a Greek and Latin scholar. He earned his law degree at the University of Pennsylvania as well. Then he started private law practice in Philadelphia and lectured on contracts, bankruptcy, and real property at his alma mater. After World War I, he was named a special deputy attorney general to prosecute individuals charged with violating the Espionage Act (he secured convictions of several German and Lithuanian publishers). President Calvin Coolidge made him a special counsel in the prosecution of the Teapot Dome case, which involved the bribery of the secretary of the interior for oil leases. In March 1930, Herbert Hoover nominated him to the Supreme Court.

In *Nebbia v New York*, Justice Roberts was joined by Chief Justice Hughes and the progressive justices, Brandeis, Cardozo, and Stone, who considered only the interests of the milk producers and upheld the law suppressing price competition.[16] Justice McReynolds wrote the dissenting opinion, which was joined by Sutherland, Van Devanter, and Butler. These supposedly reactionary justices defended the rights of consumers.

McReynolds wrote, "The Legislature cannot lawfully destroy guaranteed rights of one man with the prime purpose of enriching another, even if, for the moment, this may seem advantageous to the public. . . . Not only does the statute interfere arbitrarily with the rights of the little grocer to conduct his business according to standards long accepted, but it takes away the liberty of twelve million consumers to buy a necessity of life in an open market. It imposes direct and arbitrary burdens upon those already seriously impoverished with the alleged immediate design of affording special benefits to others. To him with less than nine cents it says—You cannot procure a quart of milk from the grocer although he is anxious to accept what you can pay and the demands of your household are urgent."[17]

THE "FOUR HORSEMEN OF REACTION" gained support on the Court as FDR increasingly asserted arbitrary power via executive orders, rather than going through the legislative process. The Congressional Research Service reported, "During his first 15 months in office, President Roosevelt signed 674 executive orders. . . . Many of these administrative regulations were needed to implement statutory policy. In its first year, the National Recovery Administration (NRA) approved hundreds of codes and released 2,998 administrative orders that approved or modified the codes. Almost 6,000 NRA press releases, some of them having a legislative effect, were issued during this period. So many orders were issued that departmental officials were often unaware of their own regulations. At one point the government discovered that it had brought an indictment and taken an appeal to the Supreme Court without realizing that the portion of the regulation on which the proceeding was based had been eliminated by an executive order."[18]

FDR's continued assaults on economic liberty began to alarm Chief Justice Hughes, and he wrote the majority opinion in *Panama Refining Co. v Ryan*, 293 U.S. 388 (1935). State and federal regulations restricted the quantities of petroleum that could be produced, and on July 11, 1933, FDR issued Executive Order 6199, which banned the interstate shipment of any excess production. Three days after this executive order, FDR issued Executive Order 6204, which authorized the secretary of the interior to carry out 6199. Anyone convicted of violating these orders could be hit with a $1,000 fine and/or a six-month prison sentence.[19] These and subsequent executive orders were related to the National Industrial Recovery Act, which had become law on June 16.

The regulations harmed many people. Panama Refining Company, which had oil and gas leases in Texas, filed a lawsuit claiming that the regulations amounted to an unconstitutional delegation of power from Congress to the executive. Amazon Petroleum filed a similar lawsuit.[20]

Justice Hughes agreed that the delegation of power violated the Constitution. He observed that the executive orders didn't offer any findings to justify the delegation of power. He didn't see any reason to assume that a president would always use this power to serve the public good. Accordingly, he concluded the power was unconstitutional.[21]

The challenge to the National Industrial Recovery Act came from the most unlikely source, a chicken producer. Joseph Schechter operated Schechter Poultry Company, and Martin, Alex, and Alan Schechter operated A.L.A. Schechter Company, both of which were slaughterhouses selling chickens to kosher markets in New York City. Schechter was convicted of violating the Code of Fair Competition for the Live Poultry Industry of the Metropolitan Area in and about the City of New York, in the District Court of the United States for the Eastern District of New York. On April 13, 1934, FDR had issued his executive order authorizing this code.

There were two key issues. First, Schechter conducted its business entirely within New York State. The company purchased chickens in New York State and sold them in New York State. Schechter wasn't involved with interstate commerce.

In the *unanimous* decision, written by Chief Justice Hughes, he noted that the Constitution's commerce clause (Article 1, section 8, clause 3) provides that "Congress shall have the power . . . to regulate commerce . . . among the several States." This had long been interpreted as a limitation on the power of the states, but all the justices believed it was also a limitation on the power of Congress, barring it from interfering with business that didn't involve interstate commerce.

The second key issue involved the delegation of legislative power to a president. Hughes wrote, "The President in approving a code may impose his own conditions, adding to or taking from what is proposed, as 'in his discretion' he thinks necessary 'to effectuate the policy' declared by the Act. Of course, he has no less liberty when he prescribes a code on his own motion or on complaint, and he is free to prescribe one if a code has not been approved. The Act provides for the creation by the President of administrative agencies to assist him, but the action or reports of such agencies, or of his other assistants—their recommendations and findings in relation to the making of codes—have no sanction beyond the will of the President, who may accept, modify or reject them as he pleases . . . the discretion of the President in approving or prescribing codes, and thus enacting laws for the government of trade and industry throughout the country, is virtually unfettered."[22]

This violated the constitutional principle of delegated, enumerated powers, the principle that the branches of the federal government had only such powers as were specifically delegated to them. As Hughes explained, "These powers of the national government are limited by the constitutional grants. Those who act under these grants are not at liberty to transcend the imposed limits because they believe that more or different power is necessary. Such assertions of extra-constitutional authority were anticipated and precluded by the explicit terms of the Tenth Amendment,—'The powers not delegated to the United States by the Constitution, nor prohibited by it to the States, are reserved to the States respectively, or to the people.' . . . We think that the code-making authority thus conferred is an unconstitutional delegation of legislative power."[23]

Hughes rejected claims that the NRA operated on the basis of voluntary cooperation: "It involves the coercive exercise of the law-making power. The codes of fair competition which the statute attempts to authorize are codes of laws. If valid, they place all persons within their reach under the obligation of positive law, binding equally those who assent and those who do not assent. Violations of the provisions of the codes are punishable as crimes. . . .

"It is not the province of the Court to consider the economic advantages or disadvantages of such a centralized system," Hughes wrote. "It is sufficient to say that the Federal Constitution does not provide for it."[24]

So, on May 27, 1935, the NIRA was struck down, and the NRA was out of business. After the Supreme Court *Schechter* decision had been published, Justice Brandeis met with two of FDR's advisers, lawyers Benjamin V. Cohen and Thomas G. Corcoran, and explained: "They change everything. The Court was unanimous. . . . The President has been living in a fool's paradise."[25]

At a press conference, FDR complained, "The whole tendency over these years has been to view the interstate commerce clause in the light of present-day civilization. The country was in the horse-and-buggy age when that clause was written and if you go back to the debates on the Federal Constitution you will find in 1787 that one of the impelling motives for putting in that clause was this: There wasn't much interstate commerce at all—probably 80 or 90 percent of the human beings in the thirteen original States were completely self-supporting within their own communities."[26]

The *Schechter* decision was a blow to FDR, but as things turned out, it was a boon for the economy. As economists Richard K.

Vedder and Lowell E. Gallaway explained, "The [1935–1936] job expansion coincided with a leveling-off in the sharp money-wage growth observed in 1933 and 1934. This was probably because one wage-increasing piece of legislation, the National Industrial Recovery Act, was found unconstitutional, and a second such piece of legislation, the National Labor Relations Act of 1935, had not yet had any real effect, as its constitutionality was still uncertain."[27]

Before the Supreme Court ruled on the NIRA, Congress passed the Bituminous Coal Conservation Act, known as the Guffey Act— which was much like the NIRA, except that it applied to coal mining. It aimed to maintain high coal prices and high wages amidst the depression. Under the act, the National Bituminous Coal Commission was established to issue a Bituminous Coal Code for enforcing coal mining cartels.[28] The act divided the coal mining industry into twenty-three districts, each ruled by three commissioners who had the power to restrict mining output and fix minimum coal prices, minimum wages, and maximum working hours. The commissioners, working with the biggest producers, set policies that presumably served the interests of these producers, even though other producers might be harmed. Every coal mining company would be subject to a 15 percent excise tax, and those that went along with the cartel would get a 90 percent rebate. Thus, any company refusing to go along would be hit with the full 15 percent tax and be at a potentially ruinous competitive disadvantage.[29]

The board of directors of Carter Coal, a Kentucky company, voted to join the government cartel so the 15 percent punitive tax could be avoided, but principal stockholder James Carter filed suit in an effort to stay out of the cartel and honor existing contracts. The Roosevelt administration defended the Guffey Act by saying that coal mining had an impact on interstate commerce and accordingly federal regulation was justified by the Constitution's commerce clause.

Justice Sutherland wrote the 5–4 majority opinion, with Justices Butler, McReynolds, Roberts, and Van Devanter concurring. The "firmly established principle is that the powers which the general government may exercise are only those specifically enumerated in the Constitution and such implied powers as are necessary and proper to carry into effect the enumerated powers," the court said in its decision, announced on May 18, 1936. "The supremacy of the Constitution as law is declared without qualification. That supremacy is absolute; the supremacy of a statute enacted by Congress is not absolute, but conditioned upon its being made in pursuance of the Constitution."[30]

Sutherland rejected the Roosevelt administration's claim that the Bituminous Coal Conservation Act was sanctioned by the Constitution's commerce clause. Mining is a local business, he observed, and the law restricted it before the products (coal) entered interstate commerce, which meant that the law couldn't be justified on the basis of the commerce clause. By contrast, in the *Schechter* case, the National Industrial Recovery Act was found to be unconstitutional because it regulated products after they left interstate commerce.

Sutherland considered the tax illegitimate: "It is very clear that the 'excise tax' is not imposed for revenue, but exacted as a penalty to compel compliance with the regulatory provisions of the act. The whole purpose of the exaction is to coerce what is called an agreement—which, of course, it is not, for it lacks the essential element of consent. One who does a thing in order to avoid a monetary penalty does not agree; he yields to compulsion precisely the same as though he did so to avoid a term in jail."[31]

Sutherland was especially concerned about the power of a majority to harm a minority: "This is legislative delegation in its most obnoxious form, for it is not even delegation to an official or an official body, presumptively disinterested, but to private persons whose interests may be and often are adverse to the interests of others in the same business. The record shows that the conditions of competition differ among the various localities. In some, coal dealers compete among themselves. In other localities, they also compete with the mechanical production of electrical energy and of natural gas. Some coal producers favor the Code; others oppose it, and the record clearly indicates that this diversity of view arises from their conflicting and even antagonistic interests."[32]

Although the text of the Bituminous Coal Conservation Act said that if one part of it were found unconstitutional, this shouldn't invalidate the entire law, Sutherland believed that the section fixing high prices and the section fixing high wages couldn't be separated. They worked together. Consequently, since there were so many problems with the price-fixing section (the wage-fixing section hadn't yet gone into effect), the entire law must be struck down.[33]

In his dissenting opinion, with which Justices Brandeis, Cardozo, and Stone concurred, Chief Justice Hughes agreed that a key provision of the Bituminous Coal Conservation Act, restricting production, was invalid because "It attempts a broad delegation of legislative power to fix hours and wages without standards or limitation. . . . (2) The provision permits a group of producers and employees, according to their own views of expediency, to make rules as to hours and wages for other producers and employees who were not parties to the agreement. Such a provision, apart from the mere question of the delegation of legislative power, is not in accord with the requirement of due process of law which under the Fifth Amendment dominates the regulations which Congress may impose. (3) The provision goes beyond any proper measure of protection of interstate commerce, and attempts a broad regulation of industry within the State."[34] Having acknowledged all this, Hughes didn't think the case should be thrown out: "If, in fixing prices, due process is violated by arbitrary, capricious or confiscatory action, judicial remedy is available."[35]

THE NEXT BIG Supreme Court case involved the Agricultural Adjustment Act, which New Dealers considered as important for reviving agriculture as the National Industrial Recovery Act was thought to be for industry. As noted in chapter 10, the idea was to tax food processors and channel the proceeds to farmers who destroyed crops, thereby reducing supplies and maintaining farm prices. Raising farm prices was viewed as the way to raise farmers' income, much as high wage rates were supposed to raise the incomes of industrial workers.

When the government billed Hoosac Mills, a bankrupt food processor, for taxes under the Agricultural Adjustment Act, the receivers disregarded them. The district court ruled the taxes were valid, the court of appeals reversed this ruling, and the case went before the Supreme Court.

The Roosevelt administration claimed that the tax was just another tax, and taxpayers couldn't refuse to pay because they disagreed with the way it was spent. But Justice Roberts, in his majority opinion, observed that the sole purpose of this tax was to pay farmers who reduced their cultivated acreage and destroyed crops, which meant it wasn't a legitimate tax: "A tax, in the general understanding of the term, and as used in the Constitution, signifies an exaction for the support of the Government. The word has never been thought to connote the expropriation of money from one group for the benefit of another."[36]

Roberts continued, "The question is not what power the Federal Government ought to have, but what powers, in fact, have been given by the people. . . . The federal union is a government of delegated powers. It has only such as are expressly conferred upon it and such as are reasonably to be implied from those granted. In this respect, we differ radically from nations where all legislative power, without restriction or limitation, is vested in a parliament or other legislative body subject to no restrictions except the discretion of its members."[37]

Did the Constitution delegate to the federal government power over agricultural production? Since agricultural production was a local activity, it couldn't be covered by the commerce clause. Nor was such power implied in the clause about enacting taxes for the "common Defense and general Welfare of the United States." The phrase "general welfare" couldn't reasonably be invoked when a tax benefits particular people (like farmers) rather than the general population. Roberts insisted that if "general welfare" were applied to whatever the government wanted to spend money on, it would gain unlimited power, and the primary purpose of the Constitution was to protect liberty by limiting government power.

To underscore the absurdity of the Agricultural Adjustment Act, Roberts considered how it would apply to other industries: "Assume that too many shoes are being manufactured throughout the nation; that the market is saturated, the price depressed, the factories running half-time, the employes suffering. Upon the principle of the statute in question, Congress might authorize the Secretary of Commerce to enter into contracts with shoe manufacturers providing that each shall reduce his output, and that the United States will pay him a fixed sum proportioned to such reduction, the money to make the payments to be raised by a tax on all retail shoe dealers or their customers.

"Suppose that there are too many garment workers in the large cities; that this results in dislocation of the economic balance. Upon the principle contended for, an excise might be laid on the manufacture of all garments manufactured, and the proceeds paid to those manufacturers who agree to remove their plants to cities having not more than a hundred thousand population. Thus, through the asserted power of taxation, the federal government, against the will of individual states, might completely redistribute the industrial population. . . . A possible result of sustaining the claimed federal power would be that every business group which thought itself underprivileged might demand that a tax be laid on its vendors or vendees, the proceeds to be appropriated to the redress of its deficiency of income."[38]

Roberts concluded: "From the accepted doctrine that the United States is a government of delegated powers, it follows that those not expressly granted, or reasonably to be implied from such as are conferred, are reserved to the states, or to the people. To forestall any suggestion to the contrary, the Tenth Amendment was adopted. The same proposition, otherwise stated, is that powers not granted are prohibited. None to regulate agricultural production is given, and therefore legislation by Congress for that purpose is forbidden."[39]

The anti–New Deal bloc was tested again in *Morehead v Tipaldo*, 298 U.S. 587, which involved a New York laundry manager who had been jailed for failing to pay the state-mandated minimum wage for women. A majority of justices (apparently including Roberts as well as Brandeis, Cardozo, Hughes, and Stone) agreed to take the case because the intention was to reverse Sutherland's 1923 majority decision in *Adkins v Children's Hospital.*

But something happened along the way, and Justice Roberts came to agree with Justices Butler, McReynolds, Sutherland, and Van Devanter that *Adkins* should be followed, and the New York State minimum wage law should be struck down. Roberts found that the fundamental provisions of the New York State minimum wage law (*Morehead*) were similar to the District of Columbia law *(Adkins),* and the circumstances were similar, too, so *Adkins* prevailed.

"The right to make contracts about one's affairs is a part of the liberty protected by the due process clause," Roberts explained. "Within this liberty are provisions of contracts between employer and employee fixing the wages to be paid. In making contracts of employment, generally speaking, the parties have equal right to obtain from each other the best terms they can by private bargaining. Legislative abridgement of that freedom can only be justified by the existence of exceptional circumstances. Freedom of contract is the general rule and restraint the exception."

Roberts suggested that the underlying purpose of the New York State minimum wage law for women was to limit competition for jobs, benefiting men. An increasing number of women had been entering the labor market. "Minimum wages for women alone," he pointed out, "would unreasonably restrain them in competition with men and tend arbitrarily to deprive them of employment and a fair chance to find work." The New York State minimum wage law for women was struck down on June 1, 1936.

Justices Sutherland, McReynolds, Van Devanter, and Butler, sometimes joined by Hughes, Roberts, and others, did a splendid job articulating vital principles of economic liberty in the worst of times. Very few authors of any era have done better. These justices faced enormous political pressure from a popular president with commanding majorities in Congress, so they deserve credit for displaying the courage of their convictions. Subsequent experience has made clear that the purported New Deal "reform" measures that these justices struck down were, in fact, prolonging the Great Depression. The economic liberty they defended, criticized as an obstacle to recovery, has been vindicated as the mainspring of human progress.

How Did Social Security Contribute to Higher Unemployment?

ONE OF THE most enduring legacies of the New Deal, Social Security, was a consequence of problems the federal government itself had caused. Because of bad government policies that brought on the Great Depression and prolonged it, millions of people lost their jobs, and those who worked for companies providing pensions no longer had pension coverage. Many companies curtailed their pension programs, and other companies went out of business. The legions of unemployed couldn't accumulate savings toward their retirement.

Although Social Security came to be seen as a bulwark of democracy, it actually originated in one of Europe's most autocratic regimes. During the 1870s, German socialists demanded that their government gain more power in the name of social justice, and German chancellor Otto von Bismarck saw that expanded government power would suit his very different purposes. In 1881, Bismarck said, "Whoever has a pension for his old age is far more content and far easier to handle than one who has no such prospect." Bismarck's biographer A. J. P. Taylor added that "Social security has certainly made the masses less independent everywhere."[1] Germany's government-run retirement system began in 1889.

Government-run pension systems spread throughout Europe. Although referred to as "social insurance," they weren't true insurance, which would have involved people voluntarily contracting for benefits based on the premiums they paid. With true insurance, premiums varied according to a policyholder's age and how much retirement income they wanted. Insurance companies invested the premiums long term in productive assets, principally stocks, bonds, and real estate, so that individuals could cover the costs of their own retirement. By contrast, every "social insurance" scheme had some people subsidizing others. Often such schemes started out or became pay-as-you-go, meaning that current taxpayers covered the costs of people currently receiving pensions. Individuals, as taxpayers, didn't contribute anything for their own retirement. The cost of their retirement became a burden for future generations. The assumption was that there would be enough taxpayers in the future to take care of all the retirees and that future generations would be willing to bear burdens. Nobody seems to have considered that such burdens might become much heavier over time if the number of retired people grew faster than the number of taxpayers. Alternatively, some countries like Denmark (in 1891) established noncontributory "social insurance," which was administered like a welfare program: It was financed out of the government's general revenues, and people could collect retirement benefits only by showing that they didn't have any other means of support.[2]

In the United States, the federal government paid pensions to Civil War veterans. Many states established pensions for their employees during the late nineteenth century. These were pay-as-you-go systems.[3] Railroads, public utilities, and steel companies started offering pensions.

Many European immigrants agitated for the same kind of government-run pension systems that they had known back home. In 1906, German immigrants established the American Association for

Labor Legislation, a branch of the International Association for Labor Legislation, which promoted government-run retirement systems. "From the early days of the movement," explained policy analyst Carolyn L. Weaver, "there was a fundamental conflict over the purpose of 'social insurance.' Was 'social insurance' fundamentally designed to prevent worker insecurity through the principle of insurance and incentive schemes or was it designed to maintain security in old age through income redistribution?" Russian immigrant Isaac Rubinow was the most prolific and influential author promoting "social insurance" as a scheme for redistributing income in the name of "social justice."[4] In 1927, the Russian-born economist Abraham Epstein formed a lobbying organization called the American Association for Old-Age Security. He wrote several books about poverty among the elderly, including *The Problem of Old Age Pensions in Industry* (1926), *Facing Old Age* (1922), and *The Challenge of the Aged* (1928).

Despite all this agitation, there wasn't much support for a government-run pension system until the Great Depression. As Weaver reported, "Even among the most industrial states, the vast majority of the elderly were dependent on neither organized private or public charity or the almshouse. Instead, they were self-supporting or supported by families and friends. . . . According to the findings of the New York Commission on Old-Age Security, for example, out of the estimated 603,700 persons over sixty-five residing in the state in 1929, nearly 90 percent were either self-supporting or voluntarily provided for by friends and families. . . . Less than 4 percent of the state's elderly were found to be dependent on organized private charity or public assistance."

Poverty among the elderly appeared to be caused primarily by low earnings during working years, which made it tough to accumulate savings. This problem lessened with the rising level of prosperity and the dramatic growth of private insurance, annuities, and pensions geared to lower-income workers. In 1911, group life insurance was introduced, providing coverage for everybody in a company and eliminating the need for medical examinations or age-related premiums.

The number of people covered by group life insurance grew twice as fast as ordinary life insurance. Finally, more and more people purchased annuities for their old age. In 1915, annuity premiums were 1 percent of life insurance premiums; annuity premiums climbed to 2.8 percent of life insurance premiums in 1929 and 15 percent in 1935.[5]

Despite the shock of the Great Depression, private pension plans continued to perform well. "Industrial pension plans not only grew steadily," Carolyn Weaver reported, "but also proved quite resilient, with certain features improving markedly. . . . The rate of failure for existing plans, moreover, was relatively modest. Of the systems operating in 1929, those that were discontinued, closed to new employees, or suspended by 1932 involved less than 3 percent of all covered employees. The large majority of these plans continued benefit payments to current pensioners. Eighty-five to 90 percent of the plans in existence in 1932 were operating normally. . . . even failing firms continued to make benefit payments as a matter of course. Trade-union pension plans, by contrast, proved to be considerably less resilient. . . ."[6]

"At least in part," Weaver continued, "these facts help explain why some five years after the onset of the depression, a bill had not yet been introduced into Congress for compulsory old-age insurance; there were simply no significant demands for such a program. As late as 1934 a leading proponent of 'social insurance' [Isaac Rubinow] conceded that the majority of the working population did not 'clamor' for 'social insurance' and that 'in practically all of Europe, it was governmental authority that was behind social insurance measures.'"[7]

THERE WAS, TO be sure, increased lobbying for a national, government-run pension system where some people would subsidize others. High unemployment during the Great Depression meant that millions of people couldn't save for their old age, and many of these people weren't eligible for pension benefits because they hadn't contributed. By mid-1934, twenty-eight states and two territories (Alaska, Hawaii) had government-run pension systems; of these, the vast majority were compulsory, with only a handful involving voluntary participation. Because of limited resources, the average monthly benefit was under $20.[8]

Louisiana Senator Huey Long, whose "Share-Our-Wealth" bill had been defeated in the Senate on March 12, 1933, introduced a variation the following year: The proceeds from confiscatory taxes were to be distributed as $30-per-month pension benefits.

Francis Townsend, a physician who worked for the Long Beach, California, health department, made the most extravagant claims for a national pension system. Many of his patients were elderly people whose savings had been wiped out. He came up with an idea and explained it in a letter to the local newspaper, generating an enormous response. In 1934, he wrote a pamphlet, *Old Age Revolving Pensions*, in which he declared that "our nation with its vast creative power needs but one important principle to be established through legislation to abolish poverty and its attendant evils forever." Townsend's "principle" was a national sales tax, the proceeds from which would pay a $200 monthly benefit for anybody over sixty who didn't have a criminal record, agreed to give up other income, and spent the entire $200 within thirty days.[9]

He went on to claim his plan would cure the Great Depression: "The money made suddenly available to the channels of trade will immediately start a new flood of buying. . . . All factories and avenues of production may be expected to start producing at full capacity and all workers called into activity at high wages, since there will be infinitely more jobs available, and many less workers to fill the jobs, the old folks having retired from competition for places as producers." Townsend promised "a marked reduction in the tax burden," since he imagined his plan would cost less than private charity.[10]

Finally, Townsend declared that people could become better human beings: "Here lies the true value of the Townsend Plan. Humanity will be forever relieved from the fear of destitution and want. The seeming need for sharp practices and greedy accumulation will disappear. Benevolence and kindly consideration for others will displace suspicion and avarice, brotherly love and tolerance will blossom into full flower, and the genial sun of human happiness will dissipate the dark clouds of distrust and gloom and despair."[11]

In 1935, Washington senator Charles Dill and Massachusetts congressman William Connery introduced a bill that would provide federal aid for states developing state-run retirement systems. The idea was that federal money would cover about 30 percent of the costs. Both the Senate Pensions Committee and the House Labor Committee approved it. But FDR was against it and used his clout with the House Rules Committee to prevent the bill from being voted on.[12]

Evidently, FDR wanted to claim credit himself for a government-run retirement system. On June 27, 1934, he signed into law the Railroad Retirement Act, which provided a government-run retirement program for railroad employees. Two days later, he issued Executive Order 6757, establishing the Committee on Economic Security to develop legislative proposals for a government-run retirement system. The committee consisted of Secretary of Labor Frances Perkins, Secretary of the Treasury Henry Morgenthau, Secretary of Agriculture Henry A. Wallace, Attorney General Homer Cummings, and Federal Emergency Relief administrator Harry L. Hopkins. Perkins chaired the committee.

The committee received assistance from a Technical Board on Economic Security and an Advisory Council on Economic Security. Both were loaded with advocates of a government-run retirement system. They could have proposed tax and legal changes to promote the expansion of private insurance, annuity, and pension systems, since those had performed well even during the depression. But, of course, the committee recommended a government-run plan, much like the welfare-type "social insurance" that had developed in Prussia.

The committee presented its report on January 15, 1935, and it recommended just about everything that had been talked about, including workers' compensation, unemployment compensation, health benefits, disability benefits, old-age benefits, survivors' benefits, and maternity benefits.

Hearings began on January 21 before the House Ways and Means Committee and on January 22 before the Senate Finance Committee. It soon became apparent that a government-run retirement system wouldn't be the bonanza that Dr. Townsend had promised. Edwin E. Witte, a University of Wisconsin economist who served as secretary of the Committee on Economic Security, testified that because of potentially high costs, a government-run retirement system would have to be scaled back. FDR, however, insisted that a government-run retirement system must be paid for by a payroll tax, which supposedly would involve contributions by employees and employers. In truth, the entire payroll tax would come out of the pockets of working people, because the tax would be part of the cost of providing a job; and if the money weren't going to the government, it would be available for employee compensation.

The Roosevelt administration proposed paying for Social Security benefits with a payroll tax, even though this would be regressive, taking a higher portion of the earnings of lower-income people than higher-income people. FDR apparently wanted a payroll tax because it made Social Security seem more like a self-financing insurance plan and politically more difficult to later repeal. Of course, Social Security wasn't insurance because a true insurance policy involved people paying premiums based on their expected life span, their health, and other risk factors and an insurance company accumulating the premiums in an investment fund that would eventually pay off the policy claim.

FDR repeatedly misrepresented Social Security as legitimate insurance. "Get these facts straight," he said. "The Act provides for two kinds of insurance for the worker. For that insurance both the employer and the worker pay premiums—just as you pay premiums on any other insurance policy. Those premiums are collected in the form of taxes. The first kind of insurance covers old age. Here the employer contributes one dollar in premium for every dollar of premium contributed by the worker; but both dollars are held by the government solely for the benefit of the worker in his old age."[13] More candidly, he was quoted as saying: "We put those payroll contributions there so as to give the contributors a legal, moral, and political right to collect their pensions. . . . With those taxes in place, no damn politician can ever scrap my social security program."

In vain did business representatives, like Samuel W. Reyburn of the National Retail Dry Goods Association, warn that by increasing the cost of employing people, payroll taxes would contribute to high unemployment. "Whatever tax you make is going to increase their expenses," he said.[14] Lloyd Peck, general manager of the National Laundryowners Association, explained, "The burden proposed for employers to carry, through a payroll tax, will act as a definite curb on business expansion, and will likely eliminate many businesses now on the verge of bankruptcy. We contend that the portion of the burden to be carried by employees will further curtail their purchasing power, thereby increasing their difficulties in meeting their actual living expenses. Therefore, his proposed social-security legislation will stifle recovery forces now at work and increase unemployment."[15]

James Emery, of the National Association of Manufacturers, added, "If you increase the cost of employment and men, the tendency is to employ a machine which would be less expensive and which would not subject you immediately to the tax. . . . it would be a tendency in industries where the labor cost is high."[16] Emery pointed out that the proposed Social Security payroll tax, like other business expenses, would be passed on to consumers, and the resulting higher prices would be a negative for employment: "General recovery depends on our ability to enlarge our production, to employ more people, and to cut down and not raise up the price of goods.

Every time we increase the price of goods in a diminishing market, we are diminishing the possibility of employing other men, because we are making it more difficult, not less, to sell goods. Until we can market goods, we cannot employ more men."[17]

Asked about the likelihood that Social Security payroll taxes would help prolong high unemployment by making it more expensive for employers to hire people, FDR admitted, "I guess you're right on the economics, but those taxes were never a problem of economics. They were politics all the way through."[18]

W. R. Williamson, an actuary with Travelers Insurance Company, also appeared before the House Ways and Means Committee, and he testified that the proposed Social Security system would incur deficits: "The amounts called for are not enough to avoid some subsidy most of the time." He warned that the deficits would go up at "a steadily increasing rate . . . because the proportion of elderly people that claim benefits steadily goes up. . . . the strain upon the plan is steadily increasing."

Kentucky congressman Fred Vinson thought Social Security would be like a private investment portfolio, but Williamson pointed out that the Social Security fund "is limited to Federal securities, and the interest on Federal securities is not like the interest on public utilities, earned by productive investment." Indeed, "Federal securities secure interest nonproductively, by taxation."[19]

THERE WAS ALSO serious concern about the possibility that if current taxpayers ended up funding the benefits of current retirees, then the retirement benefits of current taxpayers would become obligations that future generations would have to pay. Although acknowledging that Social Security would incur "a debt upon which future generations will have to pay large amounts annually," Witte also said, "While the creation of this debt will impose a burden on future generations which we do not wish to minimize, we, nevertheless, deem it advisable that the Federal Government should not pay its share of the cost of old-age annuities (the unearned part of the

annuities to persons brought into the system at the outset) currently.
. . . to pay this cost now would unfairly burden the younger part of
the present generation, which would not only pay for the cost of its
own annuities, but would also pay a large part of the annuities to
the people now middle-aged or over."[20]

Then, at the House Ways and Means Committee hearing, came
this revealing exchange which made it clear that New Dealers knew
what they were doing when they passed on liabilities to future
generations:

> MR. VINSON. Your insurance company [Travelers] would not
> think for a split second of passing on to 1965 or 1980 a bur-
> den such as is contemplated here. In other words you watch
> your step day in and month in and year in.
>
> MR. WILLIAMSON. An insurance company must main-
> tain its reserves to meet its current liabilities.
>
> MR. VINSON. That is sound economic policy, is it not?
>
> MR. WILLIAMSON. That is right.
>
> MR. VINSON. You would not suggest that we pass the
> buck on to 1965 or 1980, or even think about doing it, be-
> cause there will be 22 Congresses between now and then that
> could upset that apple cart.
>
> MR. WILLIAMSON. I think it should be well understood
> that that is exactly what is being done.[21]

The bill that emerged from the hearings had three major provisions. First, the government would collect a payroll tax on the first
$3,000 of income, which would start at 2 percent (half paid directly
by the employee and half supposedly by the employer but really by
the employee), rising to 6 percent in 1948. The tax wouldn't be deductible from the federal income tax. Exempted from having to participate and pay Social Security taxes were federal government
employees, state government employees, agricultural workers, domestic workers, and perhaps employees of nonprofit organizations.
Social Security tax revenue was intended to be enough to cover the

benefits of current retirees. Social Security tax revenue not needed for current retirees would go into an Old Age Reserve Account where it would be invested in U.S. government bonds.

Second, beginning January 1, 1942, individuals who were sixty-five and had quit work could collect monthly benefit payments. Consequently, *Social Security wouldn't do any good for elderly poor people during the Great Depression.* The aim was to build up the Old Age Reserve Account before the government started issuing benefit checks.

It certainly seemed unfair that individuals who paid into Social Security would be unable to collect benefits just because they wanted to continue working, but one of the ulterior purposes of the Social Security Act was to get older people out of the workforce and create openings for younger people who were unemployed.

Third, some miscellaneous provisions were included, presumably to help induce enough senators and representatives to vote for the Social Security Act. For fiscal year 1936, Congress appropriated $49.5 million for state-run retirement systems, $24.7 million for state assistance to dependent children, $8 million for state public health services, $3.5 million for state programs to help mothers, and $3 million for state programs assisting the blind. Such provisions suggested that even though Democrats controlled both houses of Congress, FDR believed Social Security wouldn't pass if presented by itself.[22]

Indeed, both Democrats and Republicans offered considerable opposition to the proposed Social Security Act. Montana senator Bennett Clark proposed an amendment that would have enabled employers to opt out of Social Security if their pension plans offered more generous benefits than it did. This would have meant freedom of choice for employers and employees alike, but advocates of Social Security were adamantly against freedom of choice. They wanted a monopoly.

The advocates of Social Security must have realized that private retirement plans would offer a better deal, and Social Security would be doomed if people had a choice. Wisconsin's Democratic senator Robert M. La Follette, a fixture in "progressive" politics, fumed, "If we shall adopt this amendment, the government having determined to set up a federal system of old-age insurance will provide, in its own bill creating that system, competition which in the end may destroy the federal system. . . . It would be inviting and encouraging competition with its own plan which ultimately would undermine and destroy it."[23] Defenders of the Clark amendment countered that if Social Security was going to be so great, why not give people a choice?[24]

Although Democrats controlled the Senate by a 2–1 margin, the Clark freedom of choice amendment passed by a 51–35 vote. The House was against it, however, and FDR threatened to veto the entire bill if the amendment were included. It was taken out during the House-Senate conference. FDR signed the Social Security Act into law on August 14, 1935.

THE ADVOCATES OF Social Security weren't satisfied. They wanted more. Arthur J. Altmeyer, chairman of the Social Security Board that administered Social Security, declared, "Passing the law is only, as it were, a 'curtain-raiser' in the evolution of such a program. It is already possible to distinguish at least three phases of this evolution, each with its distinctive emphasis—first, the double barreled job of setting up administrative machinery and of getting it into operation; second, the development and integration of administration and services within the present framework; and third, further expansion to liberalize existing provisions."[25]

Lest anybody think Social Security was a voluntary deal like private insurance, employers across America were required to display this notice: "Beginning January 1, 1937, your employer will be compelled by law to deduct a certain amount from your wages every payday. This is in compliance with the terms of the Social Security Act signed by President Franklin Delano Roosevelt, August 14, 1935. The deduction begins with 1 percent, and increases until it reaches 3 percent. To the amount taken from your wages, your employer is required to pay, in addition, either an equal or double amount. The combined taxes may total 9 percent of the whole payroll. This is NOT a voluntary plan."[26]

It wasn't clear, however, what the Supreme Court would do about the Social Security Act, since the Court had struck down a succession of New Deal laws. The legitimacy of the Social Security Act depended on stretching the general welfare clause. As Cato Institute analysts Peter J. Ferrara and Michael Tanner explained, "It was meant to serve as a brake on the power of Congress to tax and spend in furtherance of its enumerated powers, meaning that spending within the exercise of an enumerated power had to be for the general welfare rather than to the benefit of specific individuals or factions. Further, the court had already invalidated efforts to 'expropriate from one group for the benefit of another,' making it unlikely that taxing employers for the benefit of employees would be upheld."[27]

Meanwhile, Social Security taxes began to reduce the size of paychecks at about the same time that misguided Federal Reserve policies and the Wagner Act brought on a severe recession. Social Security became controversial because of the Old Age Reserve Account. It held money out of circulation when many people thought more consumer spending was needed to spur recovery. There were other criticisms, too. Incredibly, Abraham Epstein, who had long led the lobbying effort to have politicians get into the pension business, wrote in *Nation* magazine: "Experience everywhere indicates that politicians will hardly be able to keep their hands off such easy money."[28] Writing in *Atlantic Monthly*, insurance executive Arthur Linton called the Old Age Reserve Account "the most dangerous feature" of Social Security."[29] In *Harper's*, John T. Flynn called the reserve "a swindle and a solemn and cruel farce."[30] *American Mercury* denounced the reserve as a "gigantic slush fund."[31]

In 1939, FDR agreed to deplete the Old Age Retirement Account. He approved amendments to the Social Security Act, expanding the number of benefits and moving up by two years, to 1940, the date when monthly benefit checks would start going out. The new benefits included payments to the spouse and minor children of a retired employee ("dependents' benefits") and payments to the family of a deceased employee ("survivors' benefits"). These moves to deplete the Old Age Retirement Account ended any further pretense that Social Security was insurance. It clearly became a pay-as-you-go retirement system where current taxpayers were funding the benefits of current retirees. Nothing was being set aside to cover the future retirement benefits of current taxpayers. This burden was being pushed onto future generations.

So, during the 1930s, Social Security, through the payroll tax, increased the cost of employing people and thereby helped prolong high unemployment. Social Security monthly benefits didn't begin going out to people until after the 1930s were over. It was revealing that pro-FDR historian Robert S. McElvaine based his case for Social Security on its intentions, not its consequences: Social Security was "important as a symbolic gesture to demonstrate that Roosevelt's heart was in the right place."[32]

CHAPTER FOURTEEN

How Did New Deal Labor Laws Throw People Out of Work?

For decades, labor unions had been struggling for power, but until the 1930s they had made little headway.

Labor unions were generally based on force and violence, which long repelled a substantial number of employees as well as employers. The unions aimed to raise the wages of members above market levels, but this was possible only with strikes, which forcibly prevented employers from hiring other employees, shut down businesses, and ultimately forced employers to accept union demands. Union bosses talked about securing the "right to strike," but they didn't mean the right to quit, which everybody already had. In practice, the "right to strike" meant the right to forcibly prevent others from filling jobs that strikers had left.

Union bosses proclaimed the ideal of "collective bargaining," even described this as the essence of "industrial democracy," but what they sought was compulsory unionism—a labor market monopoly. They weren't satisfied if some of a company's employees chose to join one union, while others joined another union, and still others continued to bargain individually on their own. Union bosses were implacably opposed to labor market competition. They insisted that if a majority of a company's employees wanted to join a particular union, then it must represent 100 percent of employees, including those who didn't want to join or pay dues. The aim was a "closed shop" that made union membership a condition of employment. No union card, no job.

Until the 1920s, as far as labor issues were concerned, U.S. courts generally respected individual rights. Employers could choose their employees freely, and employees could choose among employers freely, and either could deal with a union or not as they wished. Employers who hired employees on an "at will" basis were free to let them go for any reason or no reason at all, just as "at will" employees could quit for any reason or no reason at all. Terms of employment depended on supply and demand. Because the growing American economy rapidly expanded the number of job opportunities, demand was strong for good employees, skilled and unskilled alike. Wages were in a long-term uptrend before unions had a significant impact. On the other hand, during recessions, many companies went out of business, jobs became scarcer, and people were willing to work for less so they could remain employed.

Courts frowned on organized efforts to break contracts. Individuals who had agreed to handle certain duties for a certain amount of time were held to their agreements. Union organizers were considered guilty of a civil wrong (tort) if they encouraged people to break their contracts.

When unions became violent, courts sometimes provided equity relief by issuing injunctions to stop. Often injunctions prodded police to prevent violence. Unions hated injunctions, claimed they were used all the time, and lobbied for laws that would prohibit them. But as historian Howard Dickman reported, "The number and frequency of labor injunction cases in the federal and state courts involving unions and employers after 1880 and before 1932 has been vastly overstated, to be sure; and the lion's share of injunction cases involved physical coercion of the nasty variety."[1]

Economist Sylvester Petro analyzed 524 reported federal and state injunction cases between 1880 and 1932 and found that they didn't involve peaceful primary strikes for better pay and working conditions.[2]

All these issues arose in the long struggle of the United Mine Workers in America to monopolize coal mines, a struggle that climaxed during the Great Depression. The UMW had formed in 1890 when it unionized miners in Ohio and Indiana; it then expanded into Illinois and part of Pennsylvania. These states, known as the Central Competitive Field, produced high-cost coal. Their principal competition came from lower-cost nonunion coal mines in West Virginia and other southern states. A top priority of the UMW was to unionize these mines and make their pay scales the same as those of the mines in the Central Competitive Field; doing so would eliminate the competitive advantage of the southern mines and thereby help to protect the jobs of UMW members in the Central Competitive Field. In addition, if the UMW monopolized the labor market for American coal miners, it could order a strike, shut down all the mines, and cripple the customers—such as the railroads—of the coal companies, generating additional pressure for a pro-UMW settlement.

William Green, president of UMW District 6, admitted, "We had West Virginia on the south and Pennsylvania on the east, and after four months of a strike in Eastern Ohio we had reached the danger line. We felt keenly the competition from West Virginia, and during the suspension our miners in Ohio chafed under the object lesson they had. They saw West Virginia coal go by, train-load after train-load passing their doors, when they were on strike. This coal supplied the markets that they should have had. There is no disguising the fact, something must be done to remedy this condition."[3]

The strategy was to unionize miners in West Virginia, then call strikes to demand pay scales the same as those in the Central Competitive Field; the union would keep the strikers going by paying benefits assessed from miners who were working in the Central Competitive Field.

One of their efforts involved Hitchman Coal & Coke Company in West Virginia. It began operating in 1902 with nonunion miners, but union officials threatened to shut down a unionized mine that Hitchman operators also owned, so Hitchman became a union shop on April 1, 1903. The following day, union bosses called a strike that lasted a month and a half, long enough to cause the company to default on a contract to supply coal to the Baltimore & Ohio Railroad. Then in the spring of 1904, just two days after a pay scale was agreed on with the miners, union bosses called a strike that lasted two months. In 1906, another strike was called, related not to grievances at Hitchman but to efforts at improving the union's bargaining power during a dispute in the Central Competitive Field. After two months, with the UMW not paying strike benefits, a substantial number of strikers offered to quit the union and return to work. The company, in turn, offered to pay union-scale wages but insisted it would not deal with the union. Everybody the company hired understood they were always free to join the union, but if they belonged to the union they couldn't work at Hitchman. Nonetheless, UMW organizers repeatedly tried to induce Hitchman employees to join the union. The company sought an injunction ordering the UMW to desist, and the ensuing litigation ended up before the Supreme Court.[4]

Justice Mahlon Pitney wrote the majority opinion, decided on December 10, 1917. He presented a compelling defense of freedom of association and freedom of contract. "Whatever may be the advantages of 'collective bargaining,' it is not bargaining at all, in any just sense, unless it is voluntary on both sides," he wrote. "The same liberty which enables men to form unions, and through the union to enter into agreements with employers willing to agree, entitles other men to remain independent of the union and other employers to employ no man who owes any allegiance or obligation to the union. In the latter case, as in the former, the parties are entitled to be protected by the law in the enjoyment of the benefits of any lawful agreement they may make."[5]

The Court modified and sustained the original injunction ordering the UMW to stop subverting the contract that miners had entered into with Hitchman. As long as courts curtailed threats, intimidation, and violence by the UMW, it couldn't gain a nationwide monopoly of the labor market for coal miners and eliminate the competition from southern mines.

The Railway Labor Act (1926) was a breakthrough for unions in an industry that had seen chronic union violence during the late nineteenth and early twentieth centuries. The new law secured the employees' "right to organize" and declared that employers had a "duty to bargain" with union agents. While this began to put legal pressure on employers, the law didn't outlaw company unions, which were unions for a single company, not part of a larger union. Consequently, it didn't establish the labor market monopoly that union bosses were seeking. But by the time the Railway Labor Act came before the Supreme Court, in *Texas and New Orleans Railroad Company v Brotherhood of Railway and Steamship Clerks*, 281 U.S. 548 (1930), the Great Depression was on, and prevailing opinion had advanced beyond the law. Among other things, Chief Justice Charles Evans Hughes, in his majority opinion, moved away from the *Hitchman* decision and asserted that "the carriers subject to the act have no constitutional right to interfere with the freedom of the employees in making their selections."[6]

On March 23, 1932, President Herbert Hoover signed into law the Norris-LaGuardia Anti-Injunction Act. This made so-called yellow dog contracts (which made a worker's nonunion status a condition of employment) unenforceable in U.S. courts. The conventional view was that employers demanded yellow dog contracts, but economist Morgan O. Reynolds explained that the contracts "added nothing to the acknowledged legal right of employers to discharge workers for any reason, including union activity." In fact, they served the mutual interests of employers and many workers: "In the absence of agreements to the contrary, employment relationships were 'at will' and could be terminated by either party at any time in that era. . . . waves of nonunion oaths ["yellow dog" contracts] appeared to follow outbreaks of destructive strikes and boycotts. . . . More employees would want oaths during periods of union violence because pledges could enhance the attractiveness of working conditions for those fearful of union-related conflict and violence. By this thesis, pledges could effectively reduce an employee's chances of becoming involved in a union dispute."[7]

Norris-LaGuardia, furthermore, exempted labor unions from the Sherman Antitrust Act, which meant they could act in restraint of trade and get away with it. Even when unions used violence in an effort to stop production or stop the interstate shipment of goods, they couldn't be prosecuted under the Sherman Act for acting "in restraint of trade." Finally, Norris-LaGuardia declared that federal courts couldn't protect companies and nonunion members from labor union violence by issuing injunctions to cease and desist.[8]

DESPITE THE LEGISLATIVE gains for compulsory unionism, the number of union members fell from 5 million in 1920 to under 3 million in 1933. The American Federation of Labor was in trouble, reflecting the financial problems of the United Mine Workers, the Ladies Garment Workers Union, and other members. Working union members were taxed as much as 20 percent to provide benefits for unemployed members.[9]

FDR, who had promoted compulsory unionism as assistant secretary of the navy during World War I, saw political advantages in helping the unions. For him, perhaps the most important part of the National Industrial Recovery Act had been section 7(a), drafted in the office of Senator Robert F. Wagner of New York, the most heavily unionized state. Section 7(a)(1) provided "That employees shall have the right to organize and bargain collectively through representatives of their own choosing, and shall be free from the interference, restraint, or coercion of employers of labor, or their agents, in the designation of such representatives or in self-organization or in other concerted activities for the purpose of collective bargaining or other mutual aid or protection." The phrase "of their own choosing" suggested that some employees might opt for one union, other employees might opt for a second union, and still other employees, if they chose, might wish to make their own deals with employers. In other words, this language didn't explicitly sanction a labor union monopoly.

Section 7(a)(2) said that "no employee and no one seeking employment shall be required as a condition of employment to join any company union or to refrain from joining, organizing, or assisting a labor organization of his own choosing." On the one hand, 7(a)(2) continued the ban against "yellow dog" contracts, as union bosses wished. On the other hand, it didn't ban company unions, as they certainly would have liked. Indeed, passage of the NIRA led to a dramatic increase in the number of company unions.[10]

Finally, section 7(a)(3) was the provision intended to mandate above-market compensation ("employers shall comply with the maximum hours of labor, minimum rates of pay, and other conditions of employment, approved or prescribed by the President").

On June 19, 1934, FDR issued Executive Order 6763, which took labor disputes out of the courts and established the National Labor Relations Board to handle them, since it would be more easily dominated by pro-union interests. Empowered to file complaints against employers, hold hearings, and render decisions, the NLRB was close to functioning as a prosecutor and court. If necessary, a federal court would issue an order to enforce an NLRB decision. While employers could subsequently appeal an adverse NLRB decision to a federal circuit court, the NLRB increased the odds that unions would prevail. Although section 7(a) of the NIRA twice said that employees had freedom of choice about whether to join a union, NLRB saw their mission as promoting compulsory unionism.

In the Houde Engineering case, for instance, a company talked separately with a union chosen by a majority of employees (United

Auto Workers) and another union chosen by a minority (Houde Welfare and Athletic Association). The NLRB ruled that Houde interfered with the employees' "right to organize" by not negotiating with a single union about the working conditions of all employees. The union whom a majority voted for must "constitute the exclusive agency for collective bargaining with the employer."[11]

After the Supreme Court struck down the NIRA as unconstitutional on May 27, 1935, FDR moved swiftly to salvage what he considered a crucial part of it. Meanwhile, New York Senator Robert F. Wagner Sr. revised the Labor Disputes bill that he had previously introduced in 1934.

A Washington columnist described Wagner, the congressional leader on industrial issues: "He is a widower, lives in the most exclusive hotel in Washington, and is active socially. He is immaculately groomed at all times, is short—a bit rotund—has iron gray hair and is perpetual in good humor."[12]

Wagner was born in Nastatten, Germany, in 1877, and his family emigrated to the United States when he was nine. He graduated from City College of New York (1898) and New York Law School (1900). He took to politics early on and was elected to the New York State Assembly in 1904, the state Senate in 1908. Together with Assembly Speaker Al Smith, Wagner sponsored a bill establishing a commission to investigate the tragic fire at the Triangle Shirtwaist Company, where over a hundred female garment workers had died. He was elected to the New York State Supreme Court in 1918. Eight years later, he won election to the U.S. Senate.

Rather than engage in customary attacks on Republican adversaries, Wagner focused on cultivating support for his own bills, which promoted compulsory unionism and other issues.[13] As historian George Martin noted, "He relied on facts for his speeches, had no real or contrived eccentricities to exploit and refused to play to the galleries. He was not without vanity. . . . perhaps because senator was the highest post in the federal government to which he as an immigrant could aspire, in Congress he was all work—quiet, patient, persistent and effective." Secretary of Labor Frances Perkins called him "the Chief Performer on the Hill."[14]

For help revising his Labor Disputes Bill, Wagner recruited Leon Keyserling, a lawyer whom Wagner had recruited from Jerome Frank's office of the counsel at the Agricultural Adjustment Administration. Keyserling, born in 1908 in Charleston, South Carolina, majored in economics at Columbia College and there got to know Rexford Tugwell.[15] He graduated from Harvard Law School in 1931. He taught briefly at Columbia before going to work for Frank and soon afterwards joining Wagner's staff as legislative assistant in 1933. He helped draft wage and hour provisions of the National Industrial Recovery Act.

On July 5, 1935, FDR signed into law the National Labor Relations Act, which, drafted in Senator Wagner's office, became known as the Wagner Act. Section 9 of the NLRA revived and expanded the NIRA's section 7(a), explicitly sanctioning labor union monopoly.

The Wagner Act blamed labor violence on *employers* who chose not to deal with unions. According to the opening lines of section 151, "The denial by some employers of the right of employees to organize and the refusal by some employers to accept the procedure of collective bargaining lead to strikes and other forms of industrial strife or unrest, which have the intent or the necessary effect of burdening or obstructing commerce."[16]

The Wagner Act further blamed employers for the Great Depression itself. Again, section 151 says, "The inequality of bargaining power between employees who do not possess full freedom of association or actual liberty of contract, and employers who are organized in the corporate or other forms of ownership association substantially burdens and affects the flow of commerce, and tends to aggravate recurrent business depressions, by depressing wage rates and the purchasing power of wage earners in industry and by preventing the stabilization of competitive wage rates and working conditions within and between industries."[17] It would be hard to find a non-Marxist economist today who would defend the view that employers caused the Great Depression.

Although section 7 of the Wagner Act provided that employees had "the right to form, join or assist labor organizations to bargain collectively through representatives of their own choosing . . . and shall have the right to refrain from any or all such activities," the illusion of freedom of choice was shattered by the rest of the sentence: "except to the extent that such right may be affected by an agreement requiring membership in a labor organization as a condition of employment."

The Wagner Act made it far easier for unions to secure a closed shop and gain a bargaining monopoly. The Wagner Act denied the principle of free association, a cornerstone of American liberty. Union contracts no longer involved voluntary participation, because the Wagner Act made it illegal for companies to go their own way without a union. Section 8(a) of the NLRA banned company unions, which had been permitted by section 7(a) of the National Industrial Recovery Act.

The Wagner Act made it illegal for employers to act in any way contrary to the interests of unions. Section 158 declared that "it shall be an unfair labor practice" for an employer to interfere with unionizing activities, refuse to hire somebody because they belong to a union, fire somebody because they belong to a union, or refuse to bargain with union representatives.[18] The NLRB has prosecuted managements for allegedly interfering with striking and picketing, but it has not prosecuted strikers and picketers for intimidating or actually assaulting employees who choose to work during a strike.

Even if employees go on strike, leaving their jobs, the NLRB has ruled that it is an "unfair labor practice" for an employer to hire replacements, get work done, and carry on the business. True, Supreme Court Justice Owen Roberts, writing the majority opinion in *National Labor Relations Board v Mackay Radio*, 304 U.S. 333 (1938), offered these encouraging words for freedom of association: "Nor was it an unfair labor practice to replace the striking employees with others in an effort to carry on the business. Although section 13 of the act, 29 U.S.C.A. 163, provides, 'Nothing in this Act (chapter) shall be construed so as to interfere with or impede or diminish in any way the right to strike,' it does not follow that an employer, guilty of no act denounced by the statute, has lost the right to protect and continue his business by supplying places left vacant by strikers. And he is not bound to discharge those hired to fill the places of strikers, upon the election of the latter to resume their employment, in order to create places for them. The assurance by respondent [Mackay Radio] to those who accepted employment during the strike that if they so desired their places might be permanent was not an unfair labor practice, nor was it such to reinstate only so many of the strikers as there were vacant places to be filled."[19]

Then Justice Roberts undermined what he had said by adding: "The strikers retained, under the act, the status of employees. Any such discrimination in putting them back to work is, therefore, prohibited by section 8." He then ordered the Circuit Court to enforce the NLRB's order that Mackay Radio take back the five striking workers for whom replacements had been hired.[20]

The Wagner Act provided that if 30 percent of employees signed a petition for a certification election, to determine whether a union would negotiate on behalf of all the workers, it must be held. Employers were forbidden to play any role in the process. But the Wagner Act *did not* require periodic elections to determine whether workers wanted to remain with the first union or choose to be represented by another union or no union at all. If this principle were applied to the government sector, we might never have had another election after the first one more than two centuries ago. To be sure, there were decertification procedures, but only employees could initiate them, and again employers were forbidden to play any role.

NOR WAS MUCH done about labor union racketeering. David Kendrick, program director of the National Institute for Labor

Relations Research, reported, "Local 807 of the Teamsters decided to expand their territory outside of New York City. In order to persuade truckers from outside New York City to use the local's services, members would greet the truckers with guns and charge a toll equal to one day's union wage. In some cases, the members of local 807 would drive the trucks into the city. In other cases, the members took the money and departed. In no case were the members of local 807 employed by the out-of-town trucking companies. Since these tactics at least doubled the cost of transporting goods into New York, most if not all of the local trucking companies signed contracts with local 807."[21]

Backed by New Deal labor laws and by the 1936 elections where FDR won a second term, Democrat Frank Murphy became governor of Michigan, Democrat Martin Davey became governor of Ohio, and labor union bosses planned an aggressive strategy for a monopoly of the labor market in mass-production industries. The spark was provided by the United Auto Workers, which had been formed the year before by a merger of several small auto unions. Twenty-eight-year-old Walter Reuther, a socialist visionary, had become president. The UAW quit the American Federation of Labor after it had tried to pick the autoworkers' leadership, and the new union bolted to the militant Congress of Industrial Organizations established by United Mine Workers president John L. Lewis. Mid-November, in South Bend, Indiana, about a thousand UAW members staged a sit-down strike at Bendix lasting eight days. Then came Detroit's first sit-down strike when about 1,900 UAW members held a sit-down strike at Midland Steel, which made body frames for Ford and Chrysler.[22]

At the Kelsey-Hayes Wheel Company, supplier of wheels and brake drums for Ford, Reuther, reported biographer Nelson Lichtenstein, "hoped to precipitate a series of stoppages and disruptions that would prod the company into increasing pay, slowing down the production pace, and recognizing the renewed existence of a union in the plant." On Friday, December 10, 1936, Reuther's brother Victor, who worked at the plant, suddenly announced a strike.

Kelsey-Hayes president George Kennedy agreed to increase the minimum wage rate to 75 cents an hour but insisted that higher pay be based on individual merit and that the company maintain an open shop where nonunion employees could continue working. The UAW would have none of it. The following Sunday, Lichtenstein wrote, "Reuther led five hundred Kelsey unionists over to the company-sponsored assembly at the nearby Dom Polski Hall. With the help of several husky men, Reuther hustled the company spokesmen off the platform and took over the [nonunion] association's meeting." Kelsey-Hayes maintained its open shop policy, and Reuther led a sit-down strike, seized control of the plant, and stopped production. With Christmas approaching and strikers anxious for a settlement before Christmas, Reuther accepted the company's offer and focused on a much bigger target.[23]

On December 30, 1936, 1,500 UAW members (out of 42,000 employees) seized control of Fisher Body Plant No. 1 owned by General Motors in Flint, Michigan. They stopped the assembly line and staged a sit-down strike. General Motors refused to accept a closed shop and demanded that strikers leave the plant before they would negotiate. UAW bosses countered by demanding that General Motors recognize them as the exclusive bargaining agents for everybody at the plant. CIO president John L. Lewis became involved in this struggle, revealing the GM stock holdings of a judge who had issued an injunction to end the strike. "Lewis," observed biographers Melvyn Dubofsky and Warren Van Tine, "believed that politicians reacted to power not sentiment, and that workers could advance their cause only through the exercise of power, violently if necessary, not through appeals to sympathy as oppressed Americans. . . . Power and force, then, proved central to Lewis' strategy in the General Motors conflict."[24]

Meanwhile, the UAW had begun a sit-down strike at Fisher Body Plant No. 2. Flint police tried to return the plant to its owners, but, Dubofsky and Van Tine wrote, "The sit-downers and the pickets outside fought back with hoses, cans, hinges, ice balls, and every available implement. . . . Suddenly the police halted, turned, drew their pistols and riot guns, and fired directly at their pursuers. . . . fourteen strikers and sympathizers as well as two spectators lay wounded." Governor Frank Murphy pressured General Motors to accept a deal: Strikers would leave the plants if General Motors agreed to negotiate only with the UAW about its current demands. But negotiations collapsed while strikers were still in the plants. Frances Perkins, FDR's secretary of labor, talked with Governor Murphy, General Motors president Alfred Sloan, and John L. Lewis, but the stalemate continued. Lewis publicly asked FDR to help the unions who had backed him for the presidency. Dubofsky and Tine noted that "Unable to settle the strike, federal officials fell silent about the intransigence of their friends in the labor movement but criticized publicly their enemies among the 'economic royalists.'" At a January 26 press conference, FDR denounced Sloan.[25]

While the UAW stepped up the pressure by starting a sit-down strike at Chevrolet No. 4, on February 2 Judge Paul V. Gadola issued an injunction ordering strikers to leave the Fisher plants and warned the UAW that it could be hit with a $15 million fine for resisting the injunction. Governor Murphy, however, wouldn't authorize enforcement of this order. Lewis demanded that the UAW gain a bargaining monopoly at these plants, that GM offer no better bargains with other unions or encourage the development of other unions. "Lewis acted typically," Dubofsky and Van Tine wrote. "As always, he believed that power, not principle; might, not right, prevailed. In this case, the sit-down strikers personified raw power."[26]

General Motors car production plunged from 50,000 in December 1935 to 125 during the first week of February 1936. General Motors agreed to negotiate only with the UAW on behalf of UAW members, and it wouldn't resist UAW efforts to bring all factory workers into the union. General Motors even agreed to Lewis's demand that strikers guilty of vandalism be rehired. The strikers finally left the plants on February 11, 1937.[27] During the next several months, the UAW recruited some 40,000 new members from five GM factories and several dozen smaller companies.[28]

Although John L. Lewis had prepared for a big strike against U.S. Steel, apparently the disruption of GM's business and that company's subsequent surrender convinced U.S. Steel president Benjamin Fairless that it would be better to make a deal with the year-old Steel Workers Organizing Committee. By April 1937, Firestone Tire & Rubber caved to the strong-arm tactics of the United Rubber Workers. The United Electrical Workers forced General Electric, RCA-Victor, and Philco to grant a union monopoly over employee contract bargaining. Sidney Hillman's Textile Workers Organizing Committee gained a monopoly at big textile companies like American Woolen.[29]

Unionization brought more conflict, not less. Although the Wagner Act protected union elections, economist Richard B. Freeman noted, "more workers were organized through recognition strikes during the 1934–1939 spurt than were organized through NLRB elections."[30] Union members harassed nonmembers into joining the UAW or at least paying dues. As Lichtenstein reported, "When faced with opposition of a determined sort, 'accidents' were arranged or brief stoppages instigated. Every element of the shop-floor work regime seemed up for grabs: wages, of course, but also the pace of production, the power of the shop stewards, the meaning of seniority, even the deference due company foremen outside the factory gates." There were reportedly some 170 slowdowns and wildcat strikes at GM plants between February and June 1937.

UAW tactics actually seemed to give GM a competitive advantage. The UAW gained substantial control over the operations of smaller companies. Chrysler, for instance, had more than half its car production concentrated at its Dodge Main plant, so a slowdown or strike there was devastating. GM was much bigger, with many plants, and GM responded to strikes by expanding plants to duplicate production handled elsewhere. GM had at least three plants that could produce every part in a car, so that even if most of its plants were closed by strikes, it was likely that all parts would be available, and cars would continue to be produced. If production at one plant became unreliable because of slowdowns, strikes, or other union activity, production was transferred elsewhere. To make it harder for the UAW to shut down everything, GM had almost sixty plants across the United States—in Michigan, Indiana, New York, New Jersey, and California.[31]

The UAW became so aggressive that its tactics began to backfire. A June 7, 1937, strike against a Lansing, Michigan, plant led thousands of workers to stage protests downtown, stopping traffic and occupying municipal buildings. A UAW strike shut down Consumers Power Company, and electricity was shut off for one-half million people throughout Saginaw Valley. There were fights at a Monroe, Michigan, steel plant when the UAW went on strike there. The UAW implicitly supported a sit-down strike in Pontiac, Michigan, which led GM president William Knudsen to warn, "Irresponsibility on the part of the locals, unauthorized strikes and the defiance of union officers will eventually make agreements valueless and collective bargaining impossible in practice."[32] The *New York Times* and other publications ran stories about irresponsible union bosses.[33]

ABOVE-MARKET WAGES, extorted through force or the threat of force, surely contributed to the ensuing recession. Between November 1937 and January 1938, GM dismissed a quarter of its employees. Overall U.S. car production dropped almost 50 percent. Thousands of unemployed auto workers abandoned the UAW, and by 1939 only 6 percent of GM employees were paying UAW dues. Socialists, communists, and other factions battled for control, and GM aimed to avoid recognizing any of the factions.

Walter Reuther became head of the UAW's General Motors Department, and he reaffirmed his determination to achieve a labor market monopoly. As Nelson Lichtenstein put it, his aim was to "stanch the flow of low-wage, nonunion work from the smaller, 'alley' shops that were threatening to undercut the standards the UAW had won in the big 'captive' toolrooms of the major automakers."[34]

By 1939, times were better, and the UAW could resume aggressive tactics. Reuther called a strike for 800 employees at the Fisher No. 21 shop, in Detroit. Then he called strikes at Fisher No. 23, the world's largest tool and die shop, and three other plants. In July, strikes began at Fisher No. 47, Fleetwood, Ternstedt, Cleveland, and Saginaw. Having dealt with a reported 435 strikes since 1937, GM had had enough. GM president Knudsen agreed to give the UAW a monopoly as bargaining agent for all factory employees at forty-one plants where the UAW was the only agent with a presence. Reuther wasn't, however, able to gain much in the way of wage increases. A 1940 NLRB election enabled the UAW to secure its monopoly at fifty GM plants.[35]

By 1941, the UAW turned its guns on Ford's giant plant in River Rouge, Michigan. Hundreds of UAW organizers went door-to-door, soliciting members. On April 1, 1941, some 1,200 Ford employees walked off their jobs because a UAW member had been fired. Soon an estimated 50,000 people were marching through the streets of Rouge. Picket lines blocked the five highways leading to the plant. Nonstriking employees in the plant tried twice to get out, but picketers stopped them. UAW picketers fought with nonunion workers, and some people were stabbed.[36]

Ford executive Harry Bennett appealed to FDR and Michigan governor Murray Delos Van Wagoner, but they wouldn't do anything to prevent the strikers from blocking access to the plant. It became clear that force and violence were going to carry the day. In April, the company began negotiating with the UAW, and an NLRB election went about 70 percent for the UAW. On June 20, 1941, Ford signed an agreement that gave the UAW practically everything they wanted: monopoly bargaining power at all Ford plants, monthly pay deductions for union dues and other union fees (the "checkoff"), the rehiring of 4,000 UAW members who had been fired. In return, the UAW agreed to drop Wagner Act litigation filed against Ford.[37]

White union membership expanded dramatically after passage of the Wagner Act. United Mine Workers' boss John L. Lewis and garment union bosses Sidney Hillman and David Dubinsky led drives to unionize the steel, automobile, and rubber industries. Historian Frank Freidel explained, "The Congress of Industrial Organizations (CIO) split off from the AFL by the end of 1935, and by 1937 industrial warfare was at its height. Organizers battled against company guards and sometimes against the police and rival union men, but unlike the era before the New Deal, enjoyed some protection from the National Labor Relations Board."[38]

Labor union membership soared. "In 1937," reported Morgan O. Reynolds, "the Machinists claimed 2,000 new contracts; the Auto Workers claimed all auto manufacturers, except Ford, and 300 auto parts suppliers; the Steel Workers Organizing Committee claimed 431 new contracts; Rubber Workers 100 new contracts; Textile Workers Organizing Committee over 900 new contracts; and the non-operating railroad unions 200 new contracts."[39] Altogether, labor union membership went from 2,805,000 in 1933 to 8,410,000 in 1941.[40]

A principal effect of the Wagner Act was to facilitate union strikes and violence. "Between 1922 and 1932," reported Reynolds, "there was an average of 980 work stoppages a year. After Norris-LaGuardia passed in 1932, the number of strikes doubled in 1933 to 1,695 and continued to climb to a peak of 4,740 in 1937, the same year that the Supreme Court, by a 5–4 vote in April, declared the Wagner Act to be constitutional."[41]

Wage rates went up for those who had jobs. Economists Richard K. Vedder and Lowell E. Gallaway explained, "Wages increased by 11.6 percent in 1937, the second double-digit increase in wages during the Depression. The increase for the next year was 5.2 percent. . . . If the wages theory of unemployment is valid, it is very clear that the prolonged nature of the Great Depression in the

United States was the result of rapidly rising money wages. . . . With the possible exception of the experience of the 1970s, this period probably had the largest sustained peacetime increase in money wages in the nation's history—during the nation's worst depression. . . . Government failure, not market failure, was the problem."[42]

Economists Thomas E. Hall and J. David Ferguson added, "By encouraging unionization, the Wagner Act raised the number of insiders (those with jobs) who had the incentive and ability to exclude outsiders (those without jobs). Once high wages have been negotiated, employers are less likely to hire outsiders, and thus the insiders could protect their own interests."[43] Hence, compulsory unionism contributed to higher levels of persistent unemployment.

What about black workers? They seem to have been worse off. "To the extent that the Wagner Act raised wages and labor standards beyond market levels," wrote George Mason University law professor David E. Bernstein, "it had the same effect as a minimum wage law in eliminating marginal African American jobs."[44]

By giving labor unions the monopoly power to exclusively represent employees in a workplace, the Wagner Act had the effect of excluding blacks, since the dominant unions discriminated against blacks. The Wagner Act had originally been drafted with a provision prohibiting racial discrimination, but the American Federation of Labor successfully lobbied against it, and it was dropped. AFL unions used their new power, granted by the Wagner Act, to exclude blacks on a larger scale.[45]

Initially, the CIO welcomed blacks. "The CIO's support of racial equality," Bernstein wrote, "was practical—to prevent African Americans from undercutting union wages, and to get needed African American votes during organizing drives. Although some CIO unions remained committed to egalitarianism, other unions, such as the steelworkers', lost their commitment to racial equality soon after they achieved government recognition and thus no longer needed African American members. . . . over time many CIO unions responded to pressure from the white rank and file and discriminated in subtle ways. These unions frequently excluded African Americans from apprenticeship programs that led to skilled jobs, and otherwise tried to relegate African Americans to unskilled positions."[46]

Because the U.S. Supreme Court had previously struck down the National Industrial Recovery Act and the Agricultural Adjustment Act, it was widely expected that the Wagner Act would be struck down, too, probably for stretching the Constitution's commerce clause to justify federal intervention in labor disputes. But FDR's attempt to pack the Supreme Court with additional justices of his liking apparently influenced the swing justices, namely Chief Justice Charles Evans Hughes and Owen Roberts.

CHAPTER FIFTEEN

How Did FDR's Supreme Court Subvert Individual Liberty?

IN 1936, AFTER the U.S. Supreme Court ruled that the National Industrial Recovery Act, the Agricultural Adjustment Act, and other New Deal measures were unconstitutional, it seemed that FDR would be unable to sustain his expansion of federal power.

He fumed, "Are the people of this country going to decide that their Federal Government shall in the future have no right under any implied power or any court-approved power to enter into a national economic problem? . . . we have been relegated to the horse-and-buggy definition of interstate commerce."

While having lunch with newspaper publisher Paul Block, FDR reportedly recalled how in 1911 British prime minister Henry Asquith had become frustrated by the refusal of the House of Lords to approve a government-run insurance program. Asquith threatened to expand the House of Lords with sympathizers, thereby securing enactment of his bill. FDR wondered if he might be able to expand the Supreme Court with sympathizers.

FDR began to take the court-packing scheme more seriously after his overwhelming victory in the 1936 elections. He had won

27,750,000 votes to Republican Alf Landon's 16,680,000, and he won the electoral college vote by an overwhelming 523 to 8. Democrats held three-quarters of the seats in both the Senate and the House of Representatives.

How might the court-packing scheme be sold to the public? Ironically, a key idea came from Justice James C. McReynolds, a stalwart defender of economic liberty and opponent of the New Deal. When McReynolds was attorney general under President Woodrow Wilson, he had recommended that a new judge be appointed when a sitting judge didn't retire at the legally mandated age. Although U.S. law didn't require that Supreme Court justices retire at a particular age, FDR thought that with a "court reform" law requiring that Supreme Court justices retire at seventy, he could appoint a half dozen justices to his liking, which would eliminate further legal challenges to the New Deal. "Court reform" was broadened to include lower courts with three-judge panels, because more than a hundred lower-court federal judges, as well as the Supreme Court justices, had ruled that various New Deal measures were unconstitutional.[1]

When FDR announced his plan for "court reform," however, he claimed it was needed because the justices were so decrepit that they couldn't fulfill their responsibilities. This wasn't true, and a number of FDR's advisers protested that he should be more straightforward. He disregarded their advice and unveiled his "court reform" plan on February 5, 1937. In his fireside chat of March 9, 1937, he expressed indignation that the Supreme Court objected to his key New Deal policies: "When the Congress has sought to stabilize national agriculture, to improve the conditions of labor, to safeguard business against unfair competition, to protect our national resources, and in many other ways, to serve our clearly national needs, the majority of the Court has been assuming the power to pass on the wisdom of these acts of the Congress—and to approve or disapprove the public policy written into these laws." FDR claimed that his aim was "to save the Constitution from the Court and the Court from itself."[2]

When it appeared that Democratic leaders in the House might resist "court reform," FDR decided to push it through the Senate first because members seemed likely to "stay hitched." But outraged that one branch of government (the executive) was trying to take over another (the judiciary) and thereby discard constitutional checks and balances, Virginia's Democratic senator Carter Glass denounced FDR's court-packing scheme as "a proposition which appears to me utterly destitute of moral sensibility and without parallel since the foundation of the Republic."[3] Both liberal and Democratic senators joined the opposition to court packing. Democrats Burton K. Wheeler, Harry Byrd, and Millard Tydings worked with Republicans William E. Borah, Charles L. McNary, and Arthur Vandenberg. The key issue turned out not to be the future of the New Deal but the importance of defending the separation of powers principle in the U.S. Constitution.

Hardly anybody believed FDR's claim that he was only trying to help aged justices do their job. Admirers of eighty-one-year-old liberal justice Louis Brandeis were offended. Soon, increasing numbers of New Deal supporters were expressing opposition to FDR's plan, which was being referred to as "court packing." As historian Frank Freidel observed, "Indignant though many of them had been over the anti–New Deal decisions, a considerable part of the liberals viewed the court as the bulwark of American liberties. At that very time, when European dictators were stripping populaces of their liberties, they were especially sensitive to the danger that the United States might suffer the same malign fate." Freidel added that while these people admired FDR, they were concerned that "court reform" would set a precedent that could be exploited by an unscrupulous successor.[4]

FDR began to actively campaign for his plan, claiming it would help protect the underprivileged, but Senator Wheeler countered, "Create now a political Court to echo the ideas of the executive and you have created a weapon; a weapon which in the hands of another President could . . . cut down those guarantees of liberty written by the blood of your forefathers." Though Democratic senator Pat Harrison supported the New Deal, he opposed court packing because he believed that New Deal spending had to be subject to congressional control. Vice President John Garner suggested a compromise that would enable FDR to name two or three new Supreme Court justices, but FDR rejected this, demanding the power to name six.

In March 1937, Senator Henry F. Ashurst opened hearings on FDR's court bill, and it focused opposition for weeks. Senator Wheeler presented a letter signed by Chief Justice Charles Evans Hughes and agreed to by Justices Louis Brandeis and Willis Van Devanter, asserting that the Court was properly managing its workload. The Senate had the votes to defeat FDR's plan. "Presidential pride was sorely scorched," recalled James Farley, the postmaster general and chairman of the Democratic National Committee. "For weeks and months afterward I found him fuming against the members of his own party he blamed for his bucket of bitterness."[5]

All this might have been avoided. With FDR's popularity, particularly in the months after his inauguration and the months after his overwhelming victory in the 1936 election, he might have obtained constitutional amendments to secure practically all the policies he asked for. Democrats controlled Congress and dominated state governments. "If the Constitution, intelligently and reasonably construed," wrote Justice Sutherland, "stands in the way of desirable legislation, the blame must rest upon that instrument, and not upon the court for enforcing it according to its terms. The remedy in that situation—and the only true remedy—is to amend the Constitution."

Although opinion ran against FDR after the court-packing scheme, Justices Hughes and Roberts apparently had been intimidated, and they gave up defending constitutional liberties. For starters, they abandoned the principle of enumerated powers, that the only legitimate powers of the federal government are those spelled out in the Constitution and that all other powers are reserved for the states or individuals. At the same time, these justices ignored the Ninth Amendment ("The enumeration in the Constitution, of certain rights, shall not be construed to deny or disparage others retained by the people") and the Tenth Amendment ("The powers not delegated to the United States by the Constitution, nor prohibited by it to the States, are reserved to the States respectively, or to the people"). These justices began upholding laws that asserted federal powers not mentioned anywhere in the Constitution and that according to the Ninth and Tenth Amendments should have been reserved to the states or the people. The commerce clause and the general welfare clause were stretched to permit a rapid expansion of federal power. Economic liberty, particularly freedom of contract, seemed to become a dead letter.

WHILE FDR WAS still fighting for his court bill, in May 1937, Justice Van Devanter announced he would retire from the Supreme Court. FDR wrote him a note that closed by saying, "Before you leave Washington for the summer, it would give me great personal pleasure if you would come in to see me."

James Farley told FDR. "I thought you wrote a most interesting and amusing letter, particularly the line extending the invitation to him to pay a call before he leaves."

"If I receive the resignation of a certain other judge on the bench," FDR replied, "you can be sure he won't get a similar invitation."

Farley said, "It wouldn't happen to be a certain southern gentleman answering to the name of McReynolds?"

"Still the prophet, Jim. That's exactly the one I had in mind. I'd love to write him a letter, even though he wouldn't go where I'd like to invite him to go—not yet."[6]

FDR delayed naming Arkansas Democratic senator Joseph Robinson, a conservative who had been promised the next vacancy on the Court. Then Robinson suffered a fatal heart attack, and by the time senators returned from his funeral there was solid opposition to FDR's court bill. It was referred back to the Judiciary Committee, effectively killing it.

FDR filled the Supreme Court vacancy by nominating Alabama senator Hugo L. Black. He had once belonged to the Ku Klux Klan but was well enough liked that he was confirmed without much scrutiny. When, in January 1938, Sutherland retired, FDR nominated Stanley Reed. Within three years, he nominated Felix Frankfurter, William O. Douglas, and Frank Murphy to fill additional vacancies, solidifying the FDR Court.

Justices Hughes and Roberts began the era of the FDR Court by siding with Justices Brandeis, Cardozo, and Stone. Freedom of contract was disregarded in *Wright v Vinton Branch of Mountain Trust Bank of Roanoke*, 300 U.S. 440 (March 29, 1937), where the Court upheld the Federal Farm Bankruptcy Act (Frazier-Lemke Act) of August 28, 1935, a revision of a previous law that had been struck down by the Supreme Court. This case involved a Virginia farmer who went bankrupt, defaulted on his mortgage, and wanted to retain possession of his farm. The bank that held the mortgage filed suit to take possession, was rebuffed, and appealed the case to the Supreme Court, asserting that the Frazier-Lemke Act violated the takings clause of the Fifth Amendment of the Constitution, prohibiting the taking of private property without just compensation. Justice Brandeis, writing the majority opinion, simply asserted that he didn't think the Frazier-Lemke Act made an "unreasonable modification" of the mortgage-holder's rights.

Chief Justice Hughes, writing the majority opinion in *West Coast Hotel Co. v Parrish*, 300 U.S. 379 (March 29, 1937) upheld a law making it illegal for anybody to work for less than $14.50 per forty-eight-hour week in the state of Washington. This decision overturned Justice Sutherland's 1923 decision in *Adkins v Children's Hospital*, 261 U.S. 525, defending freedom of contract. More remarkable, the Court reversed the decision from the year before in *Morehead v Tipaldo*, 298 U.S. 587 (June 1, 1936). Hughes wrote blithely, "The Constitution does not speak of freedom of contract. It speaks of liberty and prohibits the deprivation of liberty without due process of law." Robert H. Jackson, then special counsel to the

Treasury Department, exulted: "The doctrine of 'freedom of contract,' which had menaced all types of legislation to regulate the master and servant relation, had been uprooted so definitely that it could hardly be expected to thrive again."[7]

Sutherland, in the minority, affirmed his commitment to freedom of contract: "The right of a person to sell his labor upon such terms as he deems proper is, in its essence, the same as the right of the purchaser of labor to prescribe the conditions upon which he will accept such labor from the person offering to sell. In all such particulars, the employer and employee have equality of right, and any legislation that disturbs that equality is an arbitrary interference with the liberty of contract which no government can legally justify in a free land."

In *Virginian Railway Co. v Federation*, 300 U.S. 515 (March 29, 1937), the FDR Court upheld the constitutionality of the Railway Labor Act as amended in June 1934. Justice Stone, writing for the majority, ordered the railroad to negotiate with a union local of the American Federation of Labor, representing all "back shop" craft employees. Railroad managers had tried to negotiate with employees individually or through a company union, and their freedom of contract was denied.

Virginian Railway Company had maintained that because its "back shop" employees weren't engaged in interstate commerce, the Constitution's commerce clause prevented the federal government from determining who would represent whom in contract negotiations. Stone swept this objection aside by saying that labor disputes disrupt interstate commerce, and compulsory unionism would resolve labor disputes.

The National Labor Relations Act (Wagner Act) subverted the right of individuals to make their own contracts in the workplace. The FDR Court upheld the law in *National Labor Relations Board v Jones & Laughlin Steel Corp.*, 301 U.S. 1 (April 12, 1937), supporting compulsory unionism and subverting the right of individuals to make their own contracts in the workplace. Here the Beaver

Valley Lodge No. 200, affiliated with the Amalgamated Association of Iron, Steel and Tin Workers, filed a complaint that Pittsburgh-based Jones & Laughlin had fired ten employees because of their union activities. The NLRB ordered the company to rehire the individuals and pay them for the period that they had been out of work. Jones & Laughlin refused, and the NLRB petitioned the circuit court of appeals to enforce the order. The court refused, ruling that the NLRB's order "lay beyond the range of federal power." Jones & Laughlin didn't deny that it had fired the employees for their union activities, so the issue was the constitutionality of the law itself.

In his majority opinion, Hughes tried to explain away *Schechter Poultry Corporation v United States*, 295 U.S. 495 (1935), and *Carter v Carter Coal Co.*, 298 U.S. 238 (1936), in which the Court had ruled that the federal government was empowered to regulate interstate commerce, not manufacturing. Hughes asserted that the actions regulated by the Wagner Act affected interstate commerce, and therefore it was constitutional.

In his dissenting opinion, Sutherland challenged Hughes's claim that the *Jones & Laughlin* action involved interstate commerce, and Justices Butler, McReynolds, and Van Devanter concurred. Sutherland went on to reaffirm that "The right to contract is fundamental and includes the privilege of selecting those with whom one is willing to assume contractual relations. This right is unduly abridged by the act now upheld. A private owner is deprived of power to manage his own property by freely selecting those to whom his manufacturing operations are to be entrusted. We think this cannot lawfully be done in circumstances like those here disclosed. It seems clear to us that Congress has transcended the powers granted."

HAVING CEASED TO defend freedom of contract, the FDR Court found itself on a slippery slope and soon was sanctioning labor union monopolies and violence. As Morgan O. Reynolds observed, "The evolution of union power illustrates a double standard that has developed since 1932 in antitrust. Nonviolent and relatively ineffective price-fixing by businessmen, based on arguable evidence and economic theories, is vigorously prosecuted by the Department of Justice, the Federal Trade Commission, state agencies, and private plaintiffs, while industry-wide price-fixing by unionists, often accompanied by violence, is exempt from law, if not actually encouraged by government policy."[8]

In *Apex Hosiery Co. v Leader*, 310 U.S. 469 (May 27, 1940), Justice Stone wrote the Supreme Court's majority opinion that the Sherman Antitrust Act didn't apply to a labor union, even if it used violence to shut down a factory and block the interstate shipment of goods. The case involved Apex Hosiery, a Philadelphia manufacturer that employed about 2,500 people and had annual sales around $5 million. The company had eight employees belonging to the American Federation of Full Fashioned Hosiery Workers, and on May 4, 1937, they ordered a strike, the aim being to force all 2,500 employees into the union. Two days later, when the factory was shut down, the union employees, together with members of the same union who worked at other factories, gathered at the plant and demanded a closed shop—nonunion employees must either join the union or lose their jobs. When plant executives refused to force everybody into the union, as Justice Stone wrote, "acts of violence against petitioner's plant and the employees in charge of it were committed by the assembled mob." The union members "forcibly seized the plant" and held it until June 23, 1937, when the Third Circuit Court of Appeals issued an injunction ending the strike. During this period, the union changed the locks at the plant, and only strikers were given keys. Nobody could enter or leave the plant without permission of the union. The strikers damaged or destroyed several hundred thousand dollars worth of equipment. Three times the company asked the union for permission to enter the factory, remove, and ship the goods stored there and ready for shipment (130,000 dozen pairs of hosiery, worth about $800,000); and three times the union refused permission. Accordingly, Apex Hosiery filed suit in federal court, charging that the union acted in restraint of trade, outlawed by the Sherman Antitrust Act.

Justice Stone acknowledged all the union violence, the seizure of property, the stopping of production, the destruction of property, and the refusal to permit goods to enter interstate commerce, but he declared that the Sherman Antitrust Act didn't outlaw all combinations in restraint of trade—in particular, it didn't apply to unions.

United States v Hutcheson, 312 U.S. 219 (February 3, 1941), affirmed that the Sherman Antitrust Act didn't apply to labor unions. Brewer Anheuser-Busch had been caught in a jurisdictional dispute between the United Brotherhood of Carpenters and the International Association of Machinists. The two unions wanted a contract for erecting and dismantling machinery at Anheuser-Busch, and when in 1939 the company awarded the contract to the machinists, the carpenters called a strike against Anheuser-Busch and construction companies working for the brewer. Justice Felix Frankfurter wrote the majority opinion, which acknowledged that the carpenters "engaged in a deliberate campaign on a national scale to drive Anheuser-Busch from the interstate market." He maintained all this was perfectly legal.

In his dissenting opinion, Roberts, joined by Hughes, countered: "The indictment adequately charges a conspiracy to restrain trade and commerce with the specific purpose of preventing Anheuser-Busch from receiving interstate commerce commodities and materials intended for use in its plant; of preventing Borsari Corporation from obtaining materials in interstate commerce for use in performing a contract for Anheuser-Busch, and of preventing the Stocker Company from receiving materials in like manner for the construction of a building for the Gaylord Corporation. . . . Without detailing the allegations of the indictment, it is sufficient to say that they undeniably charge a secondary boycott, affecting interstate commerce. This Court, and many state tribunals, over a long period of years, have held such a secondary boycott illegal."

Hunt v Crumboch, 325 U.S. 821 (June 18, 1945), provided further sanction for union violence. Justice Hugo Black wrote the majority opinion, acknowledging, "In 1937, the respondent union called a strike of the truckers and haulers of A & P in Philadelphia for the purpose of enforcing a closed shop. The petitioner [a trucking company], refusing to unionize its business, attempted to operate during the strike. Much violence occurred. One of the union men was killed near union headquarters, and a member of the petitioner partnership was tried for the homicide and acquitted. A & P and the union entered into a closed-shop agreement whereupon all contract haulers working for A & P, including the petitioner, were notified that their employees must join and become members of the union." Because the trucker had a dispute with a union boss, he pressured A & P to cancel its contract with the trucker, and when it secured a contract with another company, the union pressured that company to cancel the contract, which it did. Black ruled that union members acted individually and therefore the union itself couldn't be found guilty of violating the Sherman Antitrust Act.

EVERY BIT AS important as the FDR Court's decisions upholding compulsory unionism were its decisions upholding Social Security. This, as already noted, involved taxing some people (younger workers) to benefit other people (those who retired), in violation of the general welfare clause, which had long been held to mean that taxpayers' money should be spent to benefit all the people, not particular individuals or factions. Justice Cardozo, writing the majority opinion in *Helvering v Davis*, 301 U.S. 619 (May 24, 1937), suggested the general welfare clause was meaningless, standing for one thing at one time and another thing at another time.

Justices McReynolds and Butler, dissenting from *Helvering*, countered by saying that the general welfare clause "is not a substantive general power to provide for the welfare of the United States, but is a limitation on the grant of power to raise money by taxes, duties, and imports." The justices continued, "If it were otherwise, all the rest of the Constitution, consisting of carefully enumerated and cautiously guarded grants of specific powers, would have been useless, if not delusive."

Further, McReynolds and Butler were "of opinion that the provisions of the act here challenged are repugnant to the Tenth
Amendment." They elaborated with separate dissenting opinions in
a related Social Security case, *Steward Machine Co. v Collector of
Internal Revenue*, 301 U.S. 548 (May 24, 1937). McReynolds expressed the enumerated powers principle when he wrote, "I cannot
find any authority in the Constitution for making the Federal Government the great almoner of public charity throughout the United
States. . . . Can it be controverted that the great mass of the business
of Government—that involved in the social relations, the internal
arrangements of the body politic, the mental and moral culture of
men, the development of local resources of wealth, the punishment
of crimes in general, the preservation of order, the relief of the needy
or otherwise unfortunate members of society—did in practice remain with the States; that none of these objects of local concern are
by the Constitution expressly or impliedly prohibited to the States,
and that none of them are by any express language of the Constitution transferred to the United States? Can it be claimed that any of
these functions of local administration and legislation are vested in
the Federal Government by any implication? I have never found
anything in the Constitution which is susceptible of such a construction. No one of the enumerated powers touches the subject, or has
even a remote analogy to it."

In yet another Social Security case, *Carmichael v Southern
Coal & Coke Co.*, 301 U.S. 495 (May 24, 1937), focusing on the
unemployment compensation component of Social Security, Sutherland expressed concern that the law violated the equal protection
clause of the Fourteenth Amendment. He wrote, "Let us suppose
that A, an employer of a thousand men, has retained all of his employees. B, an employer of a thousand men, has discharged half of
his employees. The tax is upon the pay roll of each. A, who has not
discharged a single workman, is taxed upon his pay roll twice as
much as B, although the operation of B's establishment has contributed enormously to the evil of unemployment while that of A

has contributed nothing at all. It thus results that the employer who has kept all his men at work pays twice as much toward the relief of the employees discharged by B as B himself pays." Sutherland might have added, as law professor Richard A. Epstein later pointed out, that the unemployment compensation component of Social Security effectively imposes a net tax on industries with low employee turnover and subsidizes industries with high employee turnover, which seems hard to justify by any recognized standard.[9]

Cardozo acknowledged that Social Security wasn't legitimate insurance. As he explained in *Steward Machine*, "The proceeds, when collected, go into the Treasury of the United States like internal revenue collections generally. They are not earmarked in any way." In other words, even after an individual has paid Social Security taxes for decades, he or she doesn't have a contractual claim to specific benefits. Congress could change the benefits formula at any time, and it has. By contrast, a private insurance policy is a contract specifying what premiums the insured will pay and what benefits the insured or heirs will get. If an insurance company defaults, it can be taken into court for breach of contract. Surely millions of Americans would feel more secure if their Social Security taxes bought a contractual right to collect a specific package of benefits, but they never got this from a Supreme Court that had done so much to trash freedom of contract. This position, that a taxpayer doesn't have a contractual right to collect specific Social Security benefits, was affirmed by the Supreme Court decades later, in *Flemming v Nestor*, 363 U.S. 603 (1960).

The clearest and briefest summary of the FDR Court's views came in *United States v Caroline Products*, 304 U.S. 144 (April 25, 1938). The justices distinguished between "fundamental" liberties like freedom of speech and the right to vote and "nonfundamental" liberties including property rights and freedom of contract. "Legislation that implicates fundamental rights, gets strict judicial scrutiny," observed Cato Institute constitutional scholar Roger Pilon. "By contrast, legislation that implicates nonfundamental rights gets minimal judicial scrutiny; it is presumed constitutional; the burden is on the individual to show that it is not."[10]

The FDR Court stretched the Constitution in many other cases, such as *Currin v Wallace*, 306 U.S. 1 (January 4, 1939). Here the justices ruled that the federal government could extend its power over practically anything, supposedly to promote the "general welfare." This case involved federal regulations grading tobacco sold at auctions, even though the auctions were local. Clearly, what mattered were the results sought by the FDR Court, not the Constitution that had limited government power.

In *Mulford v Smith*, 307 U.S. 38 (March 8, 1939), the FDR Court upheld the 1938 Agricultural Adjustment Act. This authorized the federal government to decree the total quantity of a crop that could be produced and how production must be allocated by state. Farmers exceeding their quotas would be hit with fines. None of these federal powers were enumerated by the Constitution.

As Roger Pilon explained, "In a nutshell, a document of delegated, enumerated, and thus limited powers became in short order a document of effectively unenumerated powers, limited only by rights that would thereafter be interpreted narrowly by conservatives on the Court and episodically by liberals on the Court. Both sides, in short, would come to ignore our roots in limited government, buying instead into the idea of vast majoritarian power—the only disagreement being over what rights might limit that power and in which circumstances."[11]

CHAPTER SIXTEEN

How Did New Deal Policies Cause the Depression of 1938?

THE BANKING ACT of 1935 had, among other things, turned the Federal Reserve System into a reasonably independent central bank.

It had been, under the 1913 Federal Reserve Act, an association of regional Federal Reserve banks supervised by a seven-member Federal Reserve Board. The Board originally had ties to the current administration, since two of the members were the secretary of the Treasury and the comptroller of the currency, and the Board met in Treasury offices. The other five members served staggered terms: one served for two years, one for four years, one for six years, one for eight years, and one for ten years. Any of the regional Federal Reserve banks could engage in open market operations that involved buying or selling gold or government securities.

The Banking Act of 1935 amended the Federal Reserve Act to set up the Board so it would have more independence from the president and Congress. After February 1, 1936, the secretary of the Treasury and the controller of the currency, with their continuing ties to the current administration, would no longer be on the Board.

Members, to be known as governors, would serve for staggered fourteen-year terms, substantially insulating the Board from political pressure. Everybody was limited to a single term. One of the governors would be a chairman, and another would be vice chairman, each serving in those capacities for a four-year term (or for the rest of the term if there were less than four years remaining). The Banking Act of 1935 established a Federal Open Market Committee consisting of the seven governors and five members selected from the regional Federal Reserve banks, which meant that the governors ought to be able to dominate the regional banks. Further, any open market operations had to be "in accordance with the direction of and regulations adopted by the Committee."

The aim was to make sure that if decisive action had to be taken, it wouldn't be thwarted by disagreement among the regional Federal Reserve banks, as had been the case between 1929 and 1933. The assumption, of course, was that the Federal Reserve Board would be smarter than the regional Federal Reserve banks. If, however, the Board made some bad calls, the consequence of the Banking Act of 1935 would be that a smaller number of people (seven Board governors) had the power to inflict harm on the entire country.

Marriner Eccles, whom FDR appointed as a Federal Reserve governor in January 1934, had demanded these changes. FDR named Eccles to be the first Federal Reserve chairman on November 15, 1934. The choice was curious, because Eccles had made clear that even with additional power he didn't believe the Federal Reserve could do much. During his House Committee on Banking testimony, Eccles borrowed a phrase of Maryland congressman Goldsborough, that "you cannot push a string," meaning the Fed couldn't help the economy much by making credit available if banks and businesses weren't willing to borrow.

The new Federal Reserve Board's first bad call came on July 14, 1936, just five and a half months after it began to operate. Banks had built up their reserves well above the minimum levels, and Fed officials became concerned the excess reserves might cause a big increase in lending and inflation. So the Board voted to increase the reserve requirement 50 percent, which meant a higher portion of reserves had to stay in the banks. For Fed chairman Eccles, a major issue was control. "We had to increase the required reserve sufficiently to bring under the direct influence of [Fed] open-market operations the reserves that remained," he wrote in his autobiography.[1]

The economy seemed to be improving as fall elections approached. After FDR won the landslide victory, and the major New Deal laws enacted in 1935 were upheld by the Supreme Court, he expected that good times would return. Indeed, the rising stock market made Treasury Secretary Morgenthau worry about inflation, and he took steps to "sterilize" the flows of gold into the United States, so they wouldn't be added to bank reserves and thereby encourage inflationary bank lending.

Experience would make clear, however, that an enduring mystery of Federal Reserve action is how long it will take to have an effect. Often symptoms of trouble don't become evident for more than a year, and the lag between action and effect can take much longer than that. The danger has always been that impatient policymakers will think they haven't done enough and compound one bad call with another. This the Federal Reserve Board did when, on January 30, 1937, it voted to increase bank reserve requirements another $33^{1/3}$ percent. Half the increase would be effective on March 6, the other half on May 1.

Then on March 12, 1937, the government bond market dropped, and interest rates moved from about 2.48 percent to 2.52 percent. This looks trivial to us; we have become accustomed to much higher interest rates and bigger fluctuations, but back then interest rates had changed little since World War I. The smallest change, particularly in the context of the Great Depression, could be a sign of trouble. Treasury Secretary Morgenthau blamed the bond market drop on the Fed's increase in reserve requirements, but Eccles insisted the drop must have reflected worries about a European war.

The bond market began dropping again on March 16, and by March 18 interest rates were up to 2.62 percent. Fed governor George Harrison thought the bond market had been making orderly adjustments, while Morgenthau and Eccles were concerned about a crisis—but the Board couldn't decide what to do. By March 27, government bond interest rates were up to 2.72 percent. After Morgenthau threatened to take action if the Fed didn't, on April 4 the Open Market Committee voted to buy as much as $250 million worth of government bonds from banks, generating downward pressure on interest rates and injecting money into the banks selling the bonds. But interest rates edged up to 2.8 percent.

The second part of the second increase in bank reserve requirements became effective May 1 as scheduled. The increases during 1936 and 1937 "removed $3.1 billion of reserves as a base for monetary expansion in a period of 9 months," noted economist Allan Meltzer. "The reduction is approximately 28 percent of the level of reserves on June 30, 1936 (shortly before the new Fed's first increase in reserve requirements). . . . In the four quarters of 1936, average M1 (currency in circulation plus demand deposits) growth was 12.8 percent, propelled by the increase in gold. Growth fell to 5 percent (annual rate) in first quarter 1937. For the remaining three-quarters of 1937, the average annual growth rate of money was 6.5 percent."[2] This reduced monetary growth was to have a depressing effect on the economy.

THE EXPANDED POWER of the Federal Reserve over the American economy did increase its potential to do harm, since power was in the hands of human beings who would always make mistakes interpreting conflicting information. As economic historian Lester V. Chandler wrote, "The increase of member bank reserve requirements in the spring of 1937 was a mistake. Federal Reserve officials were wrong in their judgment that the very large volume of excess reserves in 1936 and 1937 was 'serving no useful purpose.' They were serving the very useful purpose of satisfying the banks' continued high demand for liquidity, and of bringing pressures on banks to expand their loans and investments."[3]

Milton Friedman and Anna Jacobson Schwartz added, "The [Federal Reserve] System failed to weigh the delayed effects of the rise in reserve requirements in August 1936, and employed too blunt an instrument too vigorously; this was followed by a failure to recognize promptly that the action had misfired and that a reversal of policy was called for. All those blunders were in considerable measure a consequence of the mistaken interpretation of excess reserves and their significance."[4]

Federal Reserve policy wasn't the only factor depressing the economy. New York Stock Exchange president Charles Gay insisted that Securities and Exchange Commission chairman William O. Douglas deserved some of the blame, since Douglas had become an outspoken critic of the way Wall Street firms conducted their business. When the Justice Department was reluctant to prosecute former New York Stock Exchange president Richard Whitney for embezzlement, it was SEC chairman Douglas who fumed that there's "one law for the very powerful or wealthy and another for those of little wealth and influence." After Louis Brandeis announced his retirement from the Supreme Court, Douglas, maneuvering himself into position for a Supreme Court appointment, made a Brandeis-like speech attacking certain big businesses as "a menace to the ideals of democracy." By March 19, FDR decided he wanted Douglas to fill Brandeis's seat on the Supreme Court.[5]

New Deal labor laws, particularly the Wagner Act, which rapidly led to labor union monopolies in mass-production industries, were a factor in the 1938 recession. Payroll costs, among the biggest costs any business faces, went up. The wave of violent strikes disrupted business and imposed substantial costs on many companies. All this reduced the ability of employers to hire people, and there were severe layoffs. Moreover, industries most affected by compulsory unionism had a strong incentive to substitute machines for human labor wherever possible, which contributed to the 22 percent gain in productivity between 1933 and 1938.[6]

New Deal tax increases probably contributed to the economic collapse, because they made it more difficult for businesses to employ people. First, of course, FDR's higher taxes reduced the money available to businesses and consumers. The latest tax increases were the undistributed profits tax, enacted in March 1936, and the Social Security payroll tax, which began in 1937. The Social Security tax alone took $2 billion out of the economy.[7] Rather than cut taxes, according to biographer Ted Morgan, "FDR wanted to go after the economic royalists who did not pay their fair share of taxes."[8]

Economist Kenneth D. Roose observed that "These taxes may have been part of the process which was promoting increased uncertainty over future developments. They may have contributed to the unwillingness of investors to undertake extremely risky ventures. The risk of losing everything outweighed the gain after taxes. . . . It is unlikely that these taxes, by themselves, could have curtailed the supply of funds. Where, however, the profitability of investment was declining and where there was growing uncertainty over the future, the level of individual income taxes and capital gains taxes may have assisted in precipitating the recession by limiting profits after taxes."[9]

During the summer of 1937, businesses reported higher levels of unsold inventories—$5 billion worth, believed to be the highest level in American history.[10] Industrial production fell one-third, and durable goods production was down about 50 percent.[11] About 20 percent of workers lost their jobs, and some 10 million people were out of work. The unemployment rate approached 20 percent.[12] The stock market declined, and on October 19, 1937—which came to be called "Black Tuesday"—the Dow Jones Industrial Average plunged from 190 to 115. The decline continued into 1938, and by the end of the year stocks had declined about 50 percent from their level at year-end 1936. This period has been called a recession, but economist Mark H. Leff observed that America had suffered "the steepest nosedive in its history."[13] The National Bureau of Economic Research, which monitors statistics about inflations, depressions, and recessions, ranked this the third worst recession since World War I.[14]

Some economists claimed the economy declined because the federal government had cut government spending in 1937, after having splurged the previous year to help assure that FDR would win the election. This line of thinking implicitly suggested that the economy had become dependent on government spending and that FDR hadn't prepared a transition toward private investment and private employment.

The bottom line was a chronic low level of business investment. The National Industrial Conference Board reported that the amount of investment capital per employee was much lower in the 1930s than it had been during the 1920s. Less capital meant fewer people could be employed. Economist Roose added that low working capital was an issue during the 1937–1938 recession, as evidenced by a dramatic increase in corporate accounts payable (unpaid bills).[15]

A substantial portion of business investment was short term, as had been the case throughout the New Deal period. Economist H. Gregg Lewis observed, "The situation was dominated by the short-run outlook, and was for that reason vulnerable. All the elements of a short run boom were there, but the requirement for a sustained recovery—recovery in outlays made on the basis of a long term outlook—was lacking. Reasonable certainty as to the future was absent."[16]

Employers were wary of long-term risks, one of which was a president and Congress threatening those with "idle" capital to invest. Many economists then and now recognized how bashing employers can destroy jobs. Joseph Schumpeter wrote in his 1939 book *Business Cycles* that employers felt threatened: "They realize that they are on trial before judges who have the verdict in their pocket beforehand, that an increasing part of public opinion is impervious to their point of view, and that any particular indictment will, if successfully met, at once be replaced by another. Again, we may differ in our estimates of the importance of both of this factor and the functions it tends to paralyze, but it should not be overlooked."[17]

There were plenty of proposals for more government interference in the economy. FDR advisers Brandeis, Frankfurter, Corcoran, and Cohen cherished "reform," meaning more taxes and regulations. Treasury Secretary Henry Morgenthau recommended antitrust prosecutions of big business.[18] FDR floated the idea of reviving the defunct National Recovery Administration and its cartels. He had Adolf Berle and Rexford Tugwell try to drum up support among businesspeople and labor union bosses, but nothing much came of this. FDR resolved to push for $3.5 billion of government spending on public works and relief,[19] which seems to have helped him politically in the past, although it didn't do the economy much good. Many people thought FDR had become a convert to the theories of John Maynard Keynes. In Freidel's view, "He liked Keynes, to be sure, but did not pretend to understand his theories."[20]

Naturally, all this further alarmed the business community, undermining the confidence of anybody who might have contemplated making long-term investments. As bad news continued to come in, increasing numbers of people demanded that the government get off their backs, starting with tax cuts. FDR would hear none of it, since he had fought hard to raise taxes during the depression.

Congress passed the Fair Labor Standards Act, and it became law on June 14, 1938. It was based on the minimum wage provisions of the National Industrial Recovery Act.[21] Covering about 12 million workers, it specified a minimum wage of 25 cents per hour (soon raised to 40 cents), and it provided that nobody could work more than forty-four hours per week. Although the minimum seems low to us, it meant pay increases for about 750,000 workers, further increasing the cost of funding jobs in the depression.[22]

The Fair Labor Standards Act was devastating for the South. Politicians there had opposed the measure precisely because it would undercut their principal selling point—namely, lower labor costs—in persuading northern businesses to locate factories down South. Because a disproportionate number of black workers were in the South, they were the principal losers from this minimum wage law. As George Mason University law professor David E. Bernstein noted, "labor union leaders, who by the late 1930s were an integral part of the New Deal coalition, supported a high, uniform national minimum wage partly out of labor solidarity, but also to limit competition between unskilled nonunionized southern workers and unskilled union members. . . ."[23]

"The disemployment effects of the FLSA," Bernstein continued, "were mainly felt by unskilled African American workers in the South, who were most likely to work in jobs that paid less than the government-imposed minimum wage. The Labor Department reported in 1938 that between thirty thousand and fifty thousand workers, mostly southern African Americans, lost their jobs because of the minimum wage within two weeks of the Fair Labor Standards Act's imposition. . . . African Americans in the tobacco industry were particularly hard hit. In Wilson, North Carolina, for example, machines replaced two thousand African American tobacco stemmers in 1939."[24]

Finally, on August 20, 1937, the Federal Reserve began to act, although some Fed governors weren't convinced a depression had started. At least one Fed governor believed the "causes of the present situation were not in the monetary field." Federal Reserve banks in Chicago, Atlanta, and New York cut their discount rate to 1½ percent. This was the rate the Fed charged member banks. On September 11, the Federal Open Market Committee voted to buy as much as $300 million of securities and inject that much money into member bank reserves, but these purchases didn't begin until November. Treasury Secretary Morgenthau ended his policy of sterilizing gold in February 1938, and gold stocks could again be accounted as part of bank reserves. In April, the Fed reversed the 50 percent hike in reserve requirements that had been put into effect May 1, 1936. The money supply began to head up.[25]

The 1938 depression brought fresh opposition to New Deal policies. Apparently people were becoming weary of FDR's class-warfare
rhetoric and his attacks on "economic royalists"; in addition, there
was increasing support for tax relief. In 1939, without the president's
signature, Congress passed a bill repealing the undistributed profits
tax. The Social Security Act was amended to channel payroll taxes
right back into the economy rather than set aside funds for future retirement benefits. Current payroll taxes went to pay benefits for current retirees. The change helped reduce the negative effect of payroll
taxes, while passing retirement liabilities to future generations—and
that would become a huge financial problem.

America recovered from the 1938 depression, but unemployment remained high, the Great Depression dragged on, and increasingly FDR looked as if he didn't know what he was doing. All he
could offer was more class warfare and government controls.

CHAPTER SEVENTEEN

WHY DID
NEW DEAL LAWYERS
DISRUPT COMPANIES
EMPLOYING MILLIONS?

FDR CONTINUED BLAMING employers and investors for the Great Depression. James Farley, FDR's postmaster general and presidential campaign manager, quoted FDR as saying at a cabinet meeting, "I know that the present situation is the result of a concerted effort by big business and concentrated wealth to drive the market down just to create a situation unfavorable to me. . . . I have been around the country and know conditions are good. . . . The whole situation is being manufactured in Wall Street."[1]

New Dealers joined the attack. Harry Hopkins told the Senate's Special Committee to Investigate Unemployment and Relief that monopolies caused the recession by inflating prices and depriving the economy of needed purchasing power. Texas Democratic congressman Wright Patman railed at the "feudalistic chain store system."[2] Interior Secretary Harold Ickes condemned "America's 60 richest families."

Economic adviser Leon Henderson blamed the Great Depression on alleged business monopolists who cut production and raised prices—which is exactly what FDR's National Recovery Administration had done. On CBS radio, Henderson claimed that "many an industry, like the steel industry, has pegged its prices, thrown its employees out of jobs and ploughed under potential production"—as FDR's Agricultural Adjustment Administration had done. Assistant Attorney General Robert Jackson delivered a blistering speech in which he declared that the alleged monopolists had "priced themselves out of the market, and priced themselves into a slump." FDR reportedly told Jackson, "Bob, I'm sick and tired of sitting here kissing people's asses to get them to do what they ought to be volunteering for the Republic." FDR reportedly told Rexford Tugwell that he aimed to "scare these people [in business] into doing something."[3]

In March 1938, FDR appointed Yale University law professor Thurman Arnold to head the Antitrust Division of the Justice Department. Arnold was born in Laramie, Wyoming, in 1891. His father was a rancher and lawyer. Arnold attended Wabash College, transferred to Princeton University, and earned a law degree at Harvard Law School. Returning to Wyoming, he was elected to the state legislature in 1920, then elected mayor of Laramie. He became bored with the office and accepted an offer to serve as dean of the University of West Virginia Law School.[4] Some of his courses attracted the attention of Yale Law School dean Charles Clark, and in 1930, he started teaching at Yale Law School.

His book *The Folklore of Capitalism* (1937), a satire on antitrust laws, was a bestseller. He remarked, "The advantage of the antitrust laws is that they are sufficiently vague," meaning they gave government officials like Arnold a great deal of arbitrary power.[5] Historian Ellis W. Hawley described him as "a large man, somewhat paunchy, generally attired in a disheveled costume, and given to incessant talking in a loud voice." Hawley remarked that Arnold "was at first regarded as something of a joke, another Marx brother who had strayed into the government by mistake."[6]

Considering how passionately New Dealers condemned monopolies, it's curious that FDR didn't mount a major assault against the

Smoot-Hawley tariff that Hoover had signed into law back in June 1930. Congress did pass the Reciprocal Trade Agreements Act (1934), empowering the president to enter into tariff-reduction agreements with other countries and cut tariffs as much as 50 percent, but by 1940 the deals that were done cut tariffs only about 4 percent.[7] Tariffs were long viewed as "the mother of trusts" because they limited choices for consumers and enabled domestic companies to charge prices above world market levels.

Ironically, the Sherman Antitrust Act (1890), the New Dealers' favorite remedy for fighting monopoly, was originally enacted to provide political cover for the McKinley tariff (1890), which raised tariffs to higher levels. New York attorney Franklin Pierce explained the game in his 1913 book *The Tariff and the Trusts*: "We legalize conditions [high tariffs] out of which an evil arises and then attempt to suppress the evil by penal statutes. We provide for high duties upon foreign imports for the protection of home industries, and when a monopoly controlling the home market results therefrom, then pass penal laws punishing the monopoly. In this way our politicians prove to the great combinations who furnish campaign disbursements for political parties their fidelity to monopolistic interests, while, by the penal statute, they assure the people that they are against trusts."[8]

FDR AND HIS comrades posed as champions of competition, even though they had promoted many policies raising prices and suppressing competition. New Deal efforts to suppress competition went well beyond the wage and price codes of the National Industrial Recovery Act, the price-fixing regulations of the Agricultural Adjustment Act, the sanctions for compulsory unionism and higher wages of the National Labor Relations Act, and the minimum wage provision of the Fair Labor Standards Act.

The Communications Act (1934) established the Federal Communications Commission, which granted monopolies to a comparatively few broadcasters, while retaining the power to control speech.

Broadcasting monopolies were granted via broadcast licenses, and the FCC's licensing decisions were based not just on a broadcaster's resources but also on the FCC's approval of a broadcaster's programming. In 1940, for instance, the FCC issued a ruling, known as the "Mayflower Doctrine," against editorializing. It said "the broadcaster cannot be an advocate."[9] This policy prevailed until 1949 when the FCC adopted the "Fairness Doctrine."

The Robinson-Patman Act, amending the Clayton Antitrust Act in 1936, sought to protect small grocery stores from price competition offered by A&P, King Kullen ("World's Greatest Price Wrecker"), and other chain stores. Because A&P bought goods in large volume, it secured quantity discounts and passed these savings to consumers. The Grocery Manufacturers Association lobbied for and did much of the work drafting Robinson-Patman.[10] While the Robinson-Patman Act has also been called the Anti-Chain-Store Act, it benefited wholesalers as well as small retailers, because wholesalers didn't want chain stores buying directly from manufacturers.

The Miller-Tydings Retail Price Maintenance Act (August 17, 1937) was a related effort to protect small businesses from competition with larger, more efficient firms. Small-business lobbyists had successfully persuaded most state legislatures to enact "fair trade" laws that authorized price fixing, but the Supreme Court struck these down as violating the Sherman Antitrust Act. Congress passed, and FDR signed, Miller-Tydings, which amended the Sherman Act to let manufacturers fix the retail prices of branded merchandise and thereby stop chain stores from offering consumers great discount prices.

On June 23, 1938, FDR signed into law the Civil Aeronautics Act, which established the Civil Aeronautics Authority—this later became the Civil Aeronautics Board. It enforced a cartel, protecting existing airlines from new competition. Without a CAB certificate of "public convenience and necessity," an airline couldn't fly an interstate route. The CAB made clear its intent to suppress competition when it declared, "In the absence of particular circumstances presenting an affirmative reason for a new carrier, there appears to be no inherent desirability of increasing the present number of carriers merely for the purpose of numerically enlarging the industry."[11] During the next forty years, until airlines were deregulated in 1978, the CAB didn't issue a license for a single new interstate airline.

The CAB also had the power to fix prices and determine which airlines flew to which cities. "All passenger, cargo, and mail rates," explained economist Sam Peltzman, "while initially set by the airlines, required approval by the CAB." It maintained high fares. Nonscheduled carriers, initially exempted from CAB regulation, operated without published schedules and provided flights to whatever destinations were underserved, and they offered lower fares. The CAB-regulated airlines responded with lower-priced coach service, but they lobbied the CAB to gain jurisdiction over the "nonscheds," and it denied more and more applications to provide nonsched service, until that source of competition was virtually eliminated.[12]

Ironies aside, Thurman Arnold soon hired some 300 lawyers to file some 150 antitrust lawsuits against employers.[13] A key part of Arnold's strategy was to file both criminal and civil lawsuits simultaneously. Government attorneys could offer to drop the criminal charges if the target company agreed to make the changes they demanded and sign a consent decree. Often, too, Arnold launched a case not just against a single company but against an entire industry. He aggressively used publicity in an effort to influence public opinion against the companies and industries he was attacking.[14]

Arnold "divided the nation into 10 districts," Ellis Hawley reported. "Investigators poured into each and by the end of the year grand juries were sitting in 11 major cities and tolling off a long list of indictments. Eventually the drive produced some 99 criminal actions and 22 civil suits, a shock treatment." Arnold oversaw lawsuits against the milk, oil, tobacco, shoe machinery, tire, fertilizer, railroad, pharmaceutical, school supply, billboard, fire insurance, liquor, typewriter, and movie industries, among others. Journalist Joseph Alsop quoted Arnold as saying that he aimed "to hit hard, hit everyone, and hit them all at once."[15]

Here, as everywhere else in the New Deal, there was a lot of simplistic thinking. Arnold didn't go as far as Louis Brandeis, who seemed to disapprove of anything big, but his idea of "unfair" covered a lot of ground. For instance, he thought much honest advertising was "unfair." Raymond Moley recalled, "Mr. Arnold's point seems to be that competition becomes unfair if one party has a well-known trade name whereas a competitor has no such well-known name."[16] Arnold warned against *coercive* advertising, as if advertisers had the power to tax people or send people to jail for not buying their products.

To gain political support for his blitzkrieg of lawsuits, Arnold urged that Congress establish a body that would conduct a "thorough study of the concentration of economic power."[17] Accordingly, on June 9, the Senate passed a resolution for the Temporary National Economic Committee (TNEC). There would be twelve members, half from Congress and half from the administration. The House passed this resolution on June 14, and FDR signed it on June 16. The hearings, presided over by Wyoming senator Joseph O'Mahoney, went on for eighteen months. Altogether, 552 witnesses provided some 20,000 pages of testimony; there were 3,300 technical exhibits, and 43 special studies were written.[18] Although the TNEC generated a stupendous amount of data and publicity, it never proved that private monopoly was dominant or that it was growing or, for that matter, that private monopoly was worse than the growing sector of government monopoly. Nor did the TNEC make any clearer what should be done. Arnold himself remarked, "The recommendations of the committee were harmless, and no one ever paid any attention to them."[19]

TNEC publicity did suggest that the United States continued to be a politically risky place for businesses to make long-term investments, so the TNEC did its part to prolong the Great Depression. In

January 1940, for instance, the TNEC recommended that the Securities and Exchange Commission investigate life insurance companies. According to *Best's* magazine, which covered the field, "Many people in the industry already feared that Roosevelt and some members of Congress wanted the federal government to take over life insurance and that they were going to use Social Security to do it. The committee's report, *A Study of Legal Reserve Life Insurance Companies*, did not allay their fears."[20]

BEFORE THE TNEC hearings concluded, it had become apparent that the onslaught of antitrust lawsuits wasn't accomplishing much. In Madison Oil, one of the earliest cases, Judge Patrick Stone dismissed all charges against eleven defendants and ordered a new trial for eighteen others. The case against Aluminum Company of America dragged on for thirteen years, during which the company's market share declined as the market expanded. In the paradoxical auto financing case, Arnold went after companies that cut consumer costs. Arnold didn't achieve many victories—in the best-known cases, the big movie studios were forced to sell their theater chains, and the Pullman Company was forced to concentrate on manufacturing sleeping cars and to get out of the business of providing sleeping car services.[21]

One of the most bizarre cases involved Socony-Vacuum Oil Company (later known as Mobil), Shell Petroleum, Pure Oil, Continental Oil, and other companies indicted for having violated the Sherman Antitrust Act between February 1935 and December 1936. In particular, they allegedly "(1) conspired together to raise and fix the prices on the spot markets; (2) raised, fixed, and maintained those prices at artificially high and non-competitive levels and 'thereby intentionally increased and fixed the tank car prices of gasoline contracted to be sold . . . in interstate commerce . . . in the Mid-Western area . . . (3) exacted large sums of money from thousands of jobber contracts which made the price to the jobber dependent on the average spot market price; and (4) in turn . . .

intentionally raised the general level of retail prices prevailing in said Mid-Western area."[22]

This case was bizarre because the companies were being prosecuted for the very practices the Roosevelt administration promoted under the National Industrial Recovery Act, just months before the indictment. FDR had signed that legislation into law in June 1933. Section 9(c) "authorized the President to forbid the interstate and foreign shipment of petroleum and its products produced or withdrawn from storage in violation of state laws"—the aim being to restrict supplies and force prices up. Then on July 14, FDR issued Executive Order 6204 banning such shipments. A National Recovery Administration code for the petroleum industry was approved on August 19, and the secretary of the interior was responsible for enforcing it, so that petroleum supplies might be limited and prices maintained at above-market levels. The secretary of the interior established a Petroleum Administrative Board to advise him about how to limit supplies and maintain above-market prices.

On July 20, 1934, the NRA administrator for the Petroleum Code wrote Socony-Vacuum Oil Company vice president Charles E. Arnott, later a defendant in the antitrust lawsuit: "I am, therefore, requesting you, as Chairman of the Marketing Committee of the Planning and Coordinating Committee, to take action which we deem necessary to restore markets to their normal conditions in areas where wasteful competition has caused them to become depressed . . . and in a cooperative manner to stabilize the price level."[23]

The whole point of the National Industrial Recovery Act had been to promote cartels and fix prices and, in the process, maintain above-market wages, on the theory that such practices would help get America out of the Great Depression; it allowed its participants to apply for immunity from the Sherman Antitrust Act. Evidently the defendants never applied for immunity, which left them vulnerable to antitrust prosecution even though they did what FDR wanted them to do under the NIRA when it was still in effect. They were

accused not of fixing prices directly but of buying up "distress gasoline" from independent producers, which helped maintain prices higher than they otherwise would have been. The defendants started doing this in February 1935, and the NIRA wasn't struck down by the Supreme Court until May 27, 1935. If the defendants crossed some kind of line, it was mighty hard to see, what with FDR-sanctioned cartels and price fixing going on in over 700 industries. Apparently the defendants continued buying "distress gasoline." Legal proceedings began as if the Roosevelt administration had never promoted cartels and price fixing.

Addressing the jury, Thurman Arnold and his associate lawyers denounced the defendants as "the biggest men," "grasping men," and "malefactors of great wealth."[24] They were convicted. However, the appeals court reversed the decision, and the case then went to the Supreme Court. Justice William O. Douglas wrote the majority opinion, which reversed the appeals court and upheld the original decision against the defendants. Seemingly oblivious to everything the Roosevelt administration had done to promote price fixing, including the Agricultural Adjustment Act, the Bituminous Coal Conservation Act, the Fair Labor Standards Act, and the Civil Aeronautics Act, as well as the National Industrial Recovery Act, Douglas said, "Any combination which tampers with price structures is engaged in an unlawful activity. Even though the members of the price fixing group were in no position to control the market, to the extent that they raised, lowered, or stabilized prices they would be directly interfering with the free play of market forces."[25] Justices Hugo Black, Felix Frankfurter, Stanley Reed, and Harlan Fiske Stone concurred. Justice Owen Roberts wrote a dissenting opinion joined by Justice James McReynolds.

The antitrusters "might blame the depression upon the departure from competitive standards and suggest measures to make industrial organization correspond more closely to the competitive model," Ellis Hawley wrote. "But they could never ignore or explain away the deflationary and disruptive implications of their program."[26]

Indeed, while Arnold claimed to be a crusader for consumers, there never was a popular demand for antitrust lawsuits. His political support came primarily from smaller companies that hoped by political means to gain competitive advantages they weren't able to achieve in the marketplace. "If he pushed the cases backed by small business interests," Hawley observed, "he ran the risk of rewarding inefficiency, discouraging innovation, and forcing consumers to pay higher prices. Yet if he concentrated exclusively on consumer welfare, he ran the risk of alienating his main source of political support."[27]

ENTRY INTO WORLD War II effectively ended the antitrust crusade, as war production became the top priority, and business leaders like Edward R. Stettinius and William Knudsen were recruited to take charge. Apparently to get Arnold out of the way, FDR offered him a judgeship on the circuit court of appeals, and he resigned from the Justice Department in January 1943.

Some critics believed that Arnold's aggressive lawsuits and the endless antibusiness testimony of the Temporary National Economic Committee discouraged employers from making long-term investments needed to boost unemployment. Indeed, private investment remained low, and unemployment remained high as America mobilized for World War II. Former NRA administrator Donald Richberg voiced concern that the antitrust lawsuits threatened "industrial efficiency and stability." Historian Charles A. Beard wrote that the antitrusters were "unwittingly the foes of getting our economic machine in full motion." Raymond Moley added, "Does it help a school-boy to concentrate on his studies . . . when he knows that his mother is reorganizing his room at home—throwing out such fishing tackle, marbles, slingshots and baseballs as she considers unnecessary?"[28]

In the years since Arnold's antitrust crusade, many economists have developed estimates of industrial concentration and the extent of monopoly, concluding that there wasn't any basis for the allegations. Economist George J. Stigler estimated that in 1939 about a quarter of the U.S. economy was government-operated or -controlled, which meant it qualified as a monopoly. Stigler estimated that between 15 percent and 25 percent of the private sector (which was three-quarters of the economy) might be considered monopolistic, and there was plenty of evidence of competition in the remaining 75 percent to 85 percent of the private sector.[29] At a 1952 National Bureau of Economic Research conference called "Business Concentration and Price Policy," Harvard economists John Lintner and J. Keith Butters reported: "The best available evidence establishes a rather strong presumption that there has been no increase in over-all concentration over the last fifty-year-period and indicates that there probably has been some decrease in concentration over this period, at least so far as manufacturing is concerned."[30]

After studying available data, economists G. Warren Nutter and Henry Adler Einhorn reached similar conclusions, which were published in their book *Enterprise Monopoly in the United States, 1899–1958*. They began by analyzing the most comprehensive New Deal–era studies of industrial monopoly in the United States—namely, *The Structure of the American Economy* (1939), edited by Gardiner C. Means; *The Structure of Industry* (1941), edited by Willard L. Thorpe and Walter F. Crowder; and *Competition and Monopoly in American Industry* (1940), edited by Claire Wilcox. Nutter and Einhorn reported that available information suggested that in 1939, "(1) the effective monopolistic industries accounted for between 20 and 21 per cent of national income; (2) the workably competitive industries, between 55 and 56 per cent; (3) the governmental and 'regulated' sector, between 19 and 20 per cent; and (4) households and nonprofit enterprises, about 4 per cent. . . . workably competitive production was about two and a half to three times as prevalent as monopolistic production in the late 1930s."[31] Such findings certainly didn't correspond with the lurid allegations emerging from the Temporary National Economic Committee hearings: that monopolies dominated the American economy and caused the depression of

1938, perhaps the Great Depression itself. One might wonder why there wasn't more widespread concern about the governmental sector, which abounded with restrictions and monopolies (the Tennessee Valley Authority being only the best known).

Was private monopoly increasing or decreasing in the United States? Nutter and Einhorn, writing in 1969, reported: "There simply are no quantitative estimates of the growth of enterprise monopoly over the last fifty years. The absence of such data frequently makes it difficult to know what the debate is about. Each side tends to phrase its arguments in unverifiable terms. . . . The rise of giant corporations is more striking than is the concomitant expansion of markets. Novel monopolistic practices quickly gain notoriety, while the spreading of competitive forces passes unadvertised." Further, Nutter and Einhorn noted, "Innovation is the anathema of monopoly. Few monopolies can be stable in the face of continual changes in technology and tastes. Specific commodities cannot for long fail to have very close substitutes; technological advantages in production may dwindle away; demand conditions may frequently shift in favor of other products. The more rapidly such changes occur, the smaller the opportunity for any firm to develop a long-run monopolistic position. There seems little reason for supposing that the rate of innovation has slowed over the last half-century. In fact, evidence points toward an acceleration." The authors cited the continued robust rate of new inventions and dynamic social changes.[32]

Nutter and Einhorn then used the best available evidence to see whether it appeared likely that there was more or less monopoly in 1937 compared to 1899. They estimated that depending on standards used, the share of national income accounted for by private monopolies might have increased 1.9 percent or decreased 6.4 percent between 1899 and 1937. If results are averaged, the share of national income accounted for by monopolies falls.[33]

Nobel laureate Milton Friedman observed, "The most important fact about enterprise monopoly is its relative unimportance from the point of view of the economy as a whole." Why, then, the impression that monopoly was pervasive during the New Deal and even now? One reason is "the tendency to confuse absolute and relative size," according to Friedman. "As the economy has grown, enterprises have become larger in absolute size. This has been taken to mean that they account for a larger fraction of the market, whereas the market may have grown even faster. A second reason is that monopoly is more newsworthy and leads to more attention than competition. If individuals were asked to list the major industries in the United States, almost all would include automobile production, few would include wholesale trade. Yet wholesale trade is twice as important as automobile production. Wholesale trade is highly competitive, hence draws little attention to itself."[34]

Thus, arrogant in their ignorance, New Deal antitrust attorneys imagined they had superior knowledge about how a complex economy worked. They assumed that litigation would have the effects they intended in a timely way. All that these attorneys ended up doing was disrupting a depressed economy, making it harder for employers to recover and provide more jobs.

CHAPTER EIGHTEEN

WHAT HAVE BEEN THE EFFECTS OF THE NEW DEAL SINCE THE 1930S?

F EDERAL GOVERNMENT SPENDING and taxing, which had expanded dramatically during the New Deal, surged more than tenfold in World War II. Federal regulatory power expanded as well. It was a long time coming down.

TAXING AND SPENDING

Personal income tax rates hit 91 percent, and corporate excess profits taxes hit 95 percent.[1]

Meanwhile, on April 27, 1942, FDR issued a message to Congress in which he declared, "No American citizen ought to have a net income, after he has paid his taxes, of more than 25,000 a year."[2] The Treasury Department submitted to the House Ways and Means Committee a memorandum calling for a 100 percent tax on incomes over $25,000.[3] This is equivalent to more than $260,000 today, which doesn't sound like a big deal. People could live well on $25,000 back then and on $260,000 today. But the idea that the government had the power to set an income limit is disturbing, particularly since the trend has been for high tax rates to affect people with lower and lower incomes. Middle-class people are hit with tax rates originally aimed at the rich, simply because there are far more middle-class people. The government, like bank robbers, goes where the money is.[4]

On October 3, 1942, FDR issued an executive order "providing for the stabilizing of the national economy." Point 7 read: "In order to correct gross inequities and to provide for greater equality in contributing to the war effort, the Director is authorized to take the necessary action, and to issue the appropriate regulations, so that, insofar as practicable, no salary shall be authorized under Title III, Section 4 to the extent that it exceeds $25,000 after the payment of taxes allocable to the sum in excess of $25,000."[5]

As might be expected, such confiscatory taxes spurred people to find ways they could reduce their burdens. Businesses increased contributions to profit-sharing plans and trusts. Tax historian Randolph Paul noted that businesses "tried to deduct as repairs expenditures for improvements which should have been capitalized." In addition, "They deducted large sums said to have been paid to obtain government business, including fees paid to Washington representatives, and they attempted to deduct advertising expenses which were out of line with previous advertising budgets."[6]

Taxes made it almost impossible for living standards to recover from the Great Depression, but there wasn't much to buy anyway. Consumer goods factories had converted to producing war goods, and empty store shelves were commonplace. Practically everything was scarce. Despite the paper shortage, the government printed longer and more complicated tax forms.

Federal income tax withholding began. In March 1942, Federal Reserve Bank chairman Beardsley Ruml (who was also treasurer of R. H. Macy) published a pamphlet advocating a "Pay-as-you-go Income Tax Plan." Ruml's principal goal was to accelerate the flow of money to the government, which was spending more and more on the war. In addition, the plan was billed as a way to make paying taxes easier. At the time, the practice was to pay each year's federal income taxes the following year. Many people had a hard time coming up with the money for their single big payment, so Ruml suggested that people pay some tax out of every paycheck. This led to payroll tax withholding, which had been in effect during the Civil War and World War I. Social Security reintroduced payroll tax withholding in 1937. Since having current taxes withheld and paying the previous year's taxes in the same year would have been impossible for most people, Congress decided to offer the option of canceling 75 percent of the 1942 tax or 1943 tax, whichever was lower. The Current Tax Payment Act of 1943 was signed into law on June 9, 1943.

Tax withholding would have an unintended consequence: dramatic expansion of the Internal Revenue Service. Commissioner Guy Helvering estimated that to administer withholding for some 30 million wage earners would require hiring an estimated 11,000 more IRS agents, finding more office space, and increasing the IRS budget by about $24 million. He acknowledged, too, that the law would impose substantial costs on employers who did the government's work of collecting and remitting taxes.[7]

The World War II tax regime, supposedly "temporary," remained largely intact afterwards. It continued to be a mass tax—there was no going back to the days when only a few people had to worry about the IRS. Federal income as well as Social Security taxes continued to be withheld from paychecks. While President Truman signed the Revenue Act of 1945, which cut the top federal income tax rate from 94 percent to 86.45 percent, and there were additional modest tax reductions in the Revenue Act of 1948, taxes went up again during the Korean War.[8] Concerned about high levels of Cold War defense spending, President Eisenhower opposed tax cuts. Social Security taxes, which especially hit lower incomes, were increased.

Interestingly, it was a Democrat, not a Republican, who achieved the first big tax cuts from FDR's World War II highs. In the 1960 election campaign, John F. Kennedy talked about tax cuts as a strategy for stimulating the economy; and he won the election, in part, because the Eisenhower-Nixon administration was blamed for the recession the country was experiencing. In a speech given before the New York Economic Club on December 14, 1962, Kennedy declared, "The final and best means of strengthening demand among consumers and business is to reduce the burden on private income and the deterrents to private initiative which are imposed by our present tax system—and this administration pledged itself last summer to an across-the-board, top to bottom cut in personal and corporate income taxes. . . . I am not talking about a 'quickie' or temporary tax cut. Nor am I talking about giving the economy a mere shot in the arm, to ease some temporary complaint. I am talking about the accumulated evidence of the last five years that our present tax system . . . exerts too heavy a drag on growth in peacetime—that it siphons out of the private economy too large a share of personal and business purchasing power—that it reduces the financial incentives for personal effort, investment and risk taking."

Kennedy's viewpoint was quite a dramatic departure from that of the New Dealers, who had insisted "reform" must be the top priority even if it made recovery more difficult. Consider this letter from tax expert Richard Musgrave to Walter Heller, who served as Kennedy's chairman of the Council of Economic Advisors: "To the extent that changes in tax structure are needed to encourage investment, they should not necessarily be ruled out because they interfere with tax equity. In some cases, growth may be the overriding consideration."[9]

The Revenue Act of 1962, which Kennedy signed into law in October, offered a 7 percent investment tax credit and more attractive depreciation schedules. Spurred by the fear of another recession, which would be blamed on his administration, Kennedy presented proposals for tax rate reductions in January 1963. The result, enacted after Kennedy's assassination, was the Revenue Act of 1964, which offered the across-the-board tax cuts he had talked about. The act cut the top individual income tax rate from 91 percent to 70 percent, the corporate rate from 52 percent to 48 percent.[10]

The 1970s proved to be the undoing of Keynesian doctrines that had come into their own during the New Deal. Keynesians had claimed that government spending and inflation would bring down unemployment, but both inflation and unemployment persisted at high levels during the 1970s. "Stagflation," it was called. This brought renewed agitation for tax relief, and there were some minor tax cuts in 1975 and 1976. Then came the Revenue Act of 1978, which cut individual taxes and corporate taxes and excluded as much as 60 percent of capital gains from taxation. In 1981, President Ronald Reagan followed through on his campaign promise to cut taxes by signing into law a three-year, across-the-board 25 percent cut. His Economic Recovery Act provided that federal income tax schedules would be indexed, so that inflation wouldn't push people into higher tax brackets. The top individual income tax rate fell from 70 percent to 50 percent.[11] Reagan's Tax Reform Act of 1986 further cut tax rates and simplified the individual income tax to two brackets. In 2001, President George W. Bush pushed a potentially big tax cut through Congress, but since it is projected to come over ten years, only time will tell how much of it is realized.

FEDERAL DEPOSIT INSURANCE

Insurance on deposits looked like a great idea for a half century. Then, during the 1980s, a reported 1,043 savings and loan associations closed their doors, and taxpayers were hit with $519 billion of bailout costs,[12] which, as economist Jeffrey Rogers Hummel observed, was bigger than the combined costs of the bailing out of Lockheed, Chrysler, New York City, and Western Europe (during the 1940s via the Marshall Plan).[13]

Federal deposit insurance played a major role in the mess. Established in 1934, it originally covered a small pool of savings ($2,500). It wasn't meant to cover everything. If an individual had $100,000 deposited in a bank, but only $2,500 was covered by deposit insurance, the individual had a very strong incentive to watch for any signs that the bank was making risky loans or investments. Bankers knew that imprudent practices could result in a rapid withdrawal of deposits. But over the years, political pressures led Congress to increase fortyfold the amount of deposits covered by federal insurance—in 1980, deposits up to $100,000 were covered. When a person has $100,000 and all of it is insured at no apparent cost, there is no reason to care whether one's banker is imprudent. On the contrary, imprudent bankers could invest in crazy schemes promising above-market profits and offer above-market interest rates that attracted more and more depositors who didn't incur any risks.

Another problem with federal deposit insurance has been that covered institutions have paid the same premiums, even though the risks of these institutions varied considerably. Prudently managed institutions were overpaying, and recklessly managed institutions were subsidized—encouraged—to continue their risky practices.

Risk-graded deposit insurance premiums have been proposed for years, but the bankers' lobby is opposed. "It is ironic that some bankers attempt to estimate the market value of their customers' equity but are unwilling to have an insurance agency evaluate their own market value," observed economists George J. Benston and George G. Kaufman. "If federal deposit insurance were to be replaced by private deposit insurance, it is highly unlikely that the private firms would be willing to underwrite the insurance if they were not able to employ risk-related premiums based on market-value accounting."[14]

During the 1980s, the government compounded the problems of high deposit coverage and pricing unrelated to risk by forcing savings and loan institutions to sell their high-yield ("junk") bond holdings. This depressed prices of the bonds, triggering the collapse of many S&Ls. Ironically, the market for high-yield bonds recovered during the 1990s, confirming the original analysis by Michael

Milken and others that the interest rates on high-yield bonds more than compensated for the level of risk.

It became apparent that federal deposit insurance didn't stop bank failures. On the contrary, by providing deposit insurance below cost for banks engaged in risky practices, the federal government encouraged those practices that led to bank failures. Federal deposit insurance transferred the cost of bank failures from depositors who had profited from higher interest rates offered by the risky banks to taxpayers who were innocent third parties. No justice here.

BANKING POLICIES

Although Federal Reserve policy blunders were a major factor in the monetary contraction and the Great Depression, the New Deal didn't do anything to prevent Fed policy blunders in the future. As discussed, the Banking Act of 1935 centralized authority at the Fed, magnifying the effect of bad judgments, which were a major factor in the recession of 1938.

Laws passed since the New Deal have increased the number of policy objectives, sometimes conflicting, that the Federal Reserve must serve. Explained Anna Jacobson Schwartz, coauthor with Milton Friedman of *A Monetary History of the United States*, "The Employment Act of 1946 (Public Law 79-304), the Humphrey-Hawkins Full Employment and Balanced Growth Act of 1978 (Public Law 95-523), and the Federal Reserve's own statement of its purposes and functions encompasses at least four objectives of monetary policy: economic stability and growth, a high level of employment, stability in the purchasing power of the dollar, and reasonable balance in transactions with foreign countries. . . . Efforts to maintain the exchange value of the dollar at a given level may require money supply growth rates and interest rate changes that have undesired effects on private investment and the level of unemployment. Since the 1960s the Federal Reserve has altered money supply growth rates first to lower the unemployment rate at the cost of a higher inflation rate and subsequently to lower the inflation rate at the cost of a higher unemployment rate."[15]

Schwartz suggested that the Federal Reserve will fail if it tries to serve different, potentially conflicting objectives, but it could succeed by focusing on price stability: "Banks make contracts when they have no way of knowing whether the price level or the inflation rate that they expect will be realized. The monetary authorities make no commitment to maintain any particular price level or rate of inflation. Yet to the extent bank contracts stipulate fixed rates of future money payments to others and from others, they have arbitrary consequences when the price level or inflation rate turns out to be greater or less than anticipated. Stabilizing the price level will do more for financial stability than reforming deposit insurance or reregulating."[16]

Economists since the 1960s have confirmed that unit banking laws made the banking system more vulnerable to collapse, and in the 1980s one state after another repealed these laws. Federal Reserve Bank of New York economists Philip E. Strahan and Jith Jayaratne reported: "We find that bank efficiency improved greatly when branching restrictions were lifted. Loan losses and operating costs fell sharply, and the reduction in banks' costs was largely passed on to borrowers in the form of lower loan rates. The relaxation of state limits on interstate banking was followed also by improvements in bank performance."[17]

Similarly, it had become apparent that contrary to what New Dealers had thought, banks didn't become more risky by both taking deposits and underwriting securities. Major banks around the world had long been doing this successfully, as American city banks had done before the 1933 Glass-Steagall Act. Far from providing protection for commercial banks and investment banks by keeping these businesses separate, as Glass-Steagall had mandated, this policy actually made American banks more vulnerable to new forms of competition at home and abroad. Accordingly, political support developed for open competition. In November 1999, the Graham-Leach-Bliley Act became law, repealing Glass-Steagall.

SOCIAL SECURITY

Long considered the most important legacy of the New Deal, Social Security was a bonanza, during its early years, for those who had paid very little Social Security taxes and ended up collecting many times more in benefits. The very first Social Security check was issued to Ida Fuller of Ludlow, Vermont. Her $22 in Social Security taxes yielded more than $20,000 in benefits.[18]

But projected returns from Social Security have declined. The Congressional Research Service estimated that for people who retired in 1960 the Social Security payments they received exceeded their total tax payments in 1.1 years. People who retired in 1980 got their tax payments back in 2.8 years. Now the payback period is 12.9 years. By 2030, the payback period is estimated to be about 18 years.[19]

It has become increasingly clear that Social Security is a bad deal that is getting worse every year. For openers, although Social Security taxes have been increased more than thirty times,[20] and for perhaps three-quarters of the people Social Security is their biggest tax, nobody has a contractual right to specific Social Security benefits. Congress can and has modified the benefit formulas. Supreme Court justice John Harlan, writing the majority opinion in *Flemming v Nestor,* 363 U.S. 603 (1960), said, "A person covered by the Social Security Act has not such a right in old-age benefit payments. . . . The noncontractual interest of an employee covered by the Act cannot be soundly analogized to that of the holder of an annuity, whose rights to benefits are based on his contractual premium payments. . . . To engraft upon the Social Security system a concept of 'accrued property rights' would deprive it of the flexibility and boldness in adjustment to ever-changing conditions which it demands and which Congress probably had in mind when it expressly reserved the right to alter, amend or repeal any provision of the [Social Security] Act."[21]

Over the years, the number of recipients has been increasing faster than the number of taxpayers funding those benefits. Back in 1945, the beginning of the baby boom, forty-two taxpayers supported each Social Security recipient. Now there are only about three taxpayers supporting each Social Security recipient.[22] By the year 2030, as people born in 2000 approach their peak earning years, there will be only 1.5 taxpayers supporting each Social Security recipient, which means taxes will skyrocket, or benefits will be cut, or both.

This is a pay-as-you-go system without an investment fund yielding returns to help cover future obligations. The so-called trust fund consists of government bonds that will have to be paid off by increasingly burdened taxpayers in the future if Social Security is to remain solvent. It's likely that higher and higher Social Security taxes will trigger a tax revolt that will make benefit cuts inevitable.

Social Security has done worse than perform poorly. As set up during the New Deal, Social Security has had the effect of transferring funds from the poor to the rich. Nobel laureate Milton Friedman explained, "Persons in high income classes typically start working at a later age and so will tend to pay taxes for a shorter period. Persons in high income classes have a higher life expectancy, and so will tend to receive benefits for a longer period."[23]

A 1996 RAND Corporation study similarly reported that an individual's life span is a primary factor determining the total amount of Social Security benefits. Average Social Security benefits are lower for blacks than for whites because blacks don't live as long as whites. On average, Social Security transfers about $10,000 from blacks to whites.[24]

Blacks have fared the worst with Social Security. The rate of return for black males has been negative for the past four decades, since 1960.[25] Robert Woodson, president of the National Center for Neighborhood Enterprise, asked: "What would be the public reaction if I proposed a plan to collect monthly contributions from working black men and women, then transferred a good portion of that money to older white women? Or what would happen if I tried to sell a retirement investment plan to 24-year-old black American males that would end up paying each of them $13,400 less in benefits than they paid into my plan? Most likely, if I were successful in conning people into these schemes, I would be arrested, tried and convicted of fraud."[26]

Diversified portfolios, invested in common stocks during a typical forty-year career, have been shown to outperform Social Security by a wide margin, despite depressions, wars, and other calamities. Business professor Jeremy J. Siegel, author of *Stocks for the Long Term*, analyzed the performance of financial markets since 1802 and reported: "The total return on equities dominates all other assets. Even the cataclysmic stock crash of 1929, which caused a generation of investors to shun stocks, appears as a mere blip in the stock return index. Bear markets, which so frighten investors, pale in the context of the upward thrust of total stock returns."[27]

FARM SUBSIDIES AND RESTRICTIONS

New Deal farm programs have backfired just as Social Security has done, and they have been as tenaciously defended. Washington channeled hundreds of billions of taxpayer dollars to farmers who agreed not to grow certain crops. Marketing orders, authorized by the Agricultural Marketing Agreement Act of 1937 as amended, continue to restrict production and marketing. They are the most blatant type of interference with U.S. agricultural markets, a throwback to medieval times when guilds determined who could work in various trades, how much they could charge, and how much they could produce. Milk marketing orders, for instance, affect three-quarters of milk producers.[28] The Department of Agriculture reportedly has fined or sued thousands of farmers for violating the restrictions.[29]

Recalling Henry Wallace's policy of destroying food during the Great Depression, the kind of thing that had outraged novelist John Steinbeck, the Department of Agriculture still enforces orders that good food be left to rot when officials decide too much has been produced. This sort of thing has been going on so long it isn't news anymore, but *New York Times* reporter Ann Crittenden filed a vivid report about consequences of the New Deal in our time: "Stretching in all directions are millions and millions of navel oranges all abandoned to rot under the California sun. The oranges have been dumped under what is known as a Federal marketing order."[30]

In recent years, there have been an increasing number of legal challenges to agricultural marketing orders. For instance, in 1993 a USDA marketing order and the California Almond Board demanded that growers pay money into an advertising program. This marketing order was challenged by Cal-Almond, Inc., Dole Dried Fruit and Nut Co., Gold Hill Nut Co., Del Rio Nut Co., and James G. Crecilius dba Monte Vista Farming Co. In 1995, an administrative law judge ruled in favor of the plaintiffs, saying that among other things the marketing order violated the First Amendment right of freedom of speech.[31] Two years later, in *Glickman v Wileman Brothers & Elliott, Inc.,* 521 U.S. 457 (1997), the Supreme Court upheld the marketing orders. Justice John Paul Stevens wrote that the issue involved a "question of economic policy for Congress and the Executive Branch to resolve," not free speech. Undoubtedly, marketing orders will be challenged in other ways.

New Deal farm laws, still in effect, continue to benefit big farmers, because the programs are based on the amount of acreage a farmer has or the quantities of crops produced. As investigative reporter James Bovard observed, in a 1989 study, "the USDA gave, in direct payments to the 29,000 largest farms, an average of

$46,073—an amount that exceeded the net worth (including the value of house and cars) of over half the families in America."[32]

TENNESSEE VALLEY AUTHORITY

Hailed as a showcase project of the New Deal, the Tennessee Valley Authority has accumulated $29 billion of debt because of its failure to anticipate the demand for electricity and failure to control the cost of supplying it. There are lucrative executive perks, cozy consulting contracts, costly building leases, and much more which even the TVA's own inspector general found to be out of control. Incredibly, considering its massive debt, the TVA doesn't pay federal or state taxes—its "payments in lieu of taxes" are about half of what investor-owned utilities must pay.

The TVA remains an unaccountable government monopoly. It is exempt from more than 130 federal laws, including workplace safety laws and hydroelectric licensing laws, and hundreds of laws in the states where it operates (Alabama, Georgia, Kentucky, North Carolina, and Virginia, as well as Tennessee). The TVA is immune from civil liability lawsuits about any wrongful acts it may have committed.

Many environmentalists consider the TVA to be America's most notorious polluter. It expanded far beyond its original mandate, as bureaucracies tend to do, and built coal-fired power plants. The discharges from these make the TVA the biggest U.S. violator of the Clean Air Act. The TVA built nuclear power plants, and in 1998 Ralph Nader reported that "The TVA is by any measure the worst nuclear project in the country . . . has the poorest safety record with TVA reactors spending more time on the Nuclear Regulatory Commission's watch list than any other utility." One of the worst nuclear power accidents occurred at the TVA's Browns Ferry Unit #1 back in 1975, and that reactor has since closed.[33]

The TVA is increasingly resented as grossly unfair to the 242 million Americans who don't live in the Tennessee Valley but must subsidize it. "Taxpayers in northeastern and midwestern states, who pay some of America's highest electrical rates," observed Richard Munson, president of the Northeast-Midwest Institute, "unwittingly subsidize power bills in the Tennessee Valley. Yet at the same time, TVA uses those very subsidies and the promise of cheap electricity to lure away businesses and jobs from those same taxpayers."[34]

The TVA, however, gouges many big customers and is determined to maintain its monopoly. "TVA customers," Munson reported, "are burdened with long-term, all-requirements contracts which they can terminate only by providing a ten-year notice. These are not ten-year contracts that expire; they are rolling provisions that after each new day cannot be terminated for another ten years. The municipal utilities and rural electric cooperatives that buy power from TVA, as a result, are restricted from the benefits of competition; they cannot even obtain realistic price quotations for power to be supplied in ten years. The Federal Energy Regulatory Commission does not allow private utilities to use similar anticompetitive provisions.

"The 4-County Electric Power Association," Munson continued, "wanting lower rates, notified TVA in December 1993 that it would be seeking another power supplier":

> Earl Weeks, the Mississippi association's general manager, subsequently received some 30 bids from other electric generators, several of which would have saved the association more than $7 million annually in wholesale power costs. TVA, unwilling to lose a customer, responded aggressively. According to Weeks, TVA lobbied 4-County's biggest customers "to put pressure on us to rescind that notice." More troubling to the association manager, TVA representatives "questioned my integrity" by suggesting to customers that perhaps Earl Weeks didn't know what he was doing. But TVA's most effective tactic was to threaten cancellation of a lignite-burning power plant and elimination of the associated construction jobs and economic

development in that employment-hungry region. Not surprisingly, 4-County Electric buckled under the pressure.

The Bristol Utility Board in southwest Virginia met similar resistance when it notified TVA that it, too, wanted to leave. Angry about high industrial electricity rates, the municipal utility gave TVA "years of forewarning" that it wanted to end its 52-year relationship and to seek bids from other suppliers. TVA's price offer turned out to be the very highest of 20 bids. Therefore, Bristol in 1997 signed a contract to purchase electricity for its 15,000 residents from Cinergy of Cincinnati, Ohio, saving the local government $70 million over seven years, double the city's annual budget. TVA responded by secretly trying to sell power directly to Bristol's industrial customers for 2 percent less than the best bid (and well below what TVA had previously been charging, and well below the agency's recent bid). TVA also promptly charged Bristol $54 million for "stranded costs" investments the federal agency claimed it made with the expectation that it would continue to supply power to Bristol. Rep. Rick Boucher (D-VA), the local congressman, reacted with angry letters and volatile hearings. He complained that TVA was using tactics "to punish a former customer for exercising its legal right to obtain power from a less expensive supplier. TVA is seeking to make an example of the city of Bristol so as to discourage any other community presently served by TVA from considering the purchase of power from a TVA competitor."[35]

As for the TVA system of locks that made the Tennessee River a more navigable waterway, they were always dubious, because railroads moved bulk freight faster. Apparently railroad rates and service were attractive options for shippers: By the 1970s, when the TVA waterway system had matured, it carried only about one-seventh as much freight traffic as the estimated 3,500 miles of railroad tracks in Tennessee. The TVA waterway system long accounted for only about 0.2 percent of U.S. freight, and often there would be just one barge a day going through the locks.[36]

ANTICOMPETITIVE LAWS

Since the 1970s, a number of the New Deal anticompetitive laws have been repealed. The Retail Price Maintenance Act, prohibiting price competition from chain stores, was repealed in 1975, after the increasing variety of competition virtually made it a dead letter. Since then, consumers have saved money with the expansion of discounting. As noted earlier, the Glass-Steagall Act, preventing investment banks and commercial banks from competing with each other, was repealed in 1999. Commercial banks, which had lost more and more business to securities firms, were permitted to again offer a wide range of services and compete with other financial services firms in the United States as well as overseas.

ANTITRUST LAWS

Since the New Deal, economists have reported two major findings that have a bearing on antitrust policy. First, competition proved to be far more persistent than New Dealers had thought, with new technologies, new entrepreneurs, and changing consumer preferences undermining big businesses that seemed as if they could dominate their markets forever. All this is dramatically evident in the Fortune 500 lists, which show how, over the years, big businesses dropped in the rankings or disappeared altogether because of merger or bankruptcy.

The second major finding is that antitrust policy itself has become a major obstacle to competition. Companies that had trouble in the marketplace lobbied for antitrust action against their competitors, and antitrust officials pursued their interests by expanding their budgets, hiring more lawyers, and filing more lawsuits, even when the targets of litigation had expanded output and cut prices (monopolies were considered objectionable for restricting output and raising prices). Economist Dominick T. Armentano observed, "Businesses that innovate, market aggressively, and increase production while lowering prices have been a primary focus of antitrust enforcement. Comparatively, government licensing, certificates of public convenience, legal franchises, and foreign and domestic quotas (the real monopolistic abuse in the system) have been almost entirely immune from antitrust scrutiny."[37] Moreover, for every antitrust lawsuit filed by the government, about twenty antitrust lawsuits have been filed by private businesses seeking to defeat in the courtroom competitors whom they couldn't defeat in the marketplace.[38]

Antitrust "is a world in which competition is lauded as the basic axiom and guiding principle, yet 'too much' competition is condemned as 'cutthroat,'" wrote Alan Greenspan, before he became Federal Reserve chairman. "It is a world in which actions designed to limit competition are branded as criminal when taken by businessmen, yet praised as 'enlightened' when initiated by the government. It is a world in which the law is so vague that businessmen have no way of knowing whether specific actions will be declared illegal until they hear the judge's verdict—after the fact."[39]

THE FEDERAL GOLD MONOPOLY

As inflation rates escalated during the 1970s and world gold prices soared, more and more Americans defied FDR's gold prohibition and protected their assets with gold. Bullion coins like American double eagles, British sovereigns, and Mexican 50 pesos, which had been minted in large quantities and sold for a modest premium over their gold content, were marketed as "numismatic" coins, to avoid running afoul of the law (genuine numismatic coins commanded a substantial premium over gold content, because of rarity).

In September 1971, New Orleans investor James U. Blanchard III launched the National Committee to Legalize Gold and organized protests against gold prohibition. "On President Nixon's second in-augural," Blanchard recalled, "we hired a World War I-style biplane to carry a 50-foot sign: LEGALIZE GOLD!" People smuggled gold bars into the United States and displayed these publicly, daring Trea-sury officials to enforce the relic of law.[40] But times had changed, and President Gerald Ford gave Americans back an important part of their economic liberty by legalizing private gold ownership on De-cember 31, 1974, for the first time in forty years.

THE NEW DEAL VERSUS ECONOMIC LIBERTY

Finally, the failure of the New Deal and the subversion of economic liberty by big government have led many intellectuals to revive the views of the anti–New Deal Supreme Court justices, that constitu-tional limitations on government power were established for com-pelling reasons and must be upheld.

"What kind of people are constitutions designed to govern?" law professor Richard A. Epstein asked. "I think that the simplest answer to that question is people like you and me, people with good days and bad days. Within the context of governmental power, however, we are more worried about what people will do on their bad days than we are pleased about their behavior on their good days. A fine despot may do wonders for a while: public roads may be constructed, the trains may run on time, and the Dow may reach three thousand. But a bad despot, or a good despot turned bad, has quite the opposite effect. Our concerns go beyond potholes, train delays, and the bear market. We worry about tyranny, terror, confis-cation, segregation, imprisonment, and death. There is more to fear from the downside than there is to gain from the upside. It is not that all people will behave in irresponsible ways once they assume public office. It is enough that a few unprincipled people in high po-sitions can wreak public havoc. . . . We should set our presumption against the concentration of power in the hands of government."[41]

CHAPTER NINETEEN

WHAT CAN WE LEARN
FROM FDR'S MISTAKES?

THE GREAT DEPRESSION was probably the most important economic event in American history, and it seems likely that future historians will acknowledge what economists have reported about the actual effects of the New Deal. In that case, FDR's reputation will decline.

Regardless of the role of domestic versus international factors in bringing on the Great Depression, the New Deal did plenty to prolong high unemployment. New Deal policies were dubious when considered from the standpoint of their effects. After Americans had suffered through a catastrophic contraction for three years (1929–1933), FDR supported policies like the National Industrial Recovery Act that promoted further contraction. His executive orders helped enforce higher consumer prices when millions of Americans were unemployed and needed bargains. FDR approved the destruction of food when people were hungry. FDR signed into law higher taxes for everybody, so consumers had less money to spend, and employers had less money with which to hire people—during the worst depression in American history. New Deal labor laws empowered the most racist unions to exclude blacks and had the effect of making it illegal for many employers to hire blacks. The power of the Federal Reserve became more centralized, but this meant that the mistakes of a few people (members of the Federal Reserve Board) were likely to harm millions across the United States; and indeed the Fed's mistakes were a major cause of the depression of 1938 as well as the monetary contraction of 1929–1933. After having throttled competition with the National Industrial Recovery Act, Agricultural Adjustment Act, Bituminous Coal Conservation Act, Robinson-Patman Act, Retail Price Maintenance Act, Federal Communications Act, Civil Aeronautics Act, high corporate taxes, and other measures, New Dealers posed as defenders of competition and filed a record number of antitrust lawsuits against private employers, one effect of which was to further discourage investment needed for growth and jobs.

"Looked at now," journalist John T. Flynn wrote in 1939, the New Deal "makes a confusing picture. It was a hodge-podge of good intentions, of bold promises and glittering hopes—a desire to produce recovery, to create abundance while at the same time causing scarcity to get prices up; to help labor, to help the little business men and to help the big business men—all save a few who behaved badly to Mr. Roosevelt personally; to spend as much as possible and to tax as little as possible; to boost prices but not to diminish purchasing power; to raise wages and profits, too; to save the farmer, to save the railroads, to save anybody who could be saved with a subsidy; to make everybody happy and win everybody's good opinion and, in the process of doing this, to adopt any idea which was presented by anybody with a friendly face and which seemed at a glance to have a chance to work."[1]

Sophisticated New Dealers dismissed as simplistic those who defended individual rights, private property, and economic liberty, yet experience has revealed New Deal policies to be quite simplistic. FDR believed that if the federal government bought all the gold in the United States and as much of the gold as it could get overseas, he could push up farm prices. FDR imagined that government spending programs would end the agony of high unemployment, but he ignored the fact that government spending comes directly or indirectly from taxation, and people taxed have less money to spend or invest, offsetting the effect of spending programs. FDR assumed that taxes could be increased repeatedly without undermining incentives for people to produce, but he was mistaken. New Deal efforts to force wages above market levels made it more expensive for employers to hire people and contributed to chronic high levels of unemployment. Pro-FDR intellectuals assumed that government officials work selflessly for the public good, but as we now know, the self-interest of government officials, particularly their concern to win the next election, had a major impact on New Deal spending. FDR touted the Tennessee Valley Authority as proof that government could work wonders with electric power, ignoring subsidies from the 98 percent of American taxpayers who didn't live in the Tennessee Valley (and, as it turned out, the TVA didn't work wonders, since non-TVA southern states grew faster than TVA states).

New Dealers were naïve to assume that dictatorial power would enable them to stabilize the American economy and bring about recovery. FDR was hailed when, in his first inaugural address, he asked for "broad Executive power to wage a war against the emergency, as great as the power that would be given to me if we were in fact invaded by a foreign foe." Hugh S. Johnson, when he headed the National Recovery Administration, exercised unprecedented arbitrary power over American industry. Henry Wallace was virtually the dictator of American agriculture, dispensing subsidies, setting prices, and issuing regulations that favored some interests over others; and he went on to become FDR's running mate in 1940.

Yet what dictator ever brought prosperity by interfering with the economy? History is littered with catastrophes that occurred because dictators couldn't keep their hands off the economy. A century ago, exporting beef and wheat helped make Argentina one of the world's wealthiest nations; but by the late 1940s, after dictator Juan Perón had introduced pervasive economic controls, there were chronic beef shortages, and Argentinians had to make do with black bread. In China during the late 1950s, Mao Zedong ruthlessly enforced his orders about what people must produce, and the consequence was a famine in which as many as 30 million people died. Russia used to be a major grain exporter; but the Bolshevik Revolution and decades of Five Year Plans brought shortages of grain and just about everything else ordinary people wanted—until the economy finally collapsed, and the Soviet Union vanished from the map in 1991. Wherever there is dictatorial power over an economy, wherever economic liberty is denied, people are sure to be suffering agonies of the damned.

New Dealers assumed that individual rights, private property, and economic liberty were obstacles to recovery, but they are essential. For hundreds, if not thousands of years, there had been little improvement in living standards for ordinary people—in effect, they suffered through what seemed to be an endless depression. Then in the West during the seventeenth, eighteenth, and nineteenth centuries came great industrial revolutions that achieved unprecedented prosperity. Economic historian Fernand Braudel observed, "Markets, direct or indirect, all the many forms of trading, endlessly worked on economies, even the most quiescent, stirring them up, or as some would say, bringing them to life."[2]

As ancient restrictions on trade, business, wages, and prices were swept away, as capricious taxes and government-enforced monopolies were abolished, as private property and economic liberty were secured—millions of people began to live better than kings. Technology introduced conveniences never dreamed of before, mass production cut their costs, and long-distance transportation made them available to people throughout the West. Economic historian David S. Landes noted, for instance, "No longer was it the wealthy alone who could enjoy the comfort and hygiene of body linen; cotton made it possible for millions to wear drawers and chemises where before they had been nothing but the coarse, dirty outergarments."[3] All this was the result of spontaneous action by profit-seeking private entrepreneurs in competitive markets. "Property rights," Nobel laureate Douglass North wrote, "provided the incentives necessary for sustained growth."[4]

FDR, Louis Brandeis, and other "progressives" liked to talk about their "experiments" with the economy, but these turned out to be the same types of restrictions, like medieval guild regulations, that had blocked progress for ages. More than two centuries ago in *The Wealth of Nations*, the savvy Scotsman Adam Smith had exposed the folly of mercantilists, those who imagined that taxes, trade restrictions, government spending, and government gold hoarding would bring prosperity. Such policies were "experiments" only to the degree that New Dealers were ignorant about what had been tried and failed before.

The Great Depression was a government failure, brought on principally by Federal Reserve policies that abruptly cut the money supply; unit banking laws that made thousands of banks more vulnerable to failure; Hoover's tariffs, which throttled trade; Hoover's taxes, which took unprecedented amounts of money out of people's pockets at the worst possible time; and Hoover's other policies, which made it more difficult for the economy to recover. High unemployment lasted as long as it did because of all the New Deal policies that took more money out of people's pockets, disrupted the money supply, restricted production, harassed employers, destroyed jobs, discouraged investment, and subverted economic liberty needed for sustained business recovery.

THE FAILURE OF the New Deal contributed to some of the political catastrophes of the 1930s. Historian Gary Dean Best reflected on "the image that the depression-plagued United States projected to the world at a crucial time in international affairs." According to Best, "In the late 1930s and early 1940s, when U.S. economic strength might have given pause to potential aggressors in the world, our economic weakness furnished encouragement to them instead. From the standpoint, then, not only of our domestic history, but also of the tragic events and results of World War II, it has seemed to me that Roosevelt's failure to generate economic recovery during this critical period deserved more attention than historians have given it."[5]

A faster, sustained business recovery might well have changed history for the better. Imagine how the dramatic success of a prosperous America, during the 1930s, would have undermined political support for socialism, communism, and Nazism in other countries. Recall how the remarkable prosperity of the United States during the 1980s influenced dozens of other countries to cut their taxes and pursue deregulation. The dramatic success of Britain's privatization in the 1980s led some ninety countries to privatize government monopolies that offered poor service and lost more and more money.

It's intriguing to compare the failure of the New Deal with previous successes recovering from severe depressions. One of the most remarkable successes followed the Panic of 1837. During the next four years, the money supply fell by one-third, and prices were believed to have declined by over 40 percent. "Investment fell," reported economic historian Jeffrey Rogers Hummel, "but amazingly the economy's total output did not. Quite the contrary; it actually rose between 6 and 16 percent. This was nearly a full-employment deflation."[6] Martin Van Buren was president at the time, and his principal policies were to make government cheaper and stay out of the way of the private sector. Federal spending was cut from $37.2 million in 1837 to $24.3 million in 1840, and taxes (mainly tariff revenue) went down, too.[7]

Having gone off the gold standard during the Civil War, so that the federal government could issue as many "greenbacks" as necessary to buy war goods, the United States returned to a gold standard in 1879, and prices began a slow, steady decline that continued for two decades.[8] Falling prices have sometimes been a sign of serious trouble, and there was one contraction from 1882 to 1885, another in the 1890s.[9] The federal government was comparatively small and didn't interfere much with the economy. The best-known occupant of the White House at this time was frugal Grover Cleveland, the first Democrat elected president since the Civil War. He served two terms, 1885–1889 and 1893–1897. He didn't have a butler, press secretary, or bodyguards.[10] "On the first of every month," wrote biographer H. Paul Jeffers, "all business of government came to a halt during however much time it took the president of the United States to write personal checks for personal and household expenses."[11] Devoted to the principle that government should impose the least possible burden on taxpayers, Cleveland struggled to cut tariffs, which were then the most important and controversial federal taxes. He opposed an income tax. He vetoed a bill that would have distributed $10,000 worth of seed grain to Texas farmers who had suffered a drought. Cleveland wrote, "Federal aid in such cases encourages the expectation of paternal care on the part of the Government and weakens the sturdiness of our national character." Altogether, Cleveland vetoed more than 300 bills. Farmers resented lower agricultural prices, and there were some violent strikes, but overall income, which had begun to fall in 1892, the year Cleveland was elected to his second term, turned around and headed up in 1894.[12] The worst of the hard times appeared to be over in two years.

Commenting on this era of declining prices, Milton Friedman and Anna Jacobson Schwartz observed, "The two final decades of the nineteenth century saw a growth of population of over 2 per cent per year, rapid extension of the railroad network, essential completion of continental settlement, and an extraordinary increase both in the acreage of land in farms and the output of farm products. The number of farms rose by nearly 50 per cent, and the total value of farm lands and building, by over 60 per cent—despite the price decline. Yet at the same time, manufacturing industries were growing even more rapidly, and the Census of 1890 was the first in which the net value added by manufacturing exceeded the value of agricultural output. A feverish boom in western land swept the country during the eighties."[13]

After World War I, between May 1920 and June 1921, wholesale prices plunged almost 50 percent. Friedman and Schwartz reported, "This is, by all odds, the sharpest price decline in the period covered by our monetary series [1867–1960] . . . and perhaps also in the whole history of the United States. The only possible 'competitors' are the price declines that followed the War of 1812 and the Civil War. What was true of prices was true also of many physical magnitudes. Industrial production, employment in manufacturing, and similar series show a precipitous increase in the rate of decline in the autumn of 1920." Friedman and Schwartz added that the decline in the money supply was "the largest percentage decline in our series up to that time . . . there is only one larger decline in the subsequent record—that accompanying the contraction of 1929–1933."[14] And what did President Warren Harding do? "Harding," wrote historian Paul Johnson, "had done nothing except cut government expenditure, the last time a major industrial power treated a recession by classic laissez-faire methods, allowing wages to fall to their natural level. . . . By July 1921, it was all over and the economy was booming again."[15]

Why did the smart, well-educated, well-intentioned New Dealers back policies that prolonged the Great Depression? How could they have gone so wrong? Most of the New Dealers, as noted, were lawyers. Few among them, including FDR, had any practical business experience. They certainly seem to have overestimated the importance of their knowledge, as opposed to the knowledge of millions of ordinary people spending their own money and running their businesses. The New Dealers really came to believe that their knowledge, combined with political power, could cure the problems of the world. They thought that by issuing executive orders, passing laws, raising taxes, and redistributing money, they could make society better.

In fact, as Nobel laureate F. A. Hayek explained, prosperity depends on knowledge dispersed among millions of people about consumer wants, available resources, local business conditions, and myriad other factors. This knowledge, ever changing, is so vast that it's impossible for government policymakers to gather and assimilate. People must be free to use their knowledge, and they must have incentives to do so. Market prices must be free because they are crucial signals indicating whether things are abundant or scarce, unwanted or wanted. The most important thing government officials can do is get out of the way. Business recovery, like prosperity, comes from the ground up, not from the top down.

The "Four Horsemen of Reaction," as the anti–New Deal Supreme Court justices were sometimes called, helped promote recovery by striking down New Deal laws like the National Industrial Recovery Act and the Agricultural Adjustment Act. If the Supreme Court had continued striking down New Deal laws, the economy would have been more likely to sustain a business recovery much sooner. The relapse of 1938 might have been avoided. At the very least, a bad situation wouldn't have been made worse, as happened. Millions of Americans would have regained the dignity that comes from real, private, productive jobs, and increased output would have meant higher living standards.

THE FAILURE OF the New Deal suggests some lessons for us today. The same policies that promote prosperity also promote recovery from a recession or depression. In particular:

- The basic problem with central banks is that like socialist economic planners, they can never have more than a fraction of the vast knowledge needed to make a society work, knowledge that is dispersed in the minds of millions of people. In addition, when central bankers make mistakes—as they inevitably will, since they're human beings—these mistakes harm not just the economy in a city or a region but the entire country. Central bankers can never know how the effects of any of their policy changes will play out or how long this process might take, so changing policies is likely to make a central bank a destabilizing factor in the economy, as has been the case with the Federal Reserve System throughout most of its history. If the nation has a central bank, it should aim to keep the money supply growing consistent with the average rate of long-term economic growth. A central bank should aim to avoid monetary contractions and inflations. A central bank shouldn't change policy in an effort to influence stock markets or foreign exchange markets. This idea of aiming to make a central bank as predictable as possible, so that everybody else can better plan their lives, is the approach long favored by Nobel laureate Milton Friedman. "I've always been in favor of replacing the Fed with a computer," he explained. "In essence, a PC could determine the economy's monetary base and consistently increase it by, say, 3 percent annually." Friedman has suggested, as Nobel laureate F. A. Hayek and others have, that considering the long history of central bank blunders, it might well be better to seriously consider one of the successful alternatives to central banks.

- Deposit insurance must be priced to reflect the risks of the banks that buy it. Having the federal government provide deposit insurance inevitably introduced political pressures to offer deposit insurance at the same price for all banks, which meant subsidized banks engaged in risky practices and contributed to the instability of the banking system. It would be more prudent to have deposit insurance provided by private insurance companies, free from political influence. Economists George J. Benston and George G. Kaufman explained, "In a world without federal deposit insurance, banks would be subject to considerably greater market discipline from all depositors, shareholders, and private insurance companies if they chose to insure their deposits. As a result, banks would be likely to assume less portfolio risk and maintain higher capital-to-asset ratios."[16] One might make a case that banks, like drivers of motor vehicles, must purchase insurance, but this doesn't mean there's any reason for the government to provide it.

- Especially because taxes are the biggest burden millions of people face today, it's crucial to cut taxes. Tax cuts mean expanding economic liberty by returning money to the individuals who earned it. People are more likely to be careful about how their own money is spent than about how other people's money is spent, so giving individuals more control over their own money is likely to better promote prosperity as well as economic liberty.

- Efforts to "soak the rich" will backfire, because the investments of the rich are needed to create jobs. So tax cuts should be deep, and they should be for everyone, across the board, no conditions or limitations. There isn't any evidence that government officials possess the knowledge that would justify "targeted" tax cuts, aimed at encouraging people to do certain things which are supposedly more desirable than others.

- Public works and other "jobs" programs must be avoided because they increase the cost and burden of government, making it more difficult for the private sector to function. Moreover, "jobs" programs don't increase the total number of jobs in the economy. By increasing the tax burden, such programs merely reduce available funding for private sector jobs and replace these with government jobs. In addition, government spending is sure to be driven by the self-interest of politicians eager to buy votes for the next election, which means the programs will end up having effects very different from what was intended.

- Especially during a recession or depression, the government must not enact laws preventing prices from adjusting to circumstances. Prices are vital signals that help people decide what to produce and consume. Prices maintained above market levels will only encourage surplus production sure to burden taxpayers, as has been the case with farm programs.

- Similarly, the government must not enact laws preventing wages from adjusting to circumstances. Maintaining wages above market levels is guaranteed to maintain unemployment at high levels. Surely it's better to be employed at a lower wage than unemployed at a higher wage. Laws and regulations that make it difficult for wages to adjust to a recession or depression must be repealed.

- Labor union monopolies have been major obstacles to adjusting wages, so government support for labor union monopolies must be ended. Employers should be free to hire union or nonunion workers, and workers shouldn't be penalized if they choose not to join a union. Nonunion workers shouldn't be forced to pay union dues as a condition of employment. Nor should union workers be forced to pay for political activities they disagree with. Laws against extortion and violence should be enforced during labor disputes.

- Trade restrictions must be phased out, so that both consumers and producers will be free to choose the best, most economical suppliers wherever they might be. Some laws restrict imports from other countries, and some laws (like dairy laws) restrict trade from other states. Being free to choose alternative suppliers is also the best protection against any monopolistic practices in the U.S. market.

- Only if investors feel private property is secure will they be willing to make long-term financial commitments needed to spur recovery and boost employment. So there shouldn't be special taxes or other penalties against investors.

Of course, many of these policies would be difficult to achieve. But the right thing to do is often difficult, and if political leaders aren't going to persist, what good are they? The stakes are high, and Americans can only hope that knowledge of past mistakes, particularly the New Deal, will help remind political leaders what must be done and what must be avoided for people to prosper.

NOTES

―――→⊶⊷←―――

INTRODUCTION

1. Richard K. Vedder and Lowell E. Gallaway, *Out of Work: Unemployment and Government in Twentieth-Century America* (New York: New York University Press, 1997), p. 129.
2. Lester V. Chandler, *American Monetary Policy, 1928-1941* (New York: Harper & Row, 1971), p. 247.
3. Milton Friedman and Anna Jacobson Schwartz, *A Monetary History of the United States, 1867–1960* (Princeton: Princeton University Press, 1963), p. 493.
4. David M. Kennedy, *Freedom from Fear: The American People in Depression and War, 1929-1945* (New York: Oxford University Press, 1999), p. 361.
5. Lester V. Chandler, *America's Greatest Depression, 1929-1941* (New York: Harper & Row, 1970), p. 91.
6. *Historical Statistics of the United States from Colonial Times to the Present* (Washington, D.C.: Department of Commerce, 1974), II, p. 1107.
7. http://www.colorado.edu/AmStudies/lewis/2010/econ.htm.
8. Vedder and Gallaway, pp. 128, 131, 132.
9. Vedder and Gallaway, p. 141.
10. Thomas E. Hall and J. David Ferguson, *The Great Depression: An International Disaster of Perverse Economic Policies* (Ann Arbor: University of Michigan Press, 1998), p. 147.
11. David E. Bernstein, *Only One Place of Redress: African Americans, Labor Regulations, and the Courts from Reconstruction to the New Deal* (Durham, N.C.: Duke University Press, 2001), p. 103.
12. Michael A. Bernstein, *The Great Depression: Delayed Recovery and Economic Change in America, 1929–1939* (Cambridge: Cambridge University Press, 1987), p. 270.
13. Ellis W. Hawley, *The New Deal and the Problem of Monopoly: A Study in Economic Ambivalence* (Princeton: Princeton University Press, 1966), p. 485.

14. Hawley, p. 421.

15. "Gross Domestic Product (Millions of 1929 dollars)," National Bureau of Economic Research, NBER Series 08166. http://www.korpios.org/resurgent /GDPreal.htm; "Summary of Receipts, Outlays and Surpluses of Deficits, 1789–2004," The Budget for Fiscal Year 2000, p. 19, http://w3.access.gpo .gov/usbudget /fy2000/pdf/hist.pdf.

16. Donald R. Richberg, *My Hero: The Indiscreet Memoirs of an Eventful but Unheroic Life* (New York: Putnam's, 1954), p. 152.

17. National Archives and Records Administration, Executive Orders Disposition Tables, http://www.nara.gov/fedreg/eo.html.

18. http://newdeal.feri.org/misc/keynes2.htm.

19. Quoted in Gary Dean Best, *Pride, Prejudice, and Politics: Roosevelt Versus Recovery, 1933–1938* (Westport, Conn.: Praeger, 1991), p. 213.

CHAPTER ONE: HOW COULD SUCH BRIGHT, COMPASSIONATE PEOPLE BE WRONG?

1. Herbert Croly, *The Promise of American Life* (New York: Archon Books, 1963), pp. 22, 23, 382.

2. Samuel Eliot Morison, Henry Steele Commager, and William E. Leuchtenburg, *The Growth of the American Republic* (New York: Oxford University Press, 1980), II, p. 378.

3. Morison, Commager, and Leuchtenburg, II, p. 378.

4. Cited in Arthur A. Ekirch Jr., *Ideologies and Utopias: The Impact of the New Deal on American Thought* (Chicago: Quadrangle, 1969), p. 51.

5. Cited in Ekirch, p. 51.

6. Charles A. Beard, "The Myth of Rugged Individualism," *Harper's Magazine*, March 1931, p. 22.

7. Stuart Chase, *A New Deal* (New York: Macmillan, 1932), p. 252.

8. James T. Patterson, *Congressional Conservatism and the New Deal: The Growth of the Conservative Coalition in Congress, 1933–1939* (Lexington: University of Kentucky Press, 1967), p. 10.

9. Rixey Smith and Norman Beasley, *Carter Glass: A Biography* (New York: Da Capo, 1972), pp. 370, 406.

10. Richard T. Goldberg, "Polio," in *Franklin D. Roosevelt: His Life and Times, An Encyclopedic View,* ed. Otis L. Graham Jr. and Meghan Robinson Wander (New York: Da Capo, 1985), p. 333.

11. Henry H. Adams, *Harry Hopkins: A Biography* (New York: Putnam, 1977), p. 42.

12. George Martin, *Madam Secretary: Frances Perkins* (Boston: Houghton Mifflin, 1976), p. 213.

13. Adams, p. 47.

14. Jerry N. Hess, "Oral History Interview with Leon H. Keyserling," Truman Presidential Museum and Library, May 10, 1971, http://www.trumanlibrary.org /oralhist/keyserl2.htm.

15. Adams, p. 144.

16. Samuel I. Rosenman, *Working with Roosevelt* (New York: Harper, 1952), p. 122.

17. John Morton Blum, *Roosevelt and Morgenthau: A Revision and Condensation of From the Morgenthau Diaries* (Boston: Houghton Mifflin, 1970), p. 5.

18. Martin, pp. 58, 59.

19. Blum, p. 7.

20. Blum, pp. 11, 12.

21. Quoted in Adams, pp. 39, 40.

22. Adams, pp. 36, 37, 38.

23. Adams, pp. 41, 45.

24. Adams, p. 45.

25. Arthur M. Schlesinger Jr., *The Coming of the New Deal* (Boston: Houghton Mifflin, 1959), p. 299.

26. Martin, p. 53.

27. Martin, p. 63.

28. Martin, pp. 53, 63, 64, 68.

29. Raymond Moley, *The First New Deal* (New York: Harcourt, Brace & World, 1966), p. 17.

30. Rosenman, p. 105.

31. Moley, p. 13.

32. Cited in Jordan A. Schwarz, *The New Dealers: Power Politics in the Age of Roosevelt* (New York: Knopf, 1993), p. 158.

33. Kenneth S. Davis, *FDR: The New York Years, 1928–1933* (New York: Random House, 1994), pp. 276–277.

34. From correspondence quoted in Jordan A. Schwarz, *Liberal: Adolf A. Berle and the Vision of an American Era* (New York: Free Press, 1987), p. 38.

35. Quoted in Schwarz, *Liberal,* p. 118.

36. Quoted in Schwarz, *Liberal,* p. 207.

37. Bernard Sternsher, *Rexford Tugwell and the New Deal* (New Brunswick, N.J.: Rutgers University Press, 1964), p. 9.

38. Rexford Tugwell, Thomas Munro, and Roy E. Stryker, *American Economic Life and the Means of Its Improvement* (New York: Scribner, 1928), p. xix.

39. Tugwell, Munro, and Stryker, p. 712.

40. Arthur M. Schlesinger Jr., *The Crisis of the Old Order, 1919–1933* (Boston: Houghton Mifflin, 1957), p. 451.

41. John C. Culver and John Hyde, *American Dreamer: The Life and Times of Henry A. Wallace* (New York: Norton, 2000), p. 119.

42. Culver and Hyde, pp. 127, 128.

43. James S. Olson, *Saving Capitalism: The Reconstruction Finance Corporation and the New Deal, 1933–1940* (Princeton: Princeton University Press, 1988), p. 46.

44. Olson, p. 60.

45. Olson, p. 49.

46. *Felix Frankfurter Reminisces, Recorded in Talks with Dr. Harlan B. Phillips* (New York: Reynal, 1960), p. 242.

47. Joseph P. Lash, *Dealers and Dreamers: A New Look at the New Deal* (New York: Doubleday, 1988), p. 115.

48. Clare Cushman, ed., *The Supreme Court Justices: Illustrated Biographies, 1789–1995* (Washington, D.C.: Congressional Quarterly, 1995), p. 334.

49. Louis D. Brandeis to Felix Frankfurter, March 4, 1934, and April 1, 1934, Library of Congress, cited in Lash, p. 163.

50. *Felix Frankfurter Reminisces*, p. 247.

51. *Felix Frankfurter Reminisces*, p. 248.

52. Schwarz, *The New Dealers*, p. 126; Lash, p. 162.

53. Quoted in Lash, p. 162.

54. Laura Kalman, "Benjamin Victor Cohen," in *Franklin D. Roosevelt: His Life and Times*, p. 67.

55. Kalman, p. 67.

56. Rosenman, p. 115.

57. Schwarz, *The New Dealers*, p. 139.

58. Schwarz, *The New Dealers*, p. 140.

59. Schwarz, *The New Dealers*, p. 139.

60. Monica L. Niznik, "Thomas Gardiner Corcoran," in *Franklin D. Roosevelt: His Life and Times*, p. 83.

61. Schwarz, *The New Dealers*, p. 143.

62. Schwarz, *The New Dealers*, p. 143.

63. Linda J. Lear, "Harold LeClair Ickes," in *Franklin D. Roosevelt: His Life and Times*, p. 199.

64. T. H. Watkins, *Righteous Pilgrim: The Life and Times of Harold L. Ickes, 1874–1952* (New York: Henry Holt, 1990), pp. 1, 2.

CHAPTER TWO: WHAT CAUSED THE GREAT DEPRESSION?

1. Raburn Williams, *The Politics of Boom and Bust in Twentieth-Century America* (Minneapolis–St. Paul: West, 1994), p. 122.

2. Lester V. Chandler, *Benjamin Strong: Central Banker* (Washington, D.C.: Brookings Institution, 1958), p. 376.

3. Chandler, p. 48.

4. Priscilla Roberts, "Benjamin Strong, the Federal Reserve, and the Limits to Interwar American Nationalism," Part II, *Federal Reserve Bank of Richmond Economic Quarterly*, Spring 2000, p. 80.

5. Chandler, p. 377.
6. James S. Olson, *Saving Capitalism: The Reconstruction Finance Corporation and the New Deal, 1933–1940* (Princeton: Princeton University Press, 1988), p. 7.
7. Milton Friedman and Anna Jacobson Schwartz, *A Monetary History of the United States, 1867–1960* (Princeton: Princeton University Press, 1963), pp. 289, 290.
8. Friedman and Schwartz, pp. 299, 301.
9. Elmus Wicker, *The Banking Panics of the Great Depression* (Cambridge: Cambridge University Press, 1996), p. 5.
10. Jesse H. Jones with Edward Angly, *Fifty Billion Dollars: My Thirteen Years with the RFC, 1932–1945* (New York: Macmillan, 1951), p. 13.
11. George Benston et al., *Perspectives on Safe and Sound Banking: Past, Present, and Future* (Cambridge, Mass.: MIT Press, 1986), pp. 53–72.
12. Friedman and Schwartz, p. 352.
13. Letter from Milton Friedman to Jim Powell, June 25, 2001.
14. Nevada Department of Museums, Library and Arts, http://dmla.clan.lib.nv.us/docs/nsla/archives/gov/govbib.htm.
15. Wicker, p. 115.
16. Wicker, pp. 108–109.
17. Allan H. Meltzer, "Lessons from the Early History of the Federal Reserve," Presidential address to International Economic Society, Munich, March 17, 2000, http://www.gsia.cmu.edu/afs/andrew/gsia/meltzer/Munich.PDF.
18. Friedman and Schwartz, p. 414.
19. Merlo J. Pusey, *Eugene Meyer* (New York: Knopf, 1974), pp. 126, 193.
20. Friedman and Schwartz, p. 415.
21. See Thomas E. Hall and J. David Ferguson, *The Great Depression: An International Disaster of Perverse Economic Policies* (Ann Arbor: University of Michigan Press, 1998), pp. 77–85.
22. Friedman and Schwartz, pp. 415, 416.
23. Friedman and Schwartz, p. 419.
24. Ted Morgan, *FDR: A Biography* (New York: Simon & Schuster, 1985), pp. 484, 485. 491.
25. Kenneth S. Davis, *FDR: The New Deal Years, 1933–1937* (New York: Random House, 1986).
26. James Tobin, "The Monetary Interpretation of History: A Review Article," *American Economic Review,* June 1965, p. 85.
27. Robert. E. Lucas, Jr., "Review of Milton Friedman and Anna J. Schwartz, 'A Monetary History of the United States, 1867–1960,'" *Journal of Monetary Economics,* 1994, p. 14.
28. Peter Temin, *Did Monetary Forces Cause the Great Depression* (New York: Norton, 1976), pp. 170, 173.

29. Paul Krugman, *The Return of Depression Economics* (New York: Norton, 2000), p. 12.

30. Hall and Ferguson, pp. 84, 85.

CHAPTER THREE: WHAT DID FDR
BORROW FROM HOOVER?

1. Page Smith, *Redeeming the Time: A People's History of the 1920s and the New Deal* (New York: McGraw-Hill, 1987), p. 282.

2. Quoted in Page Smith, p. 282.

3. Jason Taylor and George Selgin, "By Our Bootstraps: Origins and Effects of the High-Wage Doctrine and the Minimum Wage," *Journal of Labor Research*, Fall 1999, p. 451.

4. Henry Ford, *My Life and Work* (Garden City, N.Y.: Doubleday, 1922), pp. 124, 125.

5. J. A. Hobson, *Rationalization and Unemployment* (London: Unwin, 1930), p. 85.

6. Irving Fisher, *The Stock Market Crash—and After* (New York: Macmillan, 1930), p. 25.

7. Murray N. Rothbard, *America's Great Depression* (Los Angeles: Nash, 1972), pp. 187, 188.

8. Quoted in Arthur A. Ekirch Jr., *Ideologies and Utopias: The Impact of the New Deal on American Thought* (Chicago: Quadrangle, 1969), p. 44.

9. Rothbard, p. 189.

10. Howard R. Smith, *Economic History of the United States* (New York: Ronald Press, 1955), p. 563.

11. Broadus Mitchell, *Depression Decade: From New Era Through New Deal, 1929–1941* (New York: Rinehart, 1947), p. 5.

12. Rothbard, pp. 201, 202, 205, 206, 209.

13. E. E. Schattschneider, *Politics, Pressures and the Tariff: A Study of Free Private Enterprise in Pressure Politics, as Shown in the 1929–1930 Revision of the Tariff* (New York: Prentice-Hall, 1935), pp. 3, 31, 140.

14. Victor A. Canto, *The Determinants and Consequences of Trade Restrictions in the U.S. Economy* (New York: Praeger, 1985), p. 2.

15. U.S. Tariff Commission, *Number of Items and Tariff Rates in the Tariff Act of 1922 as Compared with the Acts of 1930 and 1913* (Washington, D.C., 1930), cited in Schattschneider, p. 17.

16. Joseph M. Jones Jr., *Tariff Retaliation: Repercussions of the Hawley-Smoot Bill* (Philadelphia: University of Pennsylvania Press, 1934), pp. 177, 178.

17. Joseph M. Jones, pp. 232, 233.

18. *Gazette de Lausanne,* May 2, 1930, quoted in Joseph M. Jones, pp. 40, 53, 82, 83, 88, 105, 113, 167, 177, 178, 232, 233, 289.

19. Margaret S. Gordon, *Barriers to World Trade: A Study of Recent Commercial Policy* (New York: Macmillan, 1941), pp. 53, 54, 55.

20. *Historical Statistics of the United States from Colonial Times to 1970* (Washington, D.C.: U.S. Department of Commerce, 1975), p. 482.

21. Charles P. Kindleberger, *The World in Depression, 1929–1939* (Berkeley: University of California Press, 1986), p. 125

22. Sumner Welles, *A Time for Decision* (New York: Harper & Brothers, 1944), p. 46.

23. Howard R. Smith, p. 565.

24. John C. Weicher, "The Future Structure of the Housing Finance System," in *Restructuring Banking and Financial Services in America,* ed. William S. Haraf and Rose Marie Kushmeider (Washington, D.C.: American Enterprise Institute, 1988), p. 298, 299.

25. Herbert Hoover, *The Great Depression, 1929–1941* (New York: Macmillan, 1952), pp. 85, 86, 90.

26. Walter Lippmann, *Interpretations: 1931–1932,* ed. Allan Nevins (New York: Macmillan, 1933), p. 41.

27. Ida M. Tarbell, *Owen D. Young: A New Type of Industrial Leader* (New York: Macmillan, 1932), p. 228.

28. Lippmann, p. 40.

29. James S. Olson, Saving *Capitalism:, The Reconstruction Finance Corporation and the New Deal, 1933–1940* (Princeton: Princeton University Press, 1988), p. 15.

30. Rothbard, p. 262.

31. Jesse H. Jones, *My Thirteen Years with the RFC, 1932–1945* (New York: Macmillan, 1951), pp. 69–70 (Union Trust), 72–81 (Dawes).

32. Rothbard, pp. 263, 264.

33. Joseph Russell Mason, *The Determinants and Effects of Reconstruction Finance Corporation Assistance to Banks During the Great Depression,* submitted in partial fulfillment of requirements for a Doctor of Philosophy in economics at the University of Illinois, Urbana-Champaign, 1996, p. 10.

34. Rothbard, p. 265.

35. Rothbard, p. 254.

36. David T. Beito, *Taxpayers in Revolt: Tax Resistance During the Great Depression* (Chapel Hill: University of North Carolina Press, 1989), p. 6.

37. Rothbard, p. 270.

38. Cited in Beito, pp. 8, 9.

39. Beito, pp. 12, 21, 161.

40. Beito pp. 60, 61, 63, 64, 69, 71.

41. Beito, pp. 66, 67, 69.

42. Beito, pp. 72, 77, 78.

43. Rothbard, pp. 280, 284.

44. Quoted in Rothbard, p. 282.

45. Arthur M. Schlesinger Jr., *The Crisis of the Old Order, 1919–1933* (Boston: Houghton Mifflin, 1957), p. 258.

46. Schlesinger, p. 257.

47. http://www.americanpresident.org/KoTrain/Courses/HH/HH_Domestic_Affairs
.htm

CHAPTER FOUR: WHY DID NEW DEALERS BREAK UP THE STRONGEST BANKS?

1. Henry H. Adams, *Harry Hopkins: A Biography* (New York: Putnam, 1977), p. 50.

2. Lester V. Chandler, *American Monetary Policy, 1928–1941* (New York: Harper & Row, 1971), p. 260.

3. Page Smith, *Redeeming the Time: A People's History of the 1920s and the New Deal* (New York: McGraw-Hill, 1987), p. 438.

4. Chandler, *American Monetary Policy,* p. 261.

5. Jesse H. Jones with Edward Angly, *Fifty Billion Dollars: My Thirteen Years with the RFC: 1932–1945* (New York: Macmillan, 1951), p. 21.

6. James S. Olson, *Saving Capitalism: The Reconstruction Finance Corporation and the New Deal, 1933–1940* (Princeton: Princeton University Press, 1988), p. 40.

7. Jesse H. Jones, pp. 27, 29.

8. George Benston et al., *Perspectives on Safe and Sound Banking: Past, Present, and Future* (Cambridge, Mass.: MIT Press, 1986), pp. 53–72.

9. Eugene White, "Deposit Insurance," a paper presented at a World Bank seminar, http://fas-econ.rutgers.edu/home/white/Publications/article1
.html.

10. White, "Deposit Insurance."

11. Quoted in White, "Deposit Insurance."

12. Eugene N. White, "The Legacy of Deposit Insurance: The Growth, Spread, and Cost of Insuring Financial Intermediaries," National Bureau of Economic Research, Working Paper 6063 (June 1997).

13. James T. Patterson, *Congressional Conservatism and the New Deal: The Growth of the Conservative Coalition in Congress, 1933–1939* (Lexington: University of Kentucky Press, 1967), p. 18.

14. Lester V. Chandler, *Benjamin Strong: Central Banker* (Washington, D.C.: Brookings Institution, 1958), p. 163.

15. Louis D. Brandeis, *Other People's Money and How the Bankers Use It,* ed. Melvin I. Urofsky (Boston: Bedford, 1995), pp. 50, 68, 69, 70, 145.

16. George J. Benston, *The Separation of Commercial and Investment Banking: The Glass-Steagall Act Revisited and Reconsidered* (New York: Oxford University Press, 1995), p. 11.

17. Benston, p. 4.

18. Benston, pp. 31, 75, 105, 121.

19. Benston, p. 38.

20. Quoted in Benston, p. 37.

21. Benston, pp. 105, 106.
22. Benston, pp. 40–41.
23. Benston, p. 134.
24. Benston, p. 134.
25. Randall S. Kroszner and Raghurm G. Rajan, "Is the Glass-Steagall Act Justified?" *American Economic Review,* September 1994, pp. 823, 824, 825.
26. Kroszner and Rajan, pp. 827, 828.
27. Eugene N. White, "Before the Glass-Steagall Act: An Analysis of the Investment Banking Activities of National Banks," *Explorations in Economic History,* vol. 23, 1986, pp. 33, 40, 42.
28. Benston, p. 1.

CHAPTER FIVE: WHY DID FDR SEIZE EVERYBODY'S GOLD?

1. Elgin Groseclose, *Money and Man: A Survey of Monetary Experience* (New York: Ungar, 1961), pp. 75, 153.
2. "The Story of the British Gold Sovereign," http://www.24carat.co.uk /sovereignstory.html.
3. "The President Proclaims a Bank Holiday. Gold and Silver Exports and Foreign Exchange Transactions Prohibited. Proclamation No. 2039. March 6, 1933," *The Public Papers and Addresses of Franklin D. Roosevelt* (New York: Random House, 1938), II, p. 25.
4. "Gold Coin, Gold Bullion, and Gold Certificates Are Required to Be Delivered to the Government. Executive Order No. 6102. April 5, 1933," *The Public Papers and Addresses of Franklin D. Roosevelt,* II, p. 111.
5. "Fireside Chat of May 7, 1933," http://www.mhrcc.org/fdr/chat2.html.
6. Timothy Green, *The Smugglers: An Investigation into the World of the Contemporary Smuggler* (New York: Walker, 1969), p. 211.
7. Green, p. 212.
8. "Joint Resolution, To Assure Uniform Value to the Coins and Currencies of the United States," H.J. Res. 192, June 5, 1933, *The Statutes at Large of the United States of America from March 1933 to June 1934* (Washington, D.C.: Government Printing Office, 1934), XLVIII, Part 1, p. 112.
9. Raymond Moley, *The First New Deal* (New York: Harcourt, Brace & World, 1966), pp. 303, 304.
10. John Brooks, *Once in Golconda: A True Drama of Wall Street, 1920–1938* (New York: Harper & Row, 1969), p. 163.
11. Brooks, p. 163.
12. Brooks, pp. 160, 161, 162, 163.
13. James P. Warburg, *The Money Muddle* (New York: Knopf, 1934), pp. 134, 137, 138.
14. "Further Regulations on the Hoarding and Export of Gold, and on Transactions in Foreign Exchange. Executive Order No. 6260. August 28,

1933," *The Public Papers and Addresses of Franklin D. Roosevelt,* II, pp. 345–352.

15. "Address of the President Delivered from the White House, October 22, 1933, http://www.mhrcc.org/fdr/chat4.html.

16. Kenneth S. Davis, *FDR: The New Deal Years, 1933–1937* (New York: Random House, 1986), pp. 293, 294.

17. Moley, p. 304.

18. Warburg, p. 154.

19. Brooks, pp. 169, 170.

20. Brooks, pp. 171, 176.

21. http://newdeal.feri.org/misc/keynes2.htm.

22. http://newdeal.feri.org/misc/keynes2.htm.

23. Brooks, p. 177.

24. Warburg, p. 158.

25. Henry Mark Holzer, *How Americans Lost Their Right to Own Gold,* Committee for Monetary Research and Education, Monograph #35, 1981.

26. Warburg, p. 173.

CHAPTER SIX: WHY DID FDR TRIPLE TAXES DURING THE GREAT DEPRESSION?

1. "First Inaugural Address, Washington, March 4, 1933," in *The Roosevelt Reader: Selected Speeches, Messages, Press Conferences, and Letters of Franklin D. Roosevelt,* ed. Basil Rauch (New York: Rinehart, 1957), p. 90.

2. Robert M. Collins, *The Business Response to Keynes, 1929–1964* (New York: Columbia University Press, 1981), p. 38.

3. "First Inaugural Address, Washington, March 4, 1933," in *The Roosevelt Reader,* p. 92.

4. Collins, pp. 38, 48.

5. *NAM News-Letter,* April 30, 1938, p. 1, Quoted in Collins, p. 49.

6. Mario Palmieri, *The Philosophy of Fascism* (Chicago: Dante Alighieri Society, 1936), pp. 98, 99, 128, 146.

7. Sidney Ratner, *Taxation and Democracy in America* (New York: Octagon, 1980), p. 464.

8. W. Elliot Brownlee, *Federal Taxation in America: A Short History* (Cambridge: Cambridge University Press, 1996), pp. 71, 72.

9. Ratner, pp. 463, 464.

10. Ratner, p. 467.

11. Cited in Randolph E. Paul, *Taxation in the United States* (Boston: Little, Brown, 1954), p. 182.

12. Benjamin M. Anderson, *Economics and the Public Welfare: A Financial and Economic History of the United States, 1914–1946* (Indianapolis: Liberty Fund, 1980), p. 367.

13. Brownlee, p. 74.

14. Anderson, p. 369.
15. Carolyn Weber and Aaron Wildavsky, *A History of Taxation and Expenditure in the Western World* (New York: Simon & Schuster, 1986), p. 456.
16. Anderson, p. 373.
17. Alfred G. Buehler, *The Undistributed Profits Tax* (New York: 1937), p. 36, quoted in Kenneth D. Roose, *The Economics of Recession and Revival: An Interpretation of 1937–38* (New York: Archon Books, 1969), p. 213.
18. "Address of Acceptance of the Nomination for a Second Term, Philadelphia, June 27, 1936," in *The Roosevelt Reader*, pp. 150, 151.
19. John Morton Blum, *Roosevelt and Morgenthau: A Revision and Condensation of From the Morgenthau Diaries* (Boston: Houghton Mifflin, 1970), p. 166.
20. Blum, p. 170.
21. Blum, pp. 162, 163.
22. Brownlee, p. 80.
23. Title VII, Section 802(a) of the Social Security Act, http://www.ssa.gov/history/35acviii.html.
24. Mark H. Leff, *The Limits of Symbolic Reform: The New Deal and Taxation, 1933–1939* (Cambridge: Cambridge University Press, 1984), p. 4.
25. John Joseph Wallis and Wallace E. Oates, "The Impact of the New Deal on American Federalism," in *The Defining Moment: The Great Depression and the American Economy in the Twentieth Century*, ed. Michael D. Bordo, Claudia Goldin, and Eugene N. White (Chicago: University of Chicago Press, 1998), p. 171.
26. James T. Patterson, *The New Deal and the States* (Princeton: Princeton University Press, 1969), pp. 97, 98.
27. Frank Freidel, *Franklin D. Roosevelt: A Rendezvous with Destiny* (Boston: Little, Brown, 1990), pp. 166, 167.
28. Blum, p. 204.
29. Paul, pp. 214, 215.
30. Blum, p. 204.
31. Paul, p. 214.
32. Quoted in Howard Zinn, ed., *New Deal Thought* (Indianapolis: Bobbs-Merrill, 1966), p. 83.
33. Paul, p. 219.
34. Hadley Cantril, ed., *Public Opinion, 1935–1946* (Princeton: Princeton University Press, 1951), pp. 345, 346.
35. Cantril, pp. 175, 337.
36. Robert Higgs, "Regime Uncertainty: Why the Great Depression Lasted So Long and Why Prosperity Resumed After the War," *Independent Review*, Spring 1997, p. 567.
37. Lester V. Chandler, *America's Greatest Depression, 1929–1941* (New York: Harper & Row, 1970), p. 132.
38. Paul, p. 245.

CHAPTER SEVEN: WHY WAS SO MUCH NEW DEAL
RELIEF AND PUBLIC WORKS MONEY CHANNELED
AWAY FROM THE POOREST PEOPLE?

1. U.S. National Resources Planning Board, *Security, Work, and Relief Policies* (Washington, D.C.: U.S. Government Printing Office, 1942), pp. 326, 327.

2. Board of Governors of the Federal Reserve System, *Banking and Monetary Statistics* (Washington, D.C.: National Capital Press, 1943), p. 512, table 149.

3. W. L. Stoddard, "Small Business Wants Capital," *Harvard Business Review,* vol. 18, 1940, pp. 265–274.

4. Lewis Kimmel, *The Availability of Bank Credit, 1933–1938* (New York: National Industrial Conference Board, 1939).

5. Civilian Conservation Corps Museum, http://members.aol.com/famjustin/ccchis.html.

6. Don C. Reading, "New Deal Activity and the States, 1933–1939," *Journal of Economic History,* December 1973, pp. 792–810.

7. Jim F. Couch and William F. Shughart II, *The Political Economy of the New Deal* (Northampton, Mass.: Edward Elgar, 1998), p. 80.

8. Douglass V. Brown, "Helping Labor," in Douglass V. Brown et al., *The Economics of the Recovery Program* (New York: Whittlesey House, 1934), p. 78.

9. Lippmann, Walter, *Interpretations, 1933–1935,* ed. Allan Nevins (New York: Macmillan, 1936), pp. 256, 257.

10. James A. Farley, *Jim Farley's Story: The Roosevelt Years* (New York: Whittlesey House, 1948), pp. 61, 62.

11. Quoted in James S. Olson, *Saving Capitalism: The Reconstruction Finance Corporation and the New Deal, 1933–1940* (Princeton: Princeton University Press, 1988), p. 43.

12. Olson, p. 45.

13. Robert A. Caro, *The Power Broker: Robert Moses and the Fall of New York* (New York: Knopf, 1974), pp. 427, 428, 430.

14. Caro, pp. 433, 435.

15. Caro, pp. 437, 439, 440.

16. Couch and Shughart, p. 90.

17. "Federal Emergency Relief Administration," in *Franklin D. Roosevelt: His Life and Times, An Encyclopedic View,* ed. Otis L. Graham Jr. and Meghan Robinson Wander (New York: Da Capo, 1985), p. 133.

18. University of Mississippi, http://www.olemiss.edu/news/newsdesk/story505.html.

19. Jeremy Atack and Peter Passell, *A New Economic View of American History from Colonial Times to 1940* (New York: Norton, 1994), p. 670.

20. Quoted in Henry H. Adams, *Harry Hopkins: A Biography* (New York: Putnam, 1977), p. 63.

21. Kenneth S. Davis, *FDR: The New Deal Years, 1933–1937* (New York: Random House, 1986), pp. 307, 308.

22. Frank Freidel, *Franklin D. Roosevelt: A Rendezvous with Destiny* (Boston: Little, Brown, 1990), p. 135.

23. Adams, p. 62.

24. Davis, pp. 312, 313.

25. *Historical Statistics of the United States: Colonial Times to 1970* (Washington, D.C.: U.S. Department of Commerce, 1975), I, p. 126.

26. Lippmann, pp. 242, 243.

27. Coplen to Farley, December 12, 1938, OF 300, Box 104, Roosevelt Papers, quoted in James T. Patterson, *The New Deal and the States* (Princeton: Princeton University Press, 1969), pp. 82, 83.

28. Patterson, pp. 59, 83.

29. John T. Flynn, *The Roosevelt Myth* (New York: Devin-Adair, 1948), pp. 134, 135.

30. Patterson, pp. 59, 60, 82.

31. Freidel, p. 189.

32. Rixey Smith and Norman Beasley, *Carter Glass: A Biography* (New York: Da Capo, 1972), p. 370.

33. John Salmond, "National Youth Administration," in *Franklin D. Roosevelt: His Life and Times,* p. 279.

34. Leonard J. Arrington, "The New Deal in the West: A Preliminary Statistical Inquiry," *Pacific Historical Review,* August 1969, pp. 311–316.

35. Leonard J. Arrington, "Western Agriculture and the New Deal," *Agricultural History,* October 1970, pp. 337–353.

36. Reading, pp. 792–810.

37. Gavin Wright, "The Political Economy of New Deal Spending: An Econometric Analysis," *Review of Economics and Statistics,* February 1974, pp. 30–38.

38. Wright, p. 35.

39. John Joseph Wallis, "The Birth of the Old Federalism: Financing the New Deal," *Journal of Economic History,* March 1984, p. 147.

40. Gary M. Anderson and Robert D. Tollison, "Congressional Influence and Patterns of New Deal Spending, 1933–1939," *Journal of Law and Economics,* April 1991, pp. 161–175.

41. Couch and Shughart, p. 109.

42. "Shughart, Alum Write Book Revealing Roosevelt's New Deal as Vote Getter," University of Mississippi, http://www.olemiss.edu/news/newsdesk/story 505.html.

43. Couch and Shughart, pp. 190–215.

44. Couch and Shugart, pp. 215, 216.

45. Patterson, p. 72.

46. John Joseph Wallis and Daniel K. Benjamin, "Public Relief and Private Employment in the Great Depression," *Explorations in Economic History,* March 1981, p. 97.

47. Price V. Fishback, William C. Horrace, and Shawn Kantor, "The Impact of New Deal Expenditures on Local Economic Activity: An Examination of Retail Sales, 1929–1939," *National Bureau of Economic Research,* January 2001.
48. Freidel, pp. 248, 249.

CHAPTER EIGHT: WHY DIDN'T NEW DEAL SECURITIES LAWS HELP INVESTORS DO BETTER?

1. Quoted in Broadus Mitchell, *Depression Decade: From New Era Through New Deal, 1929–1941* (New York: Rinehart, 1947), p. 158.
2. Quoted in Leonard Baker, *Roosevelt and Frankfurter* (New York: n.p., 1984), p. 178, cited in Joseph P. Lash, *Dealers and Dreamers: A New Look at the New Deal* (New York: Doubleday, 1988), p. 163.
3. Raymond Moley, *The First New Deal* (New York: Harcourt, Brace & World, 1966), pp. 310, 312, 313.
4. Lester V. Chandler, *America's Greatest Depression, 1929–1941* (New York: Harper & Row, 1970), p. 159.
5. Moley, pp. 306, 315.
6. *Historical Statistics of the United States: Colonial Times to 1970* (Washington, D.C.: U.S. Department of Commerce, 1975), I, p. 126.
7. Lash, p. 169.
8. *Hall v Geiger-Jones Co.,* 242 U.S. 539 (1917).
9. Gregg A. Jarrell, "The Economic Effects of Federal Regulation of the Market for New Security Issues," *Journal of Law and Economics,* December 1981, pp. 615, 617.
10. George J. Stigler, "Public Regulation of the Securities Market," in *The Citizen and the State: Essays on Regulation* (Chicago: University of Chicago Press, 1975), p. 85.
11. Stigler, p. 85.
12. Stigler, pp. 84, 85.
13. Stigler, p. 88.
14. Jarrell, "The Economic Effects of Federal Regulation of the Market for New Security Issues," p. 666.
15. Jarrell, "The Economic Effects of Federal Regulation of the Market for New Security Issues," p. 618.
16. Gregg A. Jarrell, "Change at the Exchange: The Causes and Effects of Deregulation," *Journal of Law and Economics,* October 1984, p. 273.

CHAPTER NINE: WHY DID NEW DEALERS MAKE EVERYTHING COST MORE IN THE DEPRESSION?

1. *Time,* January 1, 1934, http://www.time.com/time/special/moy/1933.html.
2. David Loth, *Swope of GE: The Story of Gerard Swope and General Electric in American Business* (New York: Simon & Schuster, 1958), p. 3.

3. Loth, p. 206.
4. Quoted in Robert M. Collins, *The Business Response to Keynes, 1929–1964* (New York: Columbia University Press, 1981), p. 27.
5. Quoted in John T. Flynn, "Whose Child Is the NRA?" in *Forgotten Lessons: Selected Essays of John T. Flynn,* ed. Gregory P. Pavlik (Irvington-on-Hudson, N.Y.: Foundation for Economic Education, 1996), p. 13.
6. Joseph P. Lash, *Dealers and Dreamers: A New Look at the New Deal* (New York: Doubleday, 1988), pp. 116, 118, 120, 121.
7. Ellis W. Hawley, "Hugh Samuel Johnson," in *Franklin D. Roosevelt: His Life and Times, An Encyclopedic View,* ed. Otis L. Graham Jr. and Meghan Robinson Wander (New York: Da Capo, 1985), p. 219.
8. James Grant, *Bernard Baruch: The Adventures of a Wall Street Legend* (New York: Simon & Schuster, 1983), p. 173.
9. Raymond Moley, *The First New Deal* (New York: Harcourt, Brace & World, 1966), pp. 284, 285.
10. George Martin, *Madam Secretary: Frances Perkins* (Boston: Houghton Mifflin, 1976), p. 263.
11. Quoted in Collins, p. 29.
12. *New York Times,* May 21, 1933, p. 2, quoted in Collins, p. 30.
13. *Time,* January 1, 1934, http://www.time.com/time/special/moy/1933.html.
14. Kenneth S. Davis, *FDR: The New Deal Years, 1933–1937* (New York: Random House, 1986), pp. 252, 253.
15. Arthur M. Schlesinger Jr., *The Coming of the New Deal* (Boston: Houghton Mifflin, 1959), pp. 106, 115.
16. Schlesinger, p. 107.
17. Frank Freidel, *Franklin D. Roosevelt: A Rendezvous with Destiny* (Boston: Little, Brown, 1990), p. 138.
18. http://newdeal.feri.org/misc/keynes2.htm.
19. Edward Chamberlin, "Purchasing Power," in Douglass V. Brown et al., *The Economics of the Recovery Program* (New York: Whittlesey House, 1934), p. 35.
20. David E. Bernstein, *Only One Place of Redress: African Americans, Labor Regulations, and the Courts from Reconstruction to the New Deal* (Durham, N.C.: Duke University Press, 2001), pp. 86, 87, 88, 89.
21. Bernstein, pp. 90, 92, 93.
22. Edward S. Mason, "Controlling Industry," in Douglass V. Brown et al., *The Economics of the Recovery Program* (New York: Whittlesey House, 1934), p. 62.
23. Davis, pp. 248, 249.
24. Walter Lippmann, *Interpretations, 1933–1935,* ed. Allan Nevins (New York: Macmillan, 1936), p. 91.
25. Davis, pp. 249, 250, 252.

26. Quoted in Robert S. McElvaine, *The Great Depression: America, 1929–1941* (New York: Three Rivers Press, 1993), p. 160.

27. Moley, p. 293.

28. Davis, pp. 250, 251.

29. Allan Nevins and Frank Ernest Hill, *Ford: Decline and Rebirth, 1933–1962* (New York: Scribner, 1963), p. 17. Cf. 757 Industries Covered by the NRA, National Archives and Records Administration, Records of the National Recovery Administration, http://www.nara.gov/guide/rg009.html.

30. Moley, p. 292.

31. Jason E. Taylor, "The Output Effects of Government Sponsored Cartels During the New Deal," unpublished paper, University of Virginia.

32. National Archives and Records Administration, Records of the National Recovery Administration, http://www.nara.gov/guide/rg009.html.

33. Hadley Arkes, "Was the New Deal Constitutional?" a Bradley lecture at the American Enterprise Institute, January 12, 1998.

34. http://lawbooksusa.com/cconlaw/schechterpoultrycorpvunitedstates.htm.

35. Henry Hazlitt, "The Fallacies of the N.R.A.," *American Mercury,* December 1933, p. 421.

36. Hazlitt, pp. 421, 422.

37. Jim F. Couch and William F. Shughart II, *The Political Economy of the New Deal* (Northampton, Mass.: Edward Elgar, 1998), p. 78.

38. Davis, p. 286.

39. Collins, pp. 32, 33.

40. Michael A. Bernstein, *The Great Depression: Delayed Recovery and Economic Change in America, 1929–1939* (Cambridge: Cambridge University Press, 1987), pp. 201, 202.

41. Text of Executive Order 6632 at http://www.uhuh.com/laws/donncoll/eo/1934/EO6632.TXT.

42. U.S. National Recovery Review Board, "Third Report," p. 35.

43. Rixey Smith and Norman Beasley, *Carter Glass: A Biography* (New York: Da Capo, 1972), pp. 361, 362.

44. Nevins and Hill, pp. 15, 17, 18, 20.

45. Nevins and Hill, pp. 20, 22.

46. *Public Papers of President Franklin D. Roosevelt,* II, p. 143, http://www.uhuh.com/laws/donncoll/eo/1934/EO6646.TXT.

47. Nevins and Hill, pp. 20, 21.

48. Cited in Nevins and Hill, p. 23.

49. Nevins and Hill, pp. 24, 26.

50. Freidel, p. 159.

51. Leverett S. Lyon et al., *The National Recovery Administration: An Analysis and Appraisal* (Washington, D.C.: Brookings Institution, 1935), pp. 873, 874.

52. Moley, p. 295.

CHAPTER TEN: WHY DID NEW DEALERS DESTROY
ALL THAT FOOD WHEN PEOPLE WERE HUNGRY?

1. Raymond Moley, *The First New Deal* (New York: Harcourt, Brace, 1966), p. 245.
2. Broadus Mitchell, *Depression Decade: From New Era Through New Deal, 1929–1941* (New York: Rinehart, 1947), p. 186.
3. Quoted in Rixey Smith and Norman Beasley, *Carter Glass: A Biography* (New York: Da Capo, 1972), p. 365.
4. Moley, pp. 247, 248, 252, 253.
5. Moley, p. 256.
6. John C. Culver and John Hyde, *American Dreamer: A Life of Henry A. Wallace* (New York: Norton, 2000), p. 116.
7. Mitchell, pp. 186, 187.
8. Peter H. Irons, *The New Deal Lawyers* (Princeton: Princeton University Press, 1982).
9. Culver and Hyde, pp. 122, 126.
10. Clifton Luttrell, "Government Crop Programs: High Cost and Few Gains," Cato Institute Policy Analysis, July 9, 1985. http://cato.org/pubs/pas/pa056es.html
11. Clifton Luttrell, "Government Crop Programs: High Cost and Few Gains."
12. Mitchell, p. 190.
13. John T. Flynn, *The Roosevelt Myth* (New York: Devin-Adair, 1948), pp. 48, 49.
14. Ellis W. Hawley, *The New Deal and the Problem of Monopoly: A Study in Economic Ambivalence* (Princeton: Princeton University Press, 1966), pp. 193, 194.
15. Joseph P. Lash, *Dealers and Dreamers: A New Look at the New Deal* (New York: Doubleday, 1988), p. 222.
16. Price V. Fishback, William C. Horrace, and Shawn Kantor, "The Impact of New Deal Expenditures on Local Economic Activity: An Examination of Retail Sales, 1929–1939," *National Bureau of Economic Research*, January 2001, p. 20.
17. Robert S. McElvaine, *The Great Depression: America, 1929–1941* (New York: Three Rivers Press, 1993), pp. 262, 263.
18. Mitchell, p. 202.
19. Culver and Hyde, p. 125.
20. Kenneth S. Davis, *FDR: The New Deal Years, 1933–1937* (New York: Random House, 1986), p. 288.
21. Davis, pp. 299, 301.
22. Don Paarlberg, "Tarnished Gold: Fifty Years of New Deal Farm Programs," in *The New Deal and Its Legacy: Critique and Reappraisal*, ed. Robert Eden (Westport, Conn.: Greenwood Press, 1989).

23. Lee J. Alston, "Farm Foreclosures in the United States During the Interwar Period," *Journal of Economic History,* December 1983, p. 889.

24. Mitchell, p. 192.

25. Jesse H. Jones with Edward Angly, *Fifty Billion Dollars: My Thirteen Years with the RFC: 1932–1945* (New York: Macmillan, 1951), p. 93.

26. Michael McMenamin, "Tedious Fraud: Reagan's Farm Policy and the Politics of Agricultural Marketing Orders," *Cato Institute Policy Analysis,* December 6, 1983, p. 2.

27. Tom Clevenger, "A Marketing Order, How It Works," New Mexico State University, http://www.cahe.nmsu.edu/pubs/_z/z-301.html.

28. Congressional Research Service, "Farm Commodity Legislation, Chronology 1933–98," http://www.cnie.org/nle/ag-60.html.

29. Sidney Ratner, *Taxation and Democracy in America* (New York: Octagon, 1980), p. 454.

30. Rexford Tugwell, *The Stricken Land: The Story of Puerto Rico* (Garden City, N.Y.: Doubleday, 1947), p. 24.

31. Jim F. Couch and William F. Shughart II, *The Political Economy of the New Deal* (Northampton, Mass.: Edward Elgar, 1998), pp. 63, 64.

32. William E. Leuchtenburg, *Franklin D. Roosevelt and the New Deal, 1932–1940* (New York: Harper & Row, 1963), pp. 255, 256.

CHAPTER ELEVEN: HOW DID THE TENNESSEE VALLEY AUTHORITY DEPRESS THE TENNESSEE ECONOMY?

1. Richard Lowitt, *George W. Norris: The Triumph of a Progressive, 1933–1944* (Urbana: University of Illinois Press, 1978), p. 167.

2. Richard Lowitt, "George William Norris," in *Franklin D. Roosevelt: His Life and Times, An Encyclopedic View,* ed. Otis L. Graham Jr. and Meghan Robinson Wander (New York: Da Capo, 1985), p. 296.

3. James Grant, *Bernard Baruch: The Adventures of a Wall Street Legend* (New York: Simon & Schuster, 1983), pp. 163, 165, 166.

4. Broadus Mitchell, *Depression Decade: From New Era Through New Deal, 1929–1941* (New York: Rinehart, 1947), p. 341.

5. http://www.tva.gov/heritage/heritagearchive/fdr/.

6. Arthur M. Schlesinger Jr., *The Coming of the New Deal* (Boston: Houghton Mifflin, 1959), pp. 324, 325.

7. Mitchell, p. 354.

8. http://fisher.lib.virginia.edu/cgi-local/censusbin/census/cen.pl.

9. Schlesinger, p. 327.

10. Thomas K. McCraw, *Morgan vs. Lilienthal: The Feud Within the TVA* (Chicago: Loyola University Press, 1970), p. 11.

11. Schlesinger, pp. 328, 330.

12. Willson Whitman, *David Lilienthal: Public Servant in a Power Age* (New York: Henry Holt, 1948), p. 36.
13. McCraw, p. 12.
14. Mitchell, p. 355.
15. McCraw, p. 16.
16. Schlesinger, p. 328.
17. William E. Leuchtenburg, *Franklin D. Roosevelt and the New Deal, 1932–1940* (New York: Harper & Row, 1963), p. 164.
18. Whitman, pp. 44, 55.
19. Leuchtenburg, p. 165.
20. Whitman, pp. 12, 13, 27.
21. Whitman, p. 85.
22. Tennessee Valley Authority Act, http://www.chattanooga.net/cita/TVAuthority Act.html.
23. Whitman, pp. 27, 53.
24. Ellsworth Barnard, "Wendell Lewis Willkie," in *Franklin D. Roosevelt: His Life and Times*, p. 456.
25. Whitman, pp. 24, 27.
26. Whitman, p. 83.
27. William U. Chandler, *The Myth of the TVA: Conservation and Development in the Tennessee Valley, 1933–1980* (Cambridge, Mass.: Ballinger, 1984), p. 213.
28. Bonneville Dam Visitor Center interview, April 30, 2001.
29. Grand Coulee Dam, Public Affairs interview with Craig Sporangial, April 30, 2001.
30. Interview with Ed Best, TVA corporate library, Knoxville, May 1, 2001.
31. Chandler, p. 90.
32. Chandler, pp. 50, 51, 52, 53.
33. Cf. G. Warren Nutter, *The Growth of Industrial Production in the Soviet Union* (Princeton: Princeton University Press, 1962).
34. Chandler, p. 57.
35. Chandler, p. 58.
36. Chandler, pp. 58, 59.
37. Chandler, p. 73.
38. Chandler, pp. 77, 80.
39. Chandler, p. 78.
40. John R. Moore, ed., *The Economic Impact of TVA* (Knoxville: University of Tennessee Press, 1967), p. 115.
41. Interview with Ed Best, TVA corporate library, Knoxville, May 1, 2001.
42. Michael J. McDonald and John Muldowny, *TVA and the Dispossessed: The Resettlement of Population in the Norris Dam Area* (Knoxville: University of Tennessee Press, 1982), p. 264.

CHAPTER TWELVE: WHY DID THE SUPREME COURT
STRIKE DOWN EARLY NEW DEAL LAWS?

1. Clare Cushman, ed., *The Supreme Court Justices: Illustrated Biographies, 1789–1995* (Washington, D.C.: Congressional Quarterly, 1995), pp. 330, 331.
2. Cushman, p. 328.
3. Hadley Arkes, *The Return of George Sutherland: Restoring a Jurisprudence of Natural Rights* (Princeton: Princeton University Press, 1994), pp. 9, 10.
4. Joseph P. Lash, *Dealers and Dreamers: A New Look at the New Deal* (New York: Doubleday, 1988), p. 38.
5. Arkes, p. 13.
6. http://www2.law.cornell.edu/cgi-bin/foliocgi.exe/historic/query=[group+ 261+u!2Es!2E+525!3A]^[group+citemenu!3A]^[level+case+citation!3A]^ [group+notes!3A]/doc/{@121}/hit_headings/words=4/hits_only?
7. Quoted in Sutherland's majority opinion, http://laws.lp.findlaw.com/getcase /us /285/262.html.
8. http://laws.lp.findlaw.com/getcase/us/285/262.html.
9. http://laws.lp.findlaw.com/getcase/us/285/262.html.
10. http://laws.lp.findlaw.com/getcase/us/285/262.html.
11. Quoted in Justice Stephen J. Field's dissenting opinion, the *Slaughter-House Cases,* 83 U.S. 128 (1873).
12. http://www2.law.cornell.edu/cgi-bin/foliocgi.exe/historic/query=[group+ 83+u!2Es!2E+36!3A]^[group+citemenu!3A]^[level+case+citation!3A]^ [group+notes! 3A]/doc/{@361}/hit_headings/words=4/hits_only?
13. Blaisdell's first name and other details from Peter Irons, *A People's History of the Supreme Court* (New York: Viking, 1999), p. 297.
14. http://www2.law.cornell.edu/cgi-bin/foliocgi.exe/historic/query=[group+ 291+u!2Es!2E+502!3A]^[group+citemenu!3A]^[level+case+citation!3A]^ [group+notes! 3A]/doc/{@141}/hit_headings/words=4/hits_only?
15. http://www2.law.cornell.edu/cgi-bin/foliocgi.exe/historic/query=[group+ 291+u!2Es!2E+502!3A]^[group+citemenu!3A]^[level+case+citation!3A]^ [group+notes! 3A]/doc/{@1}/hit_headings/words=4/hits_only?
16. From McReynolds's separate opinion: "In New York, there are twelve million possible consumers of milk; 130,000 farms produce it. The average daily output approximates 9,500,000 quarts. For ten or fifteen years prior to 1929 or 1930, the per capita consumption steadily increased; so did the supply." "Realizing the marked improvement in milk quality, the public has tended to increase its consumption of this commodity." "In the past two years, the per capita consumption has fallen off, [possibly] 10 percent." http://www2 .law.cornell.edu/cgi-bin/foliocgi.exe/historic/query=[group+291+u!2Es!2E+ 502!3A]^[group+citemenu!3A]^[level+case+citation!3A]^[group+notes!3A]/ doc/{@1}/hit_headings /words=4/hits_only?

17. http://www2.law.cornell.edu/cgi-bin/foliocgi.exe/historic/query=[group+ 291+u!2Es!2E+502!3A]^[group+citemenu!3A]^[level+case+citation!3A]^ [group+notes! 3A]/doc/{@1}/hit_headings/words=4/hits_only?

18. Congressional Limitation of Executive Orders, Hearing Before the Subcommittee on Commercial and Administrative Law, of the Committee on the Judiciary, House of Representatives, October 28, 1999, p. 37, http://commdocs .house.gov /committees/judiciary/hju63865.000/hju63865_0.HTM.

19. http://newdeal.feri.org/court/293US388.htm.

20. http://newdeal.feri.org/court/293US388.htm.

21. http://newdeal.feri.org/court/293US388.htm.

22. http://www.tourolaw.edu/patch/Schechter/#c1.

23. http://www.tourolaw.edu/patch/Schechter/#c1.

24. http://www.tourolaw.edu/patch/Schechter/#c1.

25. Box 22, Frankfurter mss., L.C., quoted in Frank Freidel, *Franklin D. Roosevelt: A Rendezvous with Destiny* (Boston: Little, Brown, 1990), p. 161.

26. Quoted in Samuel I. Rosenman, *Working with Roosevelt* (New York: Harper, 1952), p. 111.

27. Richard K. Vedder and Lowell E. Gallaway, *Out of Work: Unemployment and Government in Twentieth-Century America* (New York: New York University Press, 1997), pp. 133, 134.

28. http://newdeal.feri.org/court/298US238.htm.

29. http://newdeal.feri.org/court/298US238.htm.

30. http://newdeal.feri.org/court/298US238.htm.

31. http://newdeal.feri.org/court/298US238.htm.

32. http://newdeal.feri.org/court/298US238.htm.

33. Kenneth S. Davis, *FDR: The New Deal Years, 1933–1937* (New York: Random House, 1986), p. 615.

34. http://newdeal.feri.org/court/298US238.htm.

35. http://newdeal.feri.org/court/298US238.htm.

36. http://www2.law.cornell.edu/cgi-bin/foliocgi.exe/historic/query=[jump!3A! 27297+u!2Es!2E+61!27]/doc/{@16928}/hit_headings/words=4/hits_only?

37. http://www2.law.cornell.edu/cgi-bin/foliocgi.exe/historic/query=[jump!3A! 27297+u!2Es!2E+61!27]/doc/{@16928}/hit_headings/words=4/hits_only?

38. http://www2.law.cornell.edu/cgi-bin/foliocgi.exe/historic/query=[jump!3A! 27297+u!2Es!2E+61!27]/doc/{@16928}/hit_headings/words=4/hits_only?

39. http://www2.law.cornell.edu/cgi-bin/foliocgi.exe/historic/query=[jump!3A! 27297+u!2Es!2E+61!27]/doc/{@16928}/hit_headings/words=4/hits_only?

CHAPTER THIRTEEN: HOW DID SOCIAL SECURITY CONTRIBUTE TO HIGHER UNEMPLOYMENT?

1. A. J. P. Taylor, *Bismarck: The Man and the Statesman* (London: Hamish Hamilton, 1955), p. 203.

2. Carolyn L. Weaver, *The Crisis in Social Security: Economic and Political Origins* (Durham, N.C.: Duke Press Policy Studies, 1982), p. 33.

3. Peter J. Ferrara and Michael Tanner, *A New Deal for Social Security* (Washington, D.C.: Cato Institute, 1998), p. 15.

4. Weaver, pp. 35, 36.

5. Weaver, pp. 42, 43, 46, 47.

6. Weaver, p. 63.

7. Weaver, p. 64.

8. Paul H. Douglas, *Social Security in the United States: An Analysis and Appraisal of the Federal Social Security Act* (New York: Whittlesey House, 1936), pp. 7, 9.

9. "The Townsend Plan in Brief," in *Old Age Revolving Pensions,* http://www.ssa.gov/history/towns5.html.

10. "Analysis of Plan," in *Old Age Revolving Pensions,* http://www.ssa.gov/history/townbrief.html

11. "Analysis of Plan," in *Old Age Revolving Pensions,* http://www.ssa.gov/history/townbrief.html

12. Douglas, pp. 9–12.

13. P. J. O'Brien, *Forward with Roosevelt* (Chicago: John Winston, 1936), pp. 92, 93.

14. Statement of Samuel W. Reyburn of the National Retail Dry Goods Association, p. 762, http://www.ssa.gov/history/pdf/hr35reyburn.pdf.

15. Statement of Lloyd Peck, General Manager of the National Laundryowners Association, Senate Finance Committee, 1935, p. 918.

16. Statement of James Emery of the National Association of Manufacturers, January 21, 1935, p. 1033, http://www.ssa.gov/history/pdf/hr35emery.pdf.

17. Statement of James Emery of the National Association of Manufacturers, January 21, 1935, p. 1036, http://www.ssa.gov/history/pdf/hr35emery.pdf.

18. Frank Freidel, *Franklin D. Roosevelt: A Rendezvous with Destiny* (Boston: Little, Brown, 1990), p. 150.

19. Statement of W. R. Williamson, Assistant Actuary, Travelers Insurance Co., Hartford, Conn., House Ways and Means Committee, January 1935, pp. 1013, 1014, http://www.ssa.gov/history/pdf/hr35williamson.pdf.

20. Statement of E. E. Witte, Executive Director, Committee on Economic Security, January 21, 1935, pp. 44–45.

21. Statement of W. R. Williamson, Assistant Actuary, Travelers Insurance Co., Hartford, Conn., House Ways and Means Committee, January 1935, p. 1014, http://www.ssa.gov/history/pdf/hr35williamson.pdf.

22. Weaver, p. 79.

23. Congressional Record, vol. 79, part 9, June 17, 1935, p. 9442.

24. Weaver, pp. 90, 91.

25. Quoted in Weaver, p. 111.

26. Social Security Board, "Notice, Deductions from Pay Start Jan. 1" (poster).
27. Ferrara and Tanner, p. 25.
28. Abraham Epstein, "Social Security Under the New Deal," *Nation,* September 4, 1935, p. 261.
29. Albert Linton, "Old-Age Security for Everybody," *Atlantic Monthly,* 1936.
30. John T. Flynn, "The Social Security Reserve Swindle," *Harper's,* February 1939.
31. *American Mercury,* December 1937, p. 390.
32. Robert S. McElvaine, *The Great Depression: America, 1929–1941* (New York: Three Rivers Press, 1993), p. 257.

CHAPTER FOURTEEN: HOW DID NEW DEAL LABOR
LAWS THROW PEOPLE OUT OF WORK?

1. Howard Dickman, *Industrial Democracy in America: Ideological Origins of National Labor Relations Policy* (LaSalle, Ill.: Open Court, 1987), p. 225.
2. Sylvester Petro, "Injunctions and Labor Disputes, 1880–1932," *Wake Forest Law Review,* June 1978, pp. 341–576.
3. Quoted in *Hitchman Coal & Coke Co. v Mitchell,* 245 U.S. 229 (1917).
4. *Hitchman Coal & Coke Co. v Mitchell,* 245 U.S. 229 (1917).
5. *Hitchman Coal & Coke Co. v Mitchell,* 245 U.S. 229 (1917).
6. *Texas and New Orleans Railroad Company v Brotherhood of Railway and Steamship Clerks,* 281 U.S. 548 (1930).
7. Morgan O. Reynolds, *Power and Privilege: Labor Unions in America* (New York: Universe Books, 1984), pp. 98, 99.
8. Reynolds, *Power and Privilege,* pp. 97, 100.
9. Morgan O. Reynolds, "An Economic Analysis of the Norris-LaGuardia Act, the Wagner Act, and the Labor Representation Industry," *Journal of Libertarian Studies,* Summer–Fall 1982, p. 245. Originally a paper presented at the 1982 meetings of the Public Choice Society of San Antonio and the 1982 meetings of the Western Economic Association in Los Angeles. Displayed at http://www .libertarianstudies.org/journals/jls/pdfs/6_3/6_3_3.pdf.
10. Dickman, p. 260.
11. Dickman, p. 261, 264, 265.
12. Quoted in George Martin, *Madam Secretary: Frances Perkins* (Boston: Houghton Mifflin, 1976), p. 381.
13. Marc Landy, "Robert Ferdinand Wagner," in *Franklin D. Roosevelt: His Life and Times, An Encyclopedic View,* ed. Otis L. Graham Jr. and Meghan Robinson Wander (New York: Da Capo, 1985), p. 439.
14. Martin, p. 381.
15. Jerry N. Hess, "Oral History Interview with Leon H. Keyserling," Truman Presidential Museum and Library, May 3, 1971, http://www.trumanlibrary .org/oralhist/keyserl1.htm.

16. U.S. Code, Title 29 (Labor), Chapter 7 (Labor-Management Relations), Subchapter II (National Labor Relations), Section 151, http://www4.law.cornell.edu/uscode/29/151.html.

17. U.S. Code, Title 29 (Labor), Chapter 7 (Labor-Management Relations), Subchapter II (National Labor Relations), Section 151, http://www4.law.cornell.edu /uscode/29/151.html.

18. U.S. Code, Title 29 (Labor), Chapter 7 (Labor-Management Relations), Subchapter II (National Labor Relations), Section 158, http://www4.law.cornell.edu /uscode/29/151.html.

19. *National Labor Relations Board v Mackay Radio,* 304 U.S. 333 (1938).

20. *National Labor Relations Board v Mackay Radio,* 304 U.S. 333 (1938).

21. David Kendrick, *Violence: Organized Labor's Unique Privilege* (Springfield, Va.: National Institute for Labor Relations Research, 1996).

22. Nelson Lichtenstein, *The Most Dangerous Man in Detroit: Walter Reuther and the Fate of American Labor* (New York: Basic, 1995), p. 63.

23. Lichtenstein, pp. 67, 69, 70, 72.

24. Melvyn Dubofsky and Warren Van Tine, *John L. Lewis: A Biography* (New York: Quadrangle, 1977), pp. 255, 257, 260.

25. Dubofsky and Van Tine, pp. 261, 264, 265.

26. Dubofsky and Van Tine, pp. 266, 267, 268.

27. Dubofsky and Van Tine, p. pp. 258, 268, 270.

28. Lichtenstein, p. 107.

29. William E. Leuchtenburg, *Franklin D. Roosevelt and the New Deal, 1932–1940* (New York: Harper & Row, 1963), p. 240.

30. Roger B. Freeman, "Spurts in Union Growth: Defining Moments and Social Processes," in *The Defining Moment: The Great Depression and the American Economy in the Twentieth Century,* ed. Michael D. Bordo, Claudia Goldin, and Eugene N. White (Chicago: University of Chicago Press, 1998), p. 281.

31. Lichtenstein, pp. 106, 107, 108.

32. Lichtenstein, p. 120.

33. Henry Kraus, *Heroes of Unwritten Story: The UAW, 1934–1939* (Urbana: University of Illinois Press, 1993), p. 303.

34. Lichtenstein, pp. 121, 122, 132, 135, 136.

35. Lichtenstein, pp. 137, 138.

36. Allan Nevins and Frank Ernest Hill, *Ford: Decline and Rebirth, 1933–1962* (New York: Scribner, 1963), pp. 159, 161, 162.

37. Nevins and Hill, pp. 164, 166.

38. Frank Freidel, *Franklin D. Roosevelt: A Rendezvous with Destiny* (Boston: Little, Brown, 1990), p. 242.

39. Reynolds, "An Economic Analysis," p. 249.

40. Clarence B. Carson, *The Welfare State, 1929–1985* (Wadley, Ala.: American Textbook Committee, 1986), p. 76.

41. Reynolds, *Power and Privilege,* p. 112.

42. Richard K. Vedder and Lowell E. Gallaway, *Out of Work: Unemployment and Government in Twentieth-Century America* (New York: New York University Press, 1997), pp. 131, 132.
43. Thomas E. Hall and J. David Ferguson, *The Great Depression: An International Disaster of Perverse Economic Policies* (Ann Arbor: University of Michigan, 1998), p. 144.
44. David E. Bernstein, *Only One Place of Redress: African Americans, Labor Regulations, and the Courts from Reconstruction to the New Deal* (Durham, N.C.: Duke University Press, 2001), p. 95.
45. Bernstein, p. 95.
46. Bernstein, p. 96.

CHAPTER FIFTEEN: HOW DID FDR'S SUPREME COURT SUBVERT INDIVIDUAL LIBERTY?

1. Frank Freidel, *Franklin D. Roosevelt: A Rendezvous with Destiny* (Boston: Little, Brown, 1990), pp. 163, 194, 222, 227, 228.
2. "Fireside Chat on the Reorganization of the Judiciary," March 9, 1937, http://www.mhric.org/fdr/chat9.html.
3. "Constitutional Immorality, Radio Address by Hon. Carter Glass, of Virginia, on March 29, 1937," in Rixey Smith and Norman Beasley, *Carter Glass: A Biography* (New York: Da Capo, 1972), p. 496.
4. Freidel, pp. 230, 231.
5. James A. Farley, *Jim Farley's Story: The Roosevelt Years* (New York: Whittlesey House, 1948), p. 95.
6. Quoted in Farley, p. 83.
7. Robert H. Jackson, *The Struggle for Judicial Supremacy: A Study of a Crisis in American Power Politics* (New York: Knopf, 1941), p. 212.
8. Morgan O. Reynolds, *Power and Privilege: Labor Unions in America* (New York: Universe Books, 1984), p. 100.
9. Richard A. Epstein, *Takings: Private Property and the Power of Eminent Domain* (Cambridge, Mass.: Harvard University Press, 1985), p. 310.
10. Roger Pilon, "A Government of Limited Powers," in *Cato Handbook for Congress* (Washington, D.C.: Cato Institute, 1995), p. 33.
11. Statement of Roger Pilon, Ph.D., J.D., Senior Fellow and Director, Center for Constitutional Studies, Cato Institute, Washington, D.C., Before the Subcommittee on Courts and Intellectual Property, Committee on the Judiciary, United States House of Representatives, May 15, 1997.

CHAPTER SIXTEEN: HOW DID NEW DEAL POLICIES CAUSE THE DEPRESSION OF 1938?

1. Marriner S. Eccles, *Beckoning Frontiers: Public and Personal Recollections* (New York: Knopf, 1951), p. 288.

2. Allan H. Meltzer, "In the Back Seat, 1933–1941," unpublished manuscript, pp. 119, 121.

3. Lester V. Chandler, *America's Greatest Depression, 1929–1941* (New York: Harper & Row, 1970), p. 180.

4. Milton Friedman and Anna Jacobson Schwartz, *A Monetary History of the United States, 1867–1960* (Princeton: Princeton University Press, 1963), p. 526.

5. Jordan A. Schwarz, *The New Dealers: Power Politics in the Age of Roosevelt* (New York: Knopf, 1993), p. 174.

6. *Historical Statistics of the United States: Colonial Times to 1970* (Washington, D.C.: U.S. Department of Commerce, 1975), p. 948.

7. Frank Freidel, *Franklin D. Roosevelt: A Rendezvous with Destiny* (Boston: Little, Brown, 1990), p. 251.

8. Ted Morgan, *FDR: A Biography* (New York: Simon & Schuster, 1985), p. 484.

9. Kenneth D. Roose, *The Economics of Recession and Revival: An Interpretation of 1937–38* (New York: Archon Books, 1969), p. 210.

10. T. H. Watkins, *The Great Depression: America in the 1930s* (Boston: Little, Brown, 1993), p. 310.

11. Mark H. Leff, *The Limits of Symbolic Reform: The New Deal and Taxation, 1933–1939* (Cambridge: Cambridge University Press, 1984), p. 209.

12. *Historical Statistics of the United States: Colonial Times to 1970,* p. 126.

13. Leff, p. 209.

14. Meltzer, p. 125.

15. Roose, p. 12.

16. H. Gregg Lewis, *An Analysis of Changes in the Demand for Steel and in Steel Prices, 1936–1939,* United States Steel Corporation, 1939, cited in Roose, p. 10.

17. Joseph Schumpeter, *Business Cycles: A Theoretical, Historical, and Statistical Analysis of the Capitalist Process,* 2 vols. (1939; reprint, Philadelphia: Porcupine Press, 1989), p. 419.

18. Freidel, p. 254.

19. Watkins, p. 311.

20. Freidel, p. 256.

21. David E. Bernstein, *Only One Place of Redress: African Americans, Labor Regulations, and the Courts from Reconstruction to the New Deal* (Durham, N.C.: Duke University Press, 2001), p. 99.

22. Morgan, p. 494.

23. Bernstein, pp. 100, 101.

24. Bernstein, p. 101.

25. Meltzer, pp. 126, 127, 128, 136, 137, 138.

CHAPTER SEVENTEEN: WHY DID NEW DEAL LAWYERS DISRUPT COMPANIES EMPLOYING MILLIONS?

1. James A. Farley, *Jim Farley's Story: The Roosevelt Years* (New York: Whittlesey House, 1948), p. 101.
2. Ellis W. Hawley, *The New Deal and the Problem of Monopoly: A Study in Economic Ambivalence* (Princeton: Princeton University Press, 1966), pp. 409, 411.
3. Joseph P. Lash, *Dealers and Dreamers: A New Look at the New Deal* (New York: Doubleday, 1988), pp. 321, 324, 325.
4. Jordan A. Schwarz, *The New Dealers: Power Politics in the Age of Roosevelt* (New York: Knopf, 1993), p. 161.
5. Thurman Arnold, *Fair Fights and Foul: A Dissenting Lawyer's Life* (New York: Harcourt, Brace & World, 1965), p. 138.
6. Hawley, p. 423.
7. Douglas A. Irwin, "From Smoot-Hawley to Reciprocal Trade Agreements: Changing the Course of U.S. Trade Policy in the 1930s," in *The Defining Moment: The Great Depression and the American Economy in the Twentieth Century,* ed. Michael D. Bordo, Claudia Goldin, and Eugene N. White (Chicago: University of Chicago Press, 1998), p. 344.
8. Franklin Pierce, *The Tariff and the Trusts* (New York: Macmillan, 1913), p. 51.
9. Mayflower Broadcasting Co., 8 FCC 330, 340 (1940).
10. The organization has bragged about doing so on its website, http://www.progressivegrocer.com/gma/history.htm.
11. Civil Aeronautics Board, Investigation of Nonscheduled Air Services, 6 CAB 1049 (1946).
12. Sam Peltzman, "CAB: Freedom from Competition," *New Individualist Review,* Spring 1963, pp. 16, 17.
13. Frank Freidel, *Franklin D. Roosevelt: A Rendezvous with Destiny* (Boston: Little, Brown, 1990), p. 257.
14. Hawley, pp. 429, 430, 431.
15. Charles E. Mueller, "Restoring America's Industrial Competitiveness," *Antitrust Law and Economics Review,* vol. 23, no. 4, http://www.home.mpinet.net/cmueller /ii-06.html.
16. Hawley, p. 434.
17. Mueller, http:L//www.home.mp9inet.net/mueller/ii-06.html.
18. Randolph E. Paul, *Taxation in the United States* (Boston: Little, Brown, 1954), p. 239.
19. Arnold, p. 140.
20. Sally Whitney, "Regulatory Battle," *Best's,* February 2000, http://www.bestreview.com/archives/2000-02/regulatory.html.
21. Hawley, pp. 433, 448, 451.

22. Opinion of Justice William O. Douglas, *U.S. v Socony-Vacuum Oil Co.*, 310 U.S. 150 (1940), X.

23. Opinion of Justice William O. Douglas, *U.S. v Socony-Vacuum Oil Co.*, 310 U.S. 150 (1940), II.

24. Opinion of Justice William O. Douglas, *U.S. v Socony-Vacuum Oil Co.*, 310 U.S. 150 (1940), n. 1.

25. Opinion of Justice William O. Douglas, *U.S. v Socony-Vacuum Oil Co.*, 310 U.S. 150 (1940).

26. Hawley, p. 486.

27. Hawley, p. 448.

28. Quoted in Hawley, pp. 444, 445.

29. George J. Stigler, *Five Lectures on Economic Problems* (London: Longmans, Green, 1949), pp. 46–65.

30. John Lintner and J. Keith Butters, "Effects of Taxes on Concentration," in *Business Concentration and Price Policy: A Conference of the Universities–National Bureau Committee for Economic Research*, ed. George J. Stigler (Princeton: Princeton University Press, 1955), p. 239.

31. G. Warren Nutter and Henry Adler Einhorn, *Enterprise Monopoly in the United States: 1899–1958* (New York: Columbia University Press, 1969), pp. 25, 30.

32. Nutter and Einhorn, p. 33.

33. Nutter and Einhorn, p. 90.

34. Milton Friedman, *Capitalism and Freedom* (Chicago: University of Chicago Press, 1962), p. 122.

CHAPTER EIGHTEEN: WHAT HAVE BEEN THE
EFFECTS OF THE NEW DEAL SINCE THE 1930s?

1. Randolph E. Paul, *Taxation in the United States* (Boston: Little, Brown, 1954), pp. 378, 380, 383.

2. http://www.ibiblio.org/pha/policy/1942/420427b.html.

3. Paul, pp. 272, 280, 281, 301, 302.

4. http://nces.ed.gov/pub2002/digest2001/tables/dt035.asp.

5. http://www.ibiblio.org/pha/policy/1942/421003a.html.

6. Paul, p. 303.

7. Paul, pp. 331, 334.

8. Jerry Tempalski, "Revenue Effects of Major Tax Bills," Office of Tax Analysis, U.S. Treasury Department, December 1998, p. 9.

9. John F. Witte, *The Politics and Development of the Federal Income Tax* (Madison: University of Wisconsin Press, 1985), p. 159.

10. Tempalski, p. 10.

11. Tempalski, p. 11.

12. Timothy Curry and Lynn Shibut, "The Cost of the Savings and Loan Crisis: Truth and Consequences," *FDIC Banking Review*, Fall 2000, p. 26.

13. Jeffrey Rogers Hummel, "Privatize Deposit Insurance," *Freeman*, July 1989.

14. George J. Benston and George G. Kaufman, "Regulating Bank Safety and Performance," in *Restructuring Banking and Financial Services in America*, ed. William S. Haraf and Rose Marie Kushmeider (Washington, D.C.: American Enterprise Institute, 1988), p. 69.

15. Anna Jacobson Schwartz, "Financial Stability and the Federal Safety Net," in *Restructuring Banking and Financial Services in America*, pp. 50, 51.

16. Schwartz, pp. 54, 55.

17. Jith Jayaratne and Philip E. Strahan, "The Benefits of Branching Deregulation," *Regulation*, vol. 22, no. 1.

18. *Personal Perspective* (LJF Insurance Services, Southport, Conn.), p. 3.

19. Gregory Bresiger, "Insecure Promise," *Financial Planning*, November 1999, p. 189.

20. Peter J. Ferrara and Michael Tanner, *A New Deal for Social Security* (Washington, D.C.: Cato Institute, 1998), pp. 45–46.

21. *Flemming v Nestor*, 363 U.S. 603, decided on June 20, 1960, and displayed at http://www.fedworld.gov/cgi-bin/waisgate?waisdocid=3856319285+2+0+0&waisactoin=retrieve.

22. Marshall N. Carter and William G. Shipman, *Promises to Keep: Saving Social Security's Dream* (Washington, D.C.: Regnery, 1996), p. 13.

23. Milton Friedman, "Second Lecture," in Wilbur J. Cohen and Milton Friedman, *Social Security: Universal or Selective* (Washington, D.C.: American Enterprise Institute, 1972), p. 35.

24. Constantijn W. A. Panis and Lee Lillard, "Socioeconomic Differentials in the Return to Social Security," RAND Corporation Working Paper Series no. 96-05, February 1996, p. 20.

25. William W. Beach and Gareth E. Davis, "Social Security's Rate of Return," Heritage Center for Data Analysis, January 15, 1998, p. 5.

26. Robert Woodson Sr., "Less Visible Burdens of Social Security," *Washington Times*, November 5, 1999, displayed at http://www.teleport.com/%7Eprf/ss/nov99/wt11-5 .html.

27. Jeremy J. Siegel, *Stocks for the Long Run: The Definitive Guide to Financial Market Returns and Long-Term Investment Strategies* (New York: McGraw-Hill, 1998), p. 5.

28. "Milk Marketing Order Statistics," Agricultural Marketing Service, U.S. Department of Agriculture, http://www.ams.usda.gov/dairy/mib/quant_util_reg _milk.htm.

29. See James Bovard, *The Farm Fiasco* (San Francisco: Institute for Contemporary Studies, 1989), p. 34.

30. Ann Crittenden, "Growers' Power in Marketing Under Attack," *New York Times*, March 25, 1981, p. 1.

31. "Ag Marketing Orders May Again Be Biggest Loser," Yuba Sutter Agribusiness, *Business to Business Journal*, 1997, http://www.otn.net/btb/agribiz/agmktg.htm.

32. Bovard, p. 45.

33. Richard Munson, "Restructure the TVA: Why the Tennessee Valley Authority Must Be Reformed," Northeast/Midwest Institute, http://www.nemw.org/tvareport.htm

34. Munson, http://www.nemw.org/tvareport.htm.

35. Munson, http://www.nemw.org/tvareport.htm.

36. William U. Chandler, *The Myth of the TVA: Conservation and Development in the Tennessee Valley, 1933–1980* (Cambridge, Mass.: Ballinger, 1984), pp. 68, 69.

37. Dominick T. Armentano, "Seven Myths of Antitrust," *Regulation*, no. 2, 1997, http://www.cato.org/pubs/regulation/reg20n2a.html.

38. Fred S. McChesney, "Antitrust," in *The Fortune Encyclopedia of Economics*, ed. David R. Henderson (New York: Warner, 1993), p. 388.

39. Alan Greenspan, "Antitrust," in *Capitalism: The Unknown Ideal*, ed. Ayn Rand (New York: New American Library, 1962), p. 56.

40. "The Golden Age," *Gold Newsletter*, November 1996, http://blanchard.stockscape.com/archive/96nov1-0.htm.

41. Richard A. Epstein, "The Mistakes of 1937," *George Mason University Law Review*, Winter 1988, pp. 5–6.

CHAPTER NINETEEN: WHAT CAN WE LEARN
FROM FDR'S MISTAKES?

1. John T. Flynn, "Mr. Hopkins and Mr. Roosevelt," *Yale Review*, June 1939, reprinted in *Forgotten Lessons: Selected Essays of John T. Flynn*, ed. Gregory P. Pavlik (Irvington-on-Hudson, N.Y.: Foundation for Economic Education, 1996), p. 42.

2. Fernand Braudel, *The Wheels of Commerce* (New York: Harper & Row, 1979), p. 49.

3. David S. Landes, *The Unbound Prometheus: Technological Change and Industrial Development in Western Europe from 1750 to the Present* (Cambridge: Cambridge University Press, 1988), p. 83.

4. Douglass C. North and Robert Paul Thomas, *The Rise of the Western World: A New Economic History* (Cambridge: Cambridge University Press, 1973), pp. 1, 157.

5. Gary Dean Best, *Pride, Prejudice, and Politics: Roosevelt Versus Recovery, 1933–1938* (New York: Praeger, 1991), p. x.

6. Jeffrey Rogers Hummel, "Martin Van Buren: The American Gladstone," in *Reassessing the Presidency,* ed. John V. Denson (Auburn, Ala.: Mises Institute, 2001), p. 191.

7. *Historical Statistics of the United States: Colonial Times to 1970* (Washington, D.C.: U.S. Department of Commerce, 1975), 335-338.

8. Milton Friedman and Anna Jacobson Schwartz, *A Monetary History of the United States, 1867–1960* (Princeton: Princeton University Press, 1963), p. 91.

9. Friedman and Schwartz, p. 92.

10. H. Paul Jeffers, *An Honest President: The Life and Times of Grover Cleveland* (New York: William Morrow, 2000), p. 137.

11. Jeffers, p. 151.

12. Friedman and Schwartz, p. 94.

13. Friedman and Schwartz, p. 93.

14. Friedman and Schwartz, p. 232.

15. Paul Johnson, *Modern Times: The World from the Twenties to the Eighties* (New York: Harper & Row, 1983), p. 216.

16. George J. Benston and George G. Kaufman, "Regulating Bank Safety and Performance," in *Restructuring Banking and Financial Services in America,* ed. William S. Haraf and Rose Marie Kushmeider (Washington, D.C.: American Enterprise Institute, 1988), p. 64.

SELECTED
BIBLIOGRAPHY

ARTICLES AND PAMPHLETS

Alston, Lee J. "Farm Foreclosures in the United States During the Interwar Period." *Journal of Economic History*, December 1983, pp. 885–902.

Amberson, William R. "The New Deal for Sharecroppers." In *New Deal Thought*, ed. Howard Zinn. Indianapolis: Bobbs-Merrill, 1966, pp. 239–243.

Anderson, B., and J. Butkiewicz. "Money, Spending, and the Great Depression." *Southern Economic Journal*, October 1980, pp. 388–403.

Anderson, Gary M., William F. Shughart II, and Robert D. Tollison. "A Public Choice Theory of the Great Contraction." *Public Choice*, October 1988, pp. 3–23.

Anderson, Gary M., and Robert D. Tollison, "Congressional Influence and Patterns of New Deal Spending, 1933–1939." *Journal of Law and Economics*, April 1991, pp. 161–175.

Arrington, Leonard J. "The New Deal in the West: A Preliminary Statistical Inquiry." *Pacific Historical Review*, August 1969, pp. 311–316.

———. "Western Agriculture and the New Deal." *Agricultural History*, October 1970, pp. 337–353.

Baird, Charles W. "Freedom and American Labor Relations Law, 1946–1996." *Freeman*, May 1996.

Ballantine, A. A. "When All the Banks Closed." *Harvard Business Review*, March 1948, pp. 129–143.

Bennett, James T., and Jason E. Taylor. "Labor Unions: Victims of their Political Success?" *Journal of Labor Research*, Spring 2001, pp. 271–273.

Bernstein, Irving. "Public Policy and the American Worker, 1933–45." *Monthly Labor Review*, October 1976, pp. 11–17.

Best, Gary Dean. "FDR's War Against Recovery." *Navigator*, July–August 2000, pp. 8–12.

Bradley, Christine M. "A Historical Perspective on Deposit Insurance Coverage." *FDIC Banking Review*, Fall 2000, pp. 1–25.

Butkeiwicz, James L. "The Impact of a Lender of Last Resort During the Great Depression: The Case of the Reconstruction Finance Corporation." *Explorations in Economic History*, April 1995, pp. 197–216.

Calomiris, Charles W. "Financial Factors in the Great Depression." *Journal of Economic Perspectives*, Spring 1993, pp. 61–85.

Calomiris, Charles W., and G. Gorton. "The Origin of Banking Panics: Models, Facts, and Bank Regulations." In *Financial Markets and Financial Crises*, ed. R. Glenn Hubbard, pp. 109–173. Chicago: University of Chicago Press, 1991.

Calomiris, Charles W., and Joseph R. Mason. "Causes of U.S. Bank Distress During the Great Depression." National Bureau of Economic Research Working Paper W7919, September 2000.

———. "Contagion and Bank Failures During the Great Depression: The June 1932 Chicago Banking Panic." National Bureau of Economic Research Working Paper W4934, November 1994.

Carosso, Vincent. "Washington and Wall Street: The New Deal and Investment Bankers, 1933–1940." *Business History Review*, vol. 64, 1970, pp. 425–445.

Kam Hon Chu. "Is Free Banking More Prone to Bank Failures Than Regulated Banking?" *Cato Journal*, vol. 16, no. 1.

Cole, Harold L., and Lee E. Ohanian. "The Great Depression in the United States from a Neoclassical Perspective." *Federal Reserve Bank of Minneapolis Quarterly Review*, Winter 1999, pp. 2–24.

Curry, Timothy, and Lynn Shibut. "The Cost of the Savings and Loan Crisis: Truth and Consequences." *FDIC Banking Review*, Fall 2000, pp. 26–35.

Darby, Michael R. "Three-and-a-Half Million U.S. Employees Have Been Mislaid: or, An Explanation of Unemployment, 1934–1941." *Journal of Political Economy*, February 1976, pp. 1–16.

De Long, J. Bradford. "'Liquidation' Cycles and the Great Depression." Unpublished draft.

Diamond, D., and P. Dybvig. "Bank Runs, Liquidity, and Deposit Insurance." *Journal of Political Economy*, June 1983, pp. 401–419.

DiLorenzo, Thomas. "The Federal Reserve and Political Corruption." *Free Market*, May 2000, pp. 1, 2.

Edwards, George W. "The Myth of the Security Affiliate." *Journal of the American Statistical Association*, vol. 37, 1942, pp. 225–232.

Epstein, Richard A. "The Mistakes of 1937." *George Mason University Law Review*, Winter 1988.

———. "The Proper Scope of the Commerce Power." *Virginia Law Review*, 1987.

Field, Alexander James. "Uncontrolled Land Development and the Duration of the Depression in the United States." *Journal of Economic History*, December 1992, pp. 785–805.

Fishback, Price V., William C. Horrace, and Shawn Kantor. "The Impact of New Deal Expenditures on Local Economic Activity: An Examination of Retail Sales, 1929–1939." *National Bureau of Economic Research*, February 2001.

Flood, Mark D. "The Great Deposit Insurance Debate." *Federal Reserve Bank of St. Louis Review*, July–August 1992, pp. 51–77.

Friedman, Milton, and Anna Jacobson Schwartz. "The Failure of the Bank of the United States: A Reappraisal: A Reply." *Explorations in Economic History*, April 1986, pp. 199–204.

Garraty, John A. "The New Deal, Nationalism Socialism, and the Great Depression." *American Historical Review*, October 1973, pp. 907–944.

Garrison, Roger W. "The Great Depression Revisited." *Independent Review*, Spring 1999, pp. 595–603.

Hamilton, D. "The Causes of the Banking Panic of 1930: Another View." *Journal of Southern History*, November 1985, pp. 581–608.

Hamilton, James D. "Monetary Factors in the Great Depression." *Journal of Monetary Economics*, vol. 19, 1987, pp. 145–169.

Hart, David M. "Antitrust and Technological Innovation in the U.S.: Ideas, Institutions, Decisions, and Impacts, 1890–2000." Unpublished paper.

Higgs, Robert. "How FDR Made the Depression Worse." *Free Market*, February 1995.

———. "Regime Uncertainty: Why the Great Depression Lasted So Long and Why Prosperity Resumed After the War." *Independent Review*, Spring 1997, pp. 561–591.

———. "The Welfare State: Promising Protection in an Age of Anxiety." *Freeman*, May 1996.

High, Stanley. "The WPA: Politicians' Playground." *Current History*, May 1939, pp. 23–25.

Hines, James R., Jr., and Richard H. Thaler. "The Flypaper Effect." *Journal of Economic Perspectives*, Fall 1995, pp. 217–226.

Hummel, Jeffrey Rogers. "Privatize Deposit Insurance." *Freeman*, July 1989.

Jacklin, C., and S. Bhattacharya. "Distinguishing Panics and Information-Based Bank Runs." *Journal of Political Economy*, June 1988, pp. 568–592.

Jarrell, Gregg A. "Change at the Exchange: The Causes and Effects of Deregulation." *Journal of Law and Economics*, October 1984, pp. 273–312.

———. "The Economic Effects of Federal Regulation of the Market for New Security Issues." *Journal of Law and Economics*, December 1981, pp. 613–675.

Jayaratne, Jith, and Philip E. Strahan. "The Benefits of Branching Deregulation." *Regulation*, vol. 22, no. 1.

Kaufman, George G. "Bank Failures, Systemic Risk, and Bank Regulation." *Cato Journal*, Spring–Summer 1996.

———. "Bank Runs: Causes, Benefits, and Costs." *Cato Journal*, Winter 1988, pp. 559–587.

Kesaris, Paul, and Joan Sherryl. *New Deal Economic Policies: F.D.R. and the Congress, 1933–1938*. Fiche collection. Bethesda, Md.: University Publications of America, 1990.

Kroszner, Randall S. "The Political Economy of the Reconstruction Finance Corporation's Bail-Out of the U.S. Banking System During the Great Depression." Unpublished draft.

Kroszner, Randall S., and Raghurm G. Rajan. "Is the Glass-Steagall Act Justified?" *American Economic Review*, September 1994.

Lee, Dwight R. *The Inflationary Impact of Labor Unions*. College Station, Tex.: Center for Education and Research in Free Enterprise, 1979.

Lucas, Robert E., Jr. "Review of Milton Friedman and Anna J. Schwartz, 'A Monetary History of the United States, 1867–1960.'" *Journal of Monetary Economics*, 1994, pp. 5–16.

Macey, Jonathan R. "Special Interest Groups Legislation and the Judicial Function: The Dilemma of Glass-Steagall." *Emory Law Journal*, Winter 1984, pp. 1–40.

Mason, Joseph R. "Do Lender of Last Resort Policies Matter? The Effects of Reconstruction Finance Corporation Assistance to Banks During the Great Depression." *Journal of Financial Services Research*, August 2001.

———. "What Do We Know About Asset Liquidation Rates? Evidence from Failed Commercial Banks During the 1930s and 1990s." Unpublished manuscript. January 2000.

Mason, Joseph R., Ali Anari, and James Kolari. "The Role of Failed-Bank Liquidation Rates in the Propagation of the U.S. Great Depression." Unpublished manuscript. May 2000.

Meltzer, Allan H. "Monetary and Other Explanations of the Start of the Great Depression." *Journal of Monetary Economics*, 1976, vol. 2, pp. 455–472.

North, Douglass. "Berle and Means." *Journal of Law and Economics*, June 1983, pp. 269–271.

Petro, Sylvester. "Sovereignty and Compulsory Public-Sector Bargaining." Reprint. *Wake Forest Law Review*, March 1974.

Reading, Don C. "New Deal Economic Activity and the States, 1933–1939." *Journal of Economic History*, December 1973, pp. 792–810.

Reynolds, Morgan O. "An Economic Analysis of the Norris-LaGuardia Act, the Wagner Act, and the Labor Representation Industry." *Journal of Libertarian Studies*, Summer–Fall 1982, pp. 227–266.

———. *The History and Economics of Labor Unions.* College Station, Tex.: Center for Education and Research in Free Enterprise.

Simons, Henry C. "Some Reflections on Syndicalism." *Journal of Labor Research*, Spring 1980.

Smiley, Gene. "Some Austrian Perspectives on Keynesian Fiscal Policy and the Recovery in the Thirties." *Review of Austrian Economics.*

Stoddard, W. L. "Small Business Wants Capital." *Harvard Business Review*, vol. 18, 1940, pp. 265–274.

Taylor, Jason E. "The Output Effects of Government Sponsored Cartels During the New Deal." Unpublished paper, University of Virginia.

Taylor, Jason E., and George Selgin. "By Our Bootstraps: Origins and Effects of the High-Wage Doctrine and the Minimum Wage." *Journal of Labor Research*, Fall 1999, pp. 447–462.

Temin, Peter. "Transmission of the Great Depression." *Journal of Economic Perspectives*, Spring 1993, pp. 87–102.

Wallis, John Joseph. "The Birth of the Old Federalism: Financing the New Deal." *Journal of Economic History*, March 1984, pp. 139–159.

———. "Employment in the Great Depression: New Data and Hypothesis." *Explorations in Economic History*, January 1989, pp. 45–72.

———. "Employment, Politics, and Economic Recovery During the Great Depression." *Review of Economics and Statistics*, August 1987, pp. 516–520.

———. "The Great Depression: Have We Learned Our Lessons?" In *Second Thoughts: The Uses of American Economic History,* ed. Donald N. McCloskey. New York: Oxford University Press, 1991.

———. "The Political Economy of New Deal Spending, Revisited, with and Without Nevada." *Explorations in Economic History*, April 1998, pp. 140–170.

———. "The Political Economy of New Federalism." *Economic Inquiry*, vol. 29, 1991, pp. 510–524.

———. "Why 1933? The Origins and Timing of National Government Growth, 1933–1940." In *The Emerging Modern Political Economy,* ed. Robert Higgs. New York: JAI Press, 1986.

Wallis, John Joseph, and Daniel K. Benjamin. "Public Relief and Private Employment in the Great Depression." *Explorations in Economic History*, March 1981, pp. 97–102.

Wallis, John Joseph, and Wallace E. Oates. "The Impact of the New Deal on American Federalism." In *The Defining Moment: The Great Depression and the American Economy in the Twentieth Century,* ed.

Michael D. Bordo, Claudia Goldin, and Eugene N. White. Chicago: University of Chicago Press, 1998.

Westerfield, Ray B. "The Banking Act of 1933." *Journal of Political Economy*, December 1933, pp. 721–749.

Wheelock, David. "Member Bank Borrowing and the Fed's Contractionary Monetary Policy During the Great Depression." *Journal of Money, Credit and Banking*, November 1990, pp. 409–426.

———. "Monetary Policy in the Great Depression." *Federal Reserve Bank of St. Louis Review*, March–April 1992, pp. 3–28.

———. "Regulation, Market Structure, and the Bank Failures of the Great Depression." *Federal Reserve Bank of St. Louis Review*, March 1995, pp. 27–38.

White, Eugene N. "Before the Glass-Steagall Act: An Analysis of the Investment Banking Activities of National Banks." *Explorations in Economic History*, vol. 23, 1986, pp. 33–35.

———. "The Legacy of Deposit Insurance: The Growth, Spread, and Cost of Insuring Financial Intermediaries." National Bureau of Economic Research, Working Paper 6063 (June 1997).

———. "The Stock Market Boom and the Crash of 1929." *Journal of Economic Perspectives*, Spring 1990.

Wicker, Elmus. "Federal Reserve Monetary Policy, 1922–33: A Reinterpretation." *Journal of Political Economy*, August 1965, pp. 325–343.

Wigmore, Barrie A. "Was the Bank Holiday of 1933 a Run of the Dollar Rather Than the Banks?" *Journal of Economic History*, September 1987, pp. 739–755.

Wright, Gavin. "The Political Economy of New Deal Spending: An Econometric Analysis." *Review of Economics and Statistics*, February 1974, pp. 30–38.

BOOKS

Adams, Henry H. *Harry Hopkins: A Biography.* New York: Putnam, 1977.

Anderson, Benjamin M. *Economics and the Public Welfare: A Financial and Economic History of the United States, 1914–1946.* Indianapolis: Liberty Fund, 1980.

Arkes, Hadley. *The Return of George Sutherland: Restoring a Jurisprudence of Natural Rights.* Princeton: Princeton University Press, 1994.

Armentano, Dominick T. *Antitrust and Monopoly: The Anatomy of a Policy Failure.* New York: John Wiley, 1982.

Arnold, Thurman. *Fair Fights and Foul: A Dissenting Lawyer's Life.* New York: Harcourt, Brace & World, 1965.

———. *The Symbols of Government.* New York: Harbinger, 1962.

Atack, Jeremy, and Peter Passell. *A New Economic View of American History from Colonial Times to 1940.* New York: Norton, 1994.

Baker, Liva. *Felix Frankfurter: A Biography.* New York: Coward-McCann, 1969.

Beito, David T. *Taxpayers in Revolt: Tax Resistance During the Great Depression.* Chapel Hill: University of North Carolina Press, 1989.

Benston, George J. *The Separation of Commercial and Investment Banking: The Glass-Steagall Act Revisited and Reconsidered.* New York: Oxford University Press, 1995.

Benston, George J., and George G. Kaufman. *Risk and Solvency Regulation of Depository Institutions: Past Policies and Current Options.* New York: Salomon Brothers Center for the Study of Financial Institutions, 1988.

Benston, George J., Robert A. Eisenbeis, Paul M. Horvitz, Edward J. Kane, and George G. Kaufman. *Perspectives on Safe and Sound Banking: Past, Present, and Future.* Cambridge, Mass.: MIT Press, 1986.

Bernstein, David E. *Only One Place of Redress: African Americans, Labor Regulations, and the Courts from Reconstruction to the New Deal.* Durham, N.C.: Duke University Press, 2001.

Bernstein, Michael A. *The Great Depression: Delayed Recovery and Economic Change in America, 1929–1939.* Cambridge: Cambridge University Press, 1987.

Best, Gary Dean. *Pride, Prejudice, and Politics: Roosevelt Versus Recovery, 1933–1938.* Westport, Conn.: Praeger, 1991.

Biles, Roger. *The South and the New Deal.* Lexington: University Press of Kentucky, 1994.

Blum, John Morton, ed. *From the Morgenthau Diaries: Years of Crisis, 1928–1938.* Boston: Houghton Mifflin, 1959.

———. *Roosevelt and Morgenthau: A Revision and Condensation of From the Morgenthau Diaries.* Boston: Houghton Mifflin, 1970.

Bordo, Michael D., Claudia Goldin, and Eugene N. White, eds. *The Defining Moment: The Great Depression and the American Economy in the Twentieth Century.* Chicago: University of Chicago Press, 1998.

Brand, Donald R. *Corporatism and the Rule of Law: A Study of the National Recovery Administration.* Ithaca, N.Y.: Cornell University Press, 1988.

Brooks, John. *Once in Golconda: A True Drama of Wall Street, 1920–1938.* New York: Harper & Row, 1969.

Brozen, Yale. *Concentration, Mergers and Public Policy.* New York: Macmillan, 1982.

Brown, Douglass V., Edward Chamberlin, Seymour E. Harris, Wassily W. Leontief, Edward S. Mason, Joseph A. Schumpeter, and Overton H.

Taylor. *The Economics of the Recovery Program*. New York: Whittlesey House, 1934.

Brownlee, W. Elliot. *Federal Taxation in America: A Short History*. Cambridge: Cambridge University Press, 1996.

Bruner, Karl, ed. *The Great Depression Revisited*. Boston: Martinus Nijhoff, 1981.

Burner, David. *Herbert Hoover: A Public Life*. New York: Knopf, 1979.

Burns, James MacGregor. *Roosevelt: The Lion and the Fox, 1882–1940*. New York: Harcourt, Brace & World, 1956.

———. *Roosevelt: The Soldier of Freedom, 1940–1945*. New York: Harcourt, Brace & World, 1970.

Carosso, Vincent. *Investment Banking in America: A History*. Cambridge, Mass.: Harvard University Press, 1970.

Carson, Clarence B. *The Welfare State, 1929–1985*. Wadley, Ala.: American Textbook Committee, 1986.

Chandler, Lester V. *American Monetary Policy, 1928–1941*. New York: Harper & Row, 1971.

———. *America's Greatest Depression, 1929–1941*. New York: Harper & Row, 1970.

———. *Benjamin Strong: Central Banker*. Washington, D.C.: Brookings Institution, 1958.

Chandler, William U. *The Myth of the TVA: Conservation and Development in the Tennessee Valley, 1933–1980*. Cambridge, Mass.: Ballinger, 1984.

Chernow, Ron. *The House of Morgan*. New York: Atlantic Monthly Press, 1990.

Collins, Robert M. *The Business Response to Keynes, 1929–1964*. New York: Columbia University Press, 1981.

Conkin, Paul K. *The New Deal*. New York: Crowell, 1969.

Couch, Jim F., and William F. Shughart II. *The Political Economy of the New Deal*. Northampton, Mass.: Edward Elgar, 1998.

Culver, John C. and John Hyde. *American Dreamer: A Life of Henry A. Wallace*. New York: Norton, 2000.

Currie, Lauchlin. *The Supply and Control of Money in the United States*. Cambridge, Mass.: Harvard University Press, 1934.

Cushman, Barry. *Rethinking the New Deal Court: The Structure of a Constitutional Revolution*. New York: Oxford University Press, 1998.

Danelski, David J., and Joseph S. Tulchin eds. *The Autobiographical Notes of Charles Evans Hughes*. Cambridge, Mass.: Harvard University Press, 1973.

Davis, Kenneth S. *FDR: Into the Storm, 1937–1940*. New York: Random House, 1993.

———. *FDR: The New Deal Years, 1933–1937*. New York: Random House, 1986.

Dearing, Charles L., et al. *The ABC of the NRA: An Analysis for the General Reader.* Washington, D.C.: Brookings Institution, 1934.

Degler, Carl N., ed. *The New Deal.* Chicago: Quadrangle Books, 1937.

Derber, Milton, and Edwin Young, eds. *Labor and the New Deal.* Madison: University of Wisconsin Press, 1961.

Dickman, Howard. *Industrial Democracy in America: Ideological Origins of National Labor Relations Policy.* LaSalle, Ill.: Open Court, 1987.

Douglas, Paul H. *Social Security in the United States: An Analysis and Appraisal of the Federal Social Security Act.* New York: Whittlesey House, 1936.

Dubofsky, Melvyn, and Warren Van Tine. *John L. Lewis: A Biography.* New York: Quadrangle, 1977.

Eccles, Marriner S. *Beckoning Frontiers: Public and Personal Recollections.* New York: Knopf, 1951.

Eden, Robert, ed. *The New Deal and Its Legacy: Critique and Reappraisal.* Westport, Conn.: Greenwood Press, 1989.

Eichengreen, Barry. *Golden Fetters.* New York: Oxford University Press, 1992.

Ekirch, Arthur A., Jr. *Ideologies and Utopias: The Impact of the New Deal on American Thought.* Chicago: Quadrangle, 1969.

Ely, James W., Jr. *The Guardian of Every Other Right: A Constitutional History of Property Rights.* New York: Oxford University Press, 1992.

Epstein, Richard A. *Takings: Private Property and the Power of Eminent Domain.* Cambridge, Mass.: Harvard University Press, 1985.

Farley, James A. *Jim Farley's Story: The Roosevelt Years.* New York: Whittlesey House, 1948.

Farr, Finis. *FDR.* New Rochelle, N.Y.: Arlington House, 1972.

Fearon, Peter. *War, Prosperity and Depression: The U.S. Economy, 1917–45.* Lawrence: University Press of Kansas, 1987.

Ferrara, Peter J. *Social Security: The Inherent Contradiction.* Washington, D.C.: Cato Institute, 1980.

Ferrara, Peter J., and Michael Tanner. *A New Deal for Social Security.* Washington, D.C.: Cato Institute, 1998.

Finegold, Kenneth, and Theda Skocpol. *State and Party in America's New Deal.* Madison: University of Wisconsin Press, 1995.

Flynn, John T. *As We Go Marching.* New York: Doubleday, Doran, 1944.

———. *Country Squire in the White House.* New York: Doubleday, Doran, 1940.

———. *The Roosevelt Myth.* New York: Devin-Adair, 1948.

Frankfurter, Felix. *Felix Frankfurter Reminisces, Recorded in Talks with Dr. Harlan B. Phillips.* New York: Reynal, 1960.

Freidel, Frank. *Franklin D. Roosevelt.* Boston: Little, Brown, 1952.

————. *Franklin D. Roosevelt: Launching of the New Deal*. Boston: Little, Brown, 1973.

————. *Franklin D. Roosevelt: The Ordeal*. Boston: Little, Brown, 1954.

————. *Franklin D. Roosevelt: A Rendezvous with Destiny*. Boston: Little, Brown, 1990.

Friedman, Milton, and Anna Jacobson Schwartz. *A Monetary History of the United States, 1867–1960*. Princeton: Princeton University Press, 1963.

Garett, Garet. *The American Story*. Chicago: Regnery, 1955.

————. *The People's Pottage*. Caldwell, Idaho: Caxton Printers, 1965.

Gordon, Margaret S. *Barriers to World Trade: A Study of Recent Commercial Policy*. New York: Macmillan, 1941.

Graham, Otis L., Jr., and Meghan Robinson Wander, eds. *Franklin D. Roosevelt: His Life and Times, An Encyclopedic View*. New York: Da Capo, 1985.

Grant, James. *Bernard Baruch: The Adventures of a Wall Street Legend*. New York: Simon & Schuster, 1983.

Gunther, John. *Roosevelt in Retrospect: A Profile in History*. New York: Harper & Row, 1950.

Hall, Thomas E., and J. David Ferguson. *The Great Depression: An International Disaster of Perverse Economic Policies*. Ann Arbor: University of Michigan Press, 1998.

Haraf, William S., and Rose Marie Kushmeider, eds. *Restructuring Banking and Financial Services in America*. Washington, D.C.: American Enterprise Institute, 1988.

Hawley, Ellis W. *The New Deal and the Problem of Monopoly: A Study in Economic Ambivalence*. Princeton: Princeton University Press, 1966.

Henderson, David R., ed. *The Fortune Encyclopedia of Economics*. New York: Warner, 1993.

Higgs, Robert. *Crisis and Leviathan: Critical Episodes in the Growth of American Government*. New York: Oxford University Press, 1987.

Hirsch, H. N. *The Enigma of Felix Frankfurter*. New York: Basic, 1981.

Hoover, Herbert. *The Cabinet and the Presidency, 1920–1933*. New York: Macmillan, 1952.

————. *The Great Depression, 1929–1941*. New York: Macmillan, 1952.

Howard, Donald S. *The WPA and Federal Relief Policy*. New York: Russell Sage Foundation, 1943.

Hughes, Jonathan R. T. *The Governmental Habit Redux: Economic Controls from Colonial Times to the Present*. Princeton: Princeton University Press, 1991.

Huthmacher, J. Joseph. *Senator Robert F. Wagner and the Rise of Urban Liberalism*. New York: Atheneum, 1968.

Ickes, Harold L. *The Secret Diaries of Harold L. Ickes: The First Thousand Days, 1933–1936*. New York: Simon & Schuster, 1953.

———. *The Secret Diary of Harold L. Ickes: The Inside Struggle, 1936–1939*. New York: Simon & Schuster, 1954.

Irons, Peter H. *A People's History of the Supreme Court*. New York: Viking, 1999.

———. *The New Deal Lawyers*. Princeton: Princeton University Press, 1982.

Johnson, Hugh S. *Blue Eagle from Egg to Earth*. Garden City, N.Y.: Doubleday, Doran, 1935.

Jones, Jesse H., with Edward Angly. *Fifty Billion Dollars: My Thirteen Years with the RFC, 1932–1945*. New York: Macmillan, 1951.

Jones, Joseph M., Jr. *Tariff Retaliation: Repercussions of the Hawley-Smoot Bill*. Philadelphia: University of Pennsylvania Press, 1934.

Josephson, Matthew. *The Money Lords: The Great Finance Capitalists, 1925–1940*. New York: Weybright & Talley, 1972.

Kennedy, David M. *Freedom from Fear: The American People in Depression and War, 1929–1945*. New York: Oxford University Press, 1999.

Kennedy, S. E. *The Banking Crisis of 1933*. Lexington: Kentucky University Press, 1973.

Kindleberger, Charles P. *The World in Depression, 1929–1939*. Berkeley: University of California Press, 1986.

Klebaner, Benjamin. *Commercial Banking in the United States: A History*. Hinsdale, Il.: Dryden, 1974.

Kroos, Herman E. *Executive Opinion: What Business Leaders Said and Thought on Economic Issues, 1920s–1960s*. Garden City, N.Y.: Doubleday, 1970.

Lash, Joseph P. *Dealers and Dreamers: A New Look at the New Deal*. New York: Doubleday, 1988.

———, ed. *From the Diaries of Felix Frankfurter*. New York: Norton, 1975.

Lebergott, Stanley. *The Americans: An Economic Record*. New York: Norton, 1984.

Leff, Mark H. *The Limits of Symbolic Reform: The New Deal and Taxation, 1933–1939*. Cambridge: Cambridge University Press, 1984.

Leuchtenburg, William E. *Franklin D. Roosevelt and the New Deal, 1932–1940*. New York: Harper & Row, 1963.

Lichtenstein, Nelson. *The Most Dangerous Man in Detroit: Walter Reuther and the Fate of American Labor*. New York: Basic, 1995.

Lippmann, Walter. *Interpretations, 1931–1932*. Ed. Allan Nevins. New York: Macmillan, 1933.

———. *Interpretations, 1933–1935*. Ed. Allan Nevins. New York: Macmillan, 1936.

Lowitt, Richard. *The New Deal and the West.* Bloomington: Indiana University Press, 1984.

Lubov, Roy. *The Struggle for Social Security: 1900–1935.* Pittsburgh: University of Pittsburgh Press, 1986.

Lynch, David. *The Concentration of Economic Power.* New York: Columbia University Press, 1946.

Lyon, Leverett S., Paul T. Homan, Lewis L. Lorwin, George Terborgh, Charles L. Dearing, and Leon C. Marshall. *The National Recovery Administration: An Analysis and Appraisal.* Washington, D.C.: Brookings Institution, 1935.

Macleish, Archibald, and E. F. Pritchard Jr., eds. *Law and Politics: Occasional Papers of Felix Frankfurter, 1913–1938.* New York: Harcourt, Brace & World, 1939.

Martin, George. *Madam Secretary: Frances Perkins.* Boston: Houghton Mifflin, 1976.

McDonald, Michael J., and John Muldowny. *TVA and the Dispossessed: The Resettlement of Population in the Norris Dam Area.* Knoxville: University of Tennessee Press, 1982.

McElvaine, Robert S. *The Great Depression: America, 1929–1941.* New York: Three Rivers Press, 1993.

Meltzer, Allan H. *A History of the Federal Reserve.* Vol. 1, 1913–1951. Chicago: University of Chicago Press, 2003.

Mertz, Paul E. *New Deal Policy and Southern Rural Poverty.* Baton Rouge: Louisiana State University Press, 1978.

Mitchell, Broadus. *Depression Decade: From New Era Through New Deal, 1929–1941.* New York: Rinehart, 1947.

Moley, Raymond. *After Seven Years.* New York: Harper, 1939.

———. *The First New Deal.* New York: Harcourt, Brace & World. 1966.

Moore, John R., ed. *The Economic Impact of TVA.* Knoxville: University of Tennessee Press, 1967.

Morgan, Ted. *FDR: A Biography.* New York: Simon & Schuster, 1985.

Morgenthau, Henry, III. *Mostly Morgenthaus: A Family History.* New York: Ticknor & Fields, 1991.

Nutter, G. Warren, and Henry Adler Einhorn. *Enterprise Monopoly in the United States, 1899–1958.* New York: Columbia University Press, 1969.

O'Brien, P. J. *Forward with Roosevelt.* Chicago: John Winston, 1936.

Ohl, John Kennedy. *Hugh S. Johnson and the New Deal.* Dekalb, Ill.: Northern Illinois University Press, 1985.

Olson, James S. *Saving Capitalism: The Reconstruction Finance Corporation and the New Deal, 1933–1940.* Princeton: Princeton University Press, 1988.

Palmieri, Mario. *The Philosophy of Fascism.* Chicago: Dante Alighieri Society, 1936.

Parrish, Michael E. *Felix Frankfurter and His Times*. New York: Free Press, 1982.

Patterson, James T. *The New Deal and the States*. Princeton: Princeton University Press, 1969.

Paul, Ellen Frankel, and Howard Dickman, eds. *Liberty, Property, and the Future of Constitutional Self-Government*. Buffalo: SUNY Press, 1990.

Paul, Randolph E. *Taxation in the United States*. Boston: Little, Brown, 1954.

Pecora, Ferdinand. *Wall Street Under Oath: The Story of Our Modern Money Managers*. New York: Simon & Schuster, 1939.

Pecora Hearings (1933, 1934), U.S. Senate, Hearings Before the Committee on Banking and Currency (available at the National Archives and Records Administration).

Pusey, Merlo J. *Charles Evans Hughes*. 2 vols. New York: Macmillan, 1952.

———. *Eugene Meyer*. New York: Knopf, 1974.

Ratner, Sidney. *Taxation and Democracy in America*. New York: Octagon, 1980.

Reynolds, Morgan O. *Power and Privilege: Labor Unions in America*. New York: Universe Books, 1984.

Richberg, Donald R. *Labor Union Monopoly*. Chicago: Regnery, 1957.

———. *My Hero: The Indiscreet Memoirs of an Eventful but Unheroic Life*. New York: Putnam's, 1954.

Robinson, Archie. *George Meany and His Times*. New York: Simon & Schuster, 1981.

Rodell, Fred. *Nine Men: A Political History of the Supreme Court from 1790 to 1955*. New York: Random House, 1955.

Roose, Kenneth D. *The Economics of Recession and Revival: An Interpretation of 1937–38*. New York: Archon Books, 1969.

Rothbard, Murray N. *America's Great Depression*. Los Angeles: Nash, 1972.

Schattschneider, E. E. *Politics, Pressures and the Tariff: A Study of Free Private Enterprise in Pressure Politics, as Shown in the 1929–1930 Revision of the Tariff*. New York: Prentice-Hall, 1935.

Schlesinger, Arthur M., Jr. *The Coming of the New Deal*. Boston: Houghton Mifflin, 1959.

———. *The Crisis of the Old Order, 1919–1933*. Boston: Houghton Mifflin, 1957.

———. *A Life in the Twentieth Century: Innocent Beginnings, 1917–1950*. Boston: Houghton Mifflin, 2000.

———. *The Politics of Upheaval*. Boston: Houghton Mifflin, 1960.

Schumpeter, Joseph. *Business Cycles: A Theoretical, Historical, and Statistical Analysis of the Capitalist Process*. 2 vols. 1939. Reprint, New York: McGraw-Hill, 1939.

Schwarz, Jordan A. *Liberal: Adolph A. Berle and the Vision of an American Era.* New York: Free Press, 1987.

———. *The New Dealers: Power Politics in the Age of Roosevelt.* New York: Knopf, 1993.

Siegan, Bernard H. *Economic Liberties and the Constitution.* Chicago: University of Chicago Press, 1981.

Simons, Henry C. *Economic Policy for a Free Society.* Chicago: University of Chicago Press, 1948.

Smiley, Gene. *The American Economy in the Twentieth Century.* Cincinnati: South-Western Publishing, 1994.

Smith, Rixey, and Norman Beasley. *Carter Glass: A Biography.* New York: Da Capo, 1972.

Sternsher, Bernard. *Rexford Tugwell and the New Deal.* New Brunswick, N.J.: Rutgers University Press, 1964.

Stigler, George J. *Lectures on Five Economic Problems.* London: Longmans, Green, 1949.

———, ed. *Business Concentration and Price Policy: A Conference of the Universities-National Bureau Committee for Economic Research.* Princeton: Princeton University Press, 1955.

Stock Exchange Practices: Report of the Committee on Banking and Currency. SEP Report. Washington, D.C.: U.S. Government Printing Office, 1934.

Tarbell, Ida M. *Owen D. Young: A New Type of Industrial Leader.* New York: Macmillan, 1932.

Temin, Peter. *Did Monetary Forces Cause the Great Depression?* New York: Norton, 1976.

———. *Lessons from the Great Depression.* Cambridge, Mass.: MIT Press, 1989.

Thieblot, Armand J., Jr., and Thomas R. Haggard. *Union Violence: The Record and the Response by Courts, Legislatures and the NLRB.* Philadelphia: University of Pennsylvania, Wharton School, Industrial Research Unit, 1983.

Timberlake, Richard. *Monetary Policy in the United States.* Chicago: University of Chicago Press, 1993.

Tugwell, Rexford G. *FDR: Architect of an Era.* New York: Macmillan, 1967.

Tyler, Gus. *The Labor Revolution.* New York: Viking, 1967.

Vedder, Richard K., and Lowell E. Gallaway. *Out of Work: Unemployment and Government in Twentieth-Century America.* New York: New York University Press, 1997.

Walter, Ingo, ed. *Deregulating Wall Street: Commercial Bank Penetration of the Corporate Securities Market.* New York: John Wiley, 1985.

Warburg, James P. *The Money Muddle*. New York: Knopf, 1934.

Warren, George F., and Frank A. Pearson. *Prices*. New York: John Wiley, 1933.

Watkins, T. H. *The Great Depression: America in the 1930s*. Boston: Little, Brown, 1993.

———. *Righteous Pilgrim: The Life and Times of Harold L. Ickes, 1874–1952*. New York: Henry Holt, 1990.

Weaver, Carolyn L. *The Crisis in Social Security: Economic and Political Origins*. Durham, N.C.: Duke University Press Policy Studies, 1982.

Weinstein, Michael M. *Recovery and Redistribution Under the NIRA*. Amsterdam: North-Holland, 1980.

Whitman, Willson. *David Lilienthal: Public Servant in a Power Age*. New York: Henry Holt, 1948.

Wicker, Elmus. *The Banking Panics of the Great Depression*. Cambridge: Cambridge University Press, 1996.

———. *Federal Reserve Monetary Policy, 1917–1933*. New York: Random House, 1966.

Wigmore, Barrie A. *The Crash and Its Aftermath*. Westport, Conn.: Greenwood Press, 1985.

Witte, John F. *The Politics and Development of the Federal Income Tax*. Madison: University of Wisconsin Press, 1985.

Zevin, B. D., ed. *Nothing to Fear: The Selected Addresses of Franklin Delano Roosevelt, 1932–1945*. Boston: Houghton Mifflin, 1946.

ACKNOWLEDGMENTS

———————

I GOT STARTED on this project because of a conversation which began in an elevator at New York's Princeton Club. I was talking with Thomas Lipscomb, who, with a quarter-century of publishing experience, suggested I consider a book about a major political personality.

Since FDR was the biggest American political personality of the twentieth century, I focused on him. In recent years, several books have been published expressing a critical view of FDR's war policies, but political historians have continued to portray him as a hero for the way he handled the Great Depression. I thought this was curious since more and more economists have concluded that his New Deal policies backfired. Their empirical evidence became the basis for this book.

Milton Friedman kindly went over the manuscript twice, offering many corrections and suggestions, and I am grateful to him. Ever since I first met him and began to follow his work almost forty years ago, he has inspired me as a scholar and as a defender of individual liberty.

Another world-class scholar, James M. Buchanan at George Mason University, offered many suggestions, too, and I appreciate his generous assistance.

My friend Sam Peltzman, a professor of economics at the University of Chicago and director of the George J. Stigler Center for the Study of the Economy and State, suggested the names of several economists who were doing important analyses of New Deal policies. His colleague Gregg A. Jarrell was particularly helpful.

Many more people than I can remember answered questions and offered helpful advice. Principal sources are acknowledged in the text, in the footnotes, and in the bibliography.

Over the years, I have drawn on material about the New Deal and the Great Depression at libraries across the country, particularly Yale University, the University of Chicago, Stanford University, the University of California (Berkeley, Los Angeles), and the Library of Congress. During the writing of this book, librarians at Westport Public Library tapped extensive interlibrary loan sources throughout Connecticut.

I appreciate the patient support of Andrea Millen Rich, publisher of Laissez Faire Books, with readers in ninety countries.

David Boaz and Ed Crane, at the Cato Institute, offered much encouragement.

I had a wonderful experience working with Crown Forum editor David Richardson and project editor Shawn Vreeland.

I want to thank Marisa, Madeline, and Rosalynd for their help during this project, and Justin and Kristin for making it all worthwhile.

—Westport, Connecticut, May 2003

INDEX

⸺━➤●◄━⸺